David James Smith was born in 1956 and has been a journalist all his working life. He writes for the *Sunday Times Magazine* and lives in Lewes, East Sussex, with his partner and their four children.

D1385720

By David James Smith

Supper with the Crippens
One Morning in Sarajevo

ONE MORNING
IN SARAJEVO

28 JUNE 1914

DAVID JAMES SMITH

PHOENIX

A PHOENIX PAPERBACK

First published in Great Britain in 2008
by Weidenfeld & Nicolson
This paperback edition published in 2009
by Phoenix,
an imprint of Orion Books Ltd,
Orion House, 5 Upper St Martin's Lane,
London WC2H 9EA

An Hachette UK company

3 5 7 9 10 8 6 4 2

Copyright © David James Smith 2008

The right of David James Smith to be identified as the author of
this work has been asserted by him in accordance with the
Copyright, Designs and Patents Act 1988.

All rights reserved. No part of this publication may be
reproduced, stored in a retrieval system, or transmitted, in
any form or by any means, electronic, mechanical,
photocopying, recording or otherwise, without the prior
permission of the copyright owner.

A CIP catalogue record for this book
is available from the British Library.

ISBN 978-0-7538-2584-6

Printed and bound in Great Britain by
Clays Ltd, St Ive plc

The Orion Publishing Group's policy is to use papers that
are natural, renewable and recyclable products and
made from wood grown in sustainable forests. The logging
and manufacturing processes are expected to conform to
the environmental regulations of the country of origin.

www.orionbooks.co.uk

For Petal

Contents

Who's Who and
How to Pronounce Them

The Serb Student Assassins
Gavrilo Princip (Printsip), also known as Gavro
Nedeljko Cabrinovic (Nedelko Chabrinovitch), also known as
   Nedjo
Trifko Grabez
Vaso Cubrilovic (Chubrilovitch)
Cvjetko Popovic (Sevyetko Popovitch)

The Muslim Assassin
Mehmed Mehmedbasic (Mehmedbashitch)

The Organizer
Danilo Ilic (Ilitch)

The Past Martyrs
Milos Obilic (Milosh Obilitch)
Bogdan Zerajic (Zerayitch)

Among the Guerillas in Belgrade
Vojin Tankosic (Voyan Tankositch)
Milan Ciganovic (Siganovitch)
Dragutin Dimitrijevic (Dimitriyevitch), also known as Apis

The Journey to Sarajevo
Rade Popovic (Rarday Popovitch)
Joca Prvanovic (Joka Pervanovitch)
Rade Grbic (Rarday Gerbitch)
Mico Micic (Mitso Mitsitch)
Jakov Milovic (Yakov Milovitch)
Obren Milosevic (Milosevitch)

Veljko Cubrilovic (Velko Chubrilovitch)
Mitar Kerovic (Kerovitch)
Blagoje Kerovic (Blagoiye)
Nedjo Kerovic
Jovo Kerovic
Cvijan Stjepanovic (Seviyan Styepanovitch)
Misko Jovanovic (Mishko Jovanovitch)

In Sarajevo
Ivo Kranjcevic (Kranychevitch)
Lazar Djukic (Jukitch)
Branko Zagorac (Zagoratch)
Marko Perin
Nikola Forkapic (Forkapitch)
Dragan Kalember
Ivan Momcinovic (Mochinovitch)
Franjo Sadilo (Franyo)
Angela Sadilo

1

June 1914 – the Dreaming Assassin

The mystic journey of Gavrilo Princip came to an end on 5 June 1914, when he finally arrived in Sarajevo after a long overland adventure across 300 kilometres of mountains and muddy passes with a heavy load of guns and bombs that he had only just succeeded in smuggling from Belgrade with considerable help from others.

He was exhausted and broke and, like many a young amateur assassin before and since, he was not thinking clearly or carefully and had no idea how best to hide himself or his intentions during the next three weeks.

He would soon be lying in bed, the weapons stashed in a Gladstone bag beneath his mattress, sleeping and dreaming of the heroic deed to come, imagining himself as a political murderer, seeing himself in his dreams, in a remarkably prescient vision, struggling with soldiers and policemen.

On 28 June he would live out his dreams and stand among the thin crowd on a street corner and fire two shots at the over-dressed passengers in an open-topped car parading down the riverside road in the centre of Sarajevo. His victims, the Heir Apparent to the Austrian imperial throne, Archduke Franz Ferdinand and his wife Sophie, would die, a world war would start and Gavrilo would become the most notorious assassin in history, but that did not mean he was a highly trained killer nor even that he had a well-devised plan.

He was not yet 20 years old and in many respects was a naive and unworldly young man, who apparently gave no thought to the need to cover his tracks against the inevitable police investigation that would ensue. Or perhaps he did give it some brief thought and deemed such a precaution unnecessary, as he planned to kill himself, in any event, and hoped to become a Serbian martyr, a suicide assassin.

On his arrival in Sarajevo, Gavrilo went first to the home of his friend Danilo Ilic, who lived with his mother, Stoja, a washerwoman, at 3 Oprkanj (Operkany) Street, a long, thin house with an overhanging roof and a front door that opened directly onto the narrow, winding lane on the edge of town.

Gavrilo said he chose to stay there because it was in a back street and Ilic was a quiet young man who did not draw attention to himself. It must have helped, too, that he did not need to make any arrangement to pay rent to Ilic's mother, especially since he had to borrow 50 crowns from Ilic to buy food.

The police would have little difficulty tracing Gavrilo's whereabouts, following the assassination, as he registered with them soon after his arrival – an obligation required of all visitors to the city – and gave Ilic's home as his lodging address, an act of unfathomable recklessness, since Ilic was not merely Gavrilo's old friend but also the chief organizer of the assassination, and remained busy even at this late state, recruiting the rest of the team of assassins.

Still, at least the two young men made sure they kept the bedroom door closed, so that Stoja, who liked to keep a tidy house, would not enter, start cleaning and discover the Gladstone bag full of weapons.

They would leave from the house on the morning of 28 June to meet their co-conspirators and take their places along the route. Soon after, the now empty Gladstone bag, still in the bedroom where it had been left, would be photographed for police records, the house too, inside and out, recorded for posterity and then all but forgotten, along with so many of the details of that day, and the events of nearly a century ago that preceded it.

Despite the relatively central location it took a while for the researcher Alex Todorovic and myself to find the house and stand before it, in the autumn of 2006. Once we had located the street the house was unmissable because it still looked almost identical to the black and white images from the police files of all those years earlier, though it was now across the road from one of Sarajevo's more elegant small hotels.

It seemed fitting that, in the end, we had stumbled across the street by chance, as almost everything about the Sarajevo assassination of 1914 was driven by fate and accident; not just the remarkable series of coincidences that morning, that delivered the Archduke and his wife to Gavrilo, virtually as sitting ducks – a hunting metaphor the Archduke might have appreciated in other circumstances – but also in the twists and turns of the loosely organized plot and the many lives it casually touched and destroyed as it ran its course.

Gavrilo, for example, had been taken to lodge with Ilic for the first time some years earlier, when still a child, the house selected more or less at random by Gavrilo's respectable older brother Jovo, a young merchant who was looking for somewhere safe and decent where Gavrilo could stay while he continued his schooling in the Bosnian capital, far from the rural world of their peasant parents.

In his attempt to do the best thing for little Gavrilo, Jovo had inadvertently set him on the path to ruin, lodging him with a fervent revolutionary, Danilo Ilic, whose fanaticism – and library of Russian socialist literature – would soon make an impression on Gavrilo.

Jovo never intended to turn his brother into a blinkered assassin. But then Gavrilo never intended to start a world war. Instead, his mind was fixed on the Serbian people and five hundred years of oppression. He acted, Gavrilo would later say, out of love for the former, and revenge for the latter; his pride, you could say, had blinded him to the wider context of history and the fatal teetering of the world's empires as they readied to implode, taking with them millions of lives.

2

Dead Babies

He was famously quiet and reserved, but even so, considering the enormity of his impact on modern history, it is ironic and quite remarkable that Gavrilo Princip left so little trace of himself behind. There are a handful of letters and inscriptions, then the testimony he gave in court and in the pre-trial inquiry, plus the unscrambled notes made by a psychiatrist during a few brief interviews in prison, and the memoirs of some associates; finally, some lines of poetry, a couplet etched into a prison wall … that's about all there is.

Much of this was pieced together by Vladimir Dedijer, forty or more years ago, for his book *The Road to Sarajevo*. Since then the transcript of the trial has finally been assembled and translated in full and we have the benefit of additional testimony from more recently released notes and papers of the family survivors of Gavrilo's co-conspirators. It does not bring Princip fully from the shadows, but it certainly now gives us a clearer idea of who he was and why he shot the Archduke.

The area of the Grahovo valley, high up on the western border of Bosnia & Hercegovina, close to Croatia, had been occupied predominantly by a rural Serb population for many hundreds of years with only the briefest breaks in continuity until the summer of 1995, during the multi-faced conflict between Serbs, Muslims and Croats.

The Croats advanced through the area driving the Serbs out as they went and razing the villages and small towns in their wake. It was said they had ploughed salt into the land to destroy its agricultural use for future years, but I can find no supporting evidence for this. The Serbs, those who survived, eventually began to return in the late 1990s and are still rebuilding their communities.

Princip was born here 100 years earlier, in the village of Obljaj, in

July 1894. Conditions and the way of life were then unforgiving and largely as they had been for several generations, so that his mother, in the final trimester of pregnancy, had spent the day, and probably all the days before this too, in the field gathering heavy bundles of newly cut straw to make hay. Then she had washed some linen in the stream and it was only after she had gone to begin milking the cow that she had begun to experience contractions and run into the house, just in time to fall on the unmade floor in front of the fire, where the baby was born.

The family home was typical of the area and the community, described as Bosnian gothic with its wooden construction and tall black roof. The interior style was mediaeval.

As one visitor, a family friend who was later to become a Princip biographer, described it, 'In the old house the doors are small, and so very low that you can enter the house only by bowing your head. Inside it is dark. The house has no windows; instead of floor only beaten earth. To the left from the door is a stone bench on which a wooden barrel for water was standing; behind this on a shelf, some cooking untensils, earthenware pots; a big round low table was hanging against the wall.

'On the other side of the door were three wooden chests, a box for keeping flour, a sieve and another shelf. Deep on the right side there was a low door leading to a small room in which stood a bed. On the left side of the main part of the house was an open hearth, burning day and night, surrounded by a low stone wall. Above it stood a verige, an iron chain hanging from the ceiling, on which were metal cauldrons hooked above the fire. Smoke went through a badza, a hole in the roof above the open fireplace. The only light in the house came through it.'

No wonder, in such basic and insanitary circumstances, that babies and children struggled to live. The newborn would be the fourth born but only the second surviving child, six years after his brother Jovo. Altogether, his parents Petar and Maria, who was known as Nana, had nine children – five boys, four girls – but six died at birth or in infancy. Only three boys lived on, the third survivor being born two years later.

Nana's mother-in-law had cut the cord with her teeth and wrapped the baby in some coarse cloth after washing him in a wooden bowl.

A fire was made, and a bed of straw prepared for mother and baby, before relatives arrived to toast the birth with plum brandy.

Princip's father, Petar, had been out at work all this time but as he came home late at night one of his young sisters came running to meet him: a scarf for me and a child for you, she called to him.

This baby, like so many of the others, was weak and not expected to last, so that a girl was sent to fetch the priest quick, for a hurried christening. Nana wanted to name the boy Spiro, for her dead brother, but the priest, not just a priest but also a renowned local military leader, did not believe in women naming children and gave his choice of name, Gavrilo, as it was the saint's day of St Gabriel.

When Gavrilo, soon shortened to Gavro, was baptised a month later a mistake was made in the registry entries. The right date – 13 July – was entered in the parish register, but the wrong date – 13 June – was entered in the civil register. This nearly got Gavrilo hanged twenty years later in 1914, as the two dates fell before and after the assassination of 28 June. If he was under 20 (as in reality he was), Gavro was too young to hang, according to Austrian law, but if he was over 20, born on 13 June, he was old enough to be executed.

Not being hanged, he went to prison, where he was hung instead in chains in solitary confinement for a long time, and then met the Viennese psychiatrist Dr Martin Pappenheim who recorded Gavro saying, 'Father a peasant but occupies himself with enterprises. Father a quiet man who does not drink. Father not occupied with political matters. No diseases in family. Scarlet fever. No bed-wetting. During school – sleep-walking – around the room.'

The priest was an important figure in the community, both because of his military leadership and because of the dominant role of the eastern Orthodox Church. Gavro's father, particularly, was a devout man who avoided swearing as well as alcohol, observed all the fasts and festivals and always attended Mass. Gavro's mother took a less pious attitude, seeing the Church in a more informal way, as part of local tradition. This must have influenced Gavro, who would later shift even further and describe himself as an atheist. His single-minded devotion was directed elsewhere; his worship that of a Serb nationalist ideal rather than a religious abstraction.

Petar worked hard and had what sounds an eccentric pastime of planting trees, not just in the grounds of his home but all around the village where he lived, Obljaj, and even on the road out, heading towards the nearby town of Bosansko Grahovo (which could be translated as Bosnian Bean).

There have been suggestions that Gavro's father was an object of amusement to others, as he took himself and his work very seriously and so invited ridicule. He had carried on the work begun by his own father, Jovo, which was a necessary sideline to the core family business of farming. Jovo used his wagon to transport passengers and mail around the region and this was taken up by Petar, who went one step further, carrying the heavy mailbag on his back in winter, when the snow was too deep for the wagon to pass. He apparently took pride in his physical prowess, once breaking his leg while stopping the horses after they had bolted while pulling the wagon on a mountain road. He also took bets (they sound more like teases or wind-ups) that he could run through the snow in the middle of winter, barefoot, dressed only in shirt and trousers, between Obljaj and another village a mile away.

Petar had presided over the demise of the Princip zadruga, the name given to a family clan in Turkish times, which had broken up in the late 1800s after his father Jovo was killed. Petar had become head of the extended family at the age of 30, and it was then that the zadruga was dissolved and the land and property divided out. Petar only had about four acres, which gave him a meadow and a harvest of corn, oats and barley, not enough to support the family for more than a couple of months of the year.

During Turkish rule the family had paid a substantial regular tribute of one third of their income to their landlord, known as a beg. The payment would only be accepted in cash, not in kind, and finding it was a constant burden.

The Princip men, Jovo and his sons, including Petar, embodied the important Serbian tradition of struggle and resistance and had joined the Serb uprising against the Turks in 1875; their families were briefly driven from their homes when the area was overrun by the Turks. The Ottoman empire had finally been losing its grip in the Balkans after 500 years of oppressive rule and even though many Serb homes had been burned during the fighting the uprising had ultimately succeeded in driving the Turks out of Bosnia.

So far as the Bosnian Serbs were concerned, however, this was only a short respite as it led directly to the Treaty of Berlin in 1878 by which the imperial powers had simply handed control of Bosnia & Hercegovina to the Austro-Hungarian empire. This had incited new uprisings and a further round of village clearances as the Austrians advanced to Sarajevo from the west.

The only difference this time had been that much of the resistance had come from Muslim insurgents, some of whom had struck alliances with the Serbs, while others chose to fight alongside the Austrians. Again homes were burnt and when Gavro's grandfather Jovo was shot and killed one Sunday afternoon in 1881 while hunting ducks and wild geese in the marshes near his home, the family believed he had been murdered by the Austrians. Gavro too was supposed to have believed this, though never mentioned his grandfather at his trial nor so much as hinted at this as a vengeful motive for the assassination.

Even in those distant days, long before the bitter wars of the 1990s, religious and ethnic differences made for fierce divisions and deeply held enmities. It was said that, during his father's lifetime, Petar had met and fallen in love with a Catholic girl. Jovo could not contemplate such a union of faiths and told Petar to stop seeing her. When Petar tried to argue, Jovo told him if he carried on he would kill him. It was only after Jovo's death that Petar met and married Maria, Nana, from a neighbouring zadruga. She was nine years younger than her husband, who was 34 when Gavro was born, but perhaps her need for escape from home was pressing as she was being mistreated by a stepmother.

The couple were said to make a contrasting pair, she being curly haired, with sharp features, a pointed chin and blessed with enough energy for two or three women, so that she seemed in some ways quite masculine, while her husband, with his slight, bony physique had softer, more feminine features.

It was reported that Gavro was the spit of his mother in childhood with the same intense blue eyes; he had also inherited her beautiful singing voice. But perhaps, as he grew older, as the photographs suggest, he took on something of his father's gentler appearance, which served to disguise the blazing spirit beneath.

There was hardship all around, from the wider picture of ethnic conflict and warfare, to the family struggles – long hours of backbreaking work with the wagon or in the fields for barely enough reward, as well as the lack of respect for Petar and Maria's estrangement from her own family. Then too, there were all those dead babies, six of them, who must have made their presence felt in the household.

Gavro seems to have been thoughtful, reserved and sentimental even as a child. The psychiatrist recorded Gavro saying about himself, 'Was not much with other schoolboys, always alone. Quiet, sentimental child. Earnest – books, art. Even as a child not particularly religious.'

He is reported to have shared the following childhood memory of evenings of community entertainment, known as selos. The tone, if a little florid, is full of loss and longing: 'The wet logs on the open fire gave the only light to the closely packed kmets and their wives, wrapped in thick smoke. If I tried to penetrate the curtain of smoke, the most that I could see were the eyes of the human beings, numerous, sad and glaring with some kind of fluid light coming from nowhere. Some kind of reproach, even threat, radiated from them, and many times since then they have awakened me from my dreams.'

Gavro would also participate in these gatherings, reading heroic Serbian poems from a collection given to him as a school prize.

One biographer noted Gavro's exceptional childhood development, walking early, alert and active. It was true he did not seem to like playing much with his mates, preferring to look after the cattle and watch the peasants at work. Even before he started school he liked to play at being a schoolboy, lugging around a bag full of old books.

But he could be rough too in his play with other children, often hitting the bigger boys and being especially determined if he thought there was some injustice. His mother was reported as saying he read a lot and was always silent, 'but every blow he received he would return twofold.'

Gavro had his mother to thank for his schooling, as his father wanted him out in the fields guarding his sheep. He started school aged nine and finished at 13 when his brother, who was already prospering in a new life out of the valley, took an interest in Gavro's education.

The brother, Jovo, was only 20. He was apparently too busy to find time to study himself, or to get caught up in the student rebellions. Perhaps he was oblivious to them and so never stopped to think what influence this new world might have on his brother.

Jovo had left home and Grahovo at 15 and gone, according to a Serbian proverb, to seek food at the urge of his stomach. He had settled in the town of Hadzici, 20 kilometres south-west of Sarajevo, trying a variety of jobs before joining a lumber transport company carrying felled trees out of the forest. Hadzici was a centre for the timber industry and Jovo soon started out on his own with teams of horses to pull the wagons. He had plans for a saw mill. He sent money home and was ready to pay for the schooling of both his brothers, Gavro and 11-year-old Nikola. It is possible that Jovo was determined to escape his impoverished agrarian origins and, having got away, was equally determined to rescue Gavro and Nikola too.

When he read that the Military School in Sarajevo was looking for healthy 14-year-olds who would receive free schooling, food and uniforms if they joined, Jovo apparently thought this the perfect opportunity for Gavro. Petar travelled down with Gavro to the city, a three-day horse-ride. On arrival, Gavro allegedly refused to stay at an inn because it was run by 'strangely dressed' Muslims, an unfamiliar sight back in the valley.

For the first time, Gavro was going shopping for new underwear and shirts. The storekeeper knew the family and did not want to see Gavro go to military school. He supposedly said, do not give the child to an institution where he will be uprooted and become an executioner of his own people … if you want to listen to me as a friend, send him to the Merchants' School.

Various Princips in the extended family around Grahovo had served as frontier guards or gendarmes for both the Turks and the Austrians. Late in the evening of 28 June 1914, Petar and Nana would be woken from their sleep by a gendarme relative, ordering them to the police station because it was being reported that Gavro had murdered 'Verdinanda', as the kmets called Archduke Ferdinand.

How history might have been altered if Gavro had followed in the family tradition and taken up arms for the Austrians, instead of against them. But his brother Jovo took the storekeeper's advice to heart and enrolled Gavro at the Merchants' School, perhaps envisioning a bright future for his brother as a businessman like himself.

Jovo made enquiries in the town for a place where Gavro might live while he was at the school and was told to try the widow Stoja Ilic at 3 Oprkanj Street in the winding back lanes of Sarajevo. He agreed to pay a month's rent in advance and an understanding was reached. Gavro shared a room with Stoja's only child, her son Danilo, who was four years older than Gavro and already in possession of a stirring collection of socialist and revolutionary literature that Gavro would soon being reading for himself.

When Gavro first arrived there, in late 1907, Danilo had already passed through and graduated from the Merchants' School and had not yet moved on to Teachers' College. It was an unsettled period in his life while he sought a job he enjoyed, working both as a newsboy and a prompter in a travelling theatre. He would spend time on the railways as a porter and on the shores of the Sava river as a longshoreman, so that by the time he started teacher training he was four years older than the other students.

His father, a cobbler, had died when he was five years old and his mother, while not remarrying, had taken in laundry to support her only child through school and then begun offering lodgings at her home. She was, and obviously needed to be, a thrifty woman, who saved money where and when she could. Her son brought little money into the home and often suffered from poor health, a stomach ulcer, it was said, at one stage, and other, apparently quite serious illnesses which incapacitated him for several weeks at a time. Perhaps they were stress related, an entirely undiagnosed phenomenon at the time.

Unfortunately for Gavro his brother could not keep paying the rent to Stoja Ilic, so he had to leave the house and move in with his brother in Hadzici, travelling daily from there to the Merchants' School in Sarajevo. He did not make a good impression with Jovo's wife and her mother, who thought he sat about reading too much, and ought to be more helpful around the house or in assisting Jovo with his business.

Gavro must have been unsettled in his first year away from home, as he cited this, to the psychiatrist Pappenheim, as the year when he was sleep-walking around the room, before being woken up. He said it only happened during this one year, a sign, surely, of some emotional disturbance.

It also quickly became apparent that Gavro was not destined to pursue a career in business. His new friends at school and in Sarajevo were becoming politicized and socially aware under the hated Austrian regime. They disapproved of bourgeois, capitalist pursuits and being at a Merchants' School was something of an embarrassment. This apparently caused tensions with his brother Jovo, because of course it was Jovo's money that was paying for Gavro's schooling, and Jovo's way of life was now being criticized by implication.

The focus of the students' detestation was the Carsija, the business district of Sarajevo. Gavro would later say if he could force the whole Carsija into a box of matches he would set it alight.

After three years he asked to switch to the classical high school in Tuzla and his brother relented, as this too offered opportunites for a professional future in the law or medicine. Jovo even hired a scholar to help Gravo through the entrance exams. He entered the school, it was said, with a copy of Caesar under his arm. Tuzla was a seedbed for many of the radical students, though Gavro was initially too shy or insecure to participate and give his opinions in the political debates. He was said to lack self-confidence, did not like being called Gavrica – little Gavro – and wanted to be thought of in more heroic terms.

After a while, it appears, Gavro learned to shield his insecurities behind a veneer of cynicism, becoming more vocal and, as a peer said, radiating energy and determination. He could be stubborn, if not pigheaded, and quick-witted, with jokes and retorts. In one discussion about youth leaders a student said of one of them that he was a brave man and Gavro immediately said, we are all brave men too.

He preferred the company of older, more mature boys and though he did not drink or smoke as some did, he liked to play billiards and often got into arguments over the play, sometimes lashing out with a cue in a fit of temper, before calming down and apologizing. Among the students in Tuzla, albeit nearly three years Gavro's junior, was Vaso Cubrilovic, who described Gavro to Vladimir Dedijer as a 'stuha', a restless spirit. Billiards was played in some cafés which were supposed to be out of bounds to the students, so Gavro was already bucking the system. He was also showing contempt for the Church, eating a meat dish during a fast and getting into trouble with his religious teachers. He was nearly expelled for missing classes and complained he was mistreated by his professors. He transferred back to the high school in Sarajevo where he soon became involved in the 'first lines' of the students in their nationalist demonstrations against the Habsburgs.

Gavro told Pappenheim he had been an excellent student up until the 5th grade, probably around 1911, when he fell in love and began to have ideals. He had known the girl in class but it was an idealized love as they never kissed and though the love did not vanish he never wrote to her. This must have been another girl, not Vukosava, the sister of Nedjo Cabrinovic, to whom he did write letters. He refused to discuss his romantic affairs further with Pappenheim.

He cited 1911, the year he turned 17, as a 'critical' point in his young life. He began reading anarchist, socialist and nationalist pamphlets and 'belles lettres', such as Alexander Dumas and Walter Scott, as well as 'the weeklies', with their detective stories, such as Sherlock Holmes and Nick Carter. A fellow student would say, 'Gavrilo always claimed that no one knew literature better than he and that he was the best among us in that field.' Gavro bought the books himself. He was broke, often starving, throughout his whole life, but he could always find money for books.

Gavro himself said to Pappenheim he was always alone, in the library reading, talking to no one, not much with other schoolboys. I wonder if, at the time of the prison interviews, at this desperate final stage of his life, when he really was alone and facing – if not yearning for – death, Gavro romanticized and exaggerated his earlier social isolation, as it seems that he was well known to many other students, albeit that they would think of him as quiet and reserved.

There was some cachet among them, as Dedijer pointed out, not just in being well-read, but in writing eloquent prose and poetry too. Gavro wrote some poetry for himself but apparently lacked confidence in its worth. In 1911 he wrote a long entry in a tourist visitors' book at a lodge in the mountains outside Hadzici. It is the most substantial piece of writing he left and was dated 25 June 1911, three years and three days before the assassination. It was signed, 'Gavrilo Princip, Fifth Grade, The Sarajevo High School'.

In many ways it is a lush description of a vivid day in a young man's life; an idyllic walk in the hills bringing with it a rush of senses; plus there is a hint, a foreshadowing of the darkness to come. Perhaps it is a little gaudy and repetitive in its adolescent descriptions and awkward attempts at poetic turns of phrase:

Gone are the days of annoyance and boredom behind the dirty scribbled desks – holidays are here. After three days of celebration at home, we decided to enliven these hot and boring days – and travel somewhere – let us go to the Bjelasnica Mountain and beyond; no sooner said than done. We left Hadzici at sunset when the western sun was blazing in purple splendour, when the numberless rays of the blood-red sun filled the whole sky and when the whole of nature was preparing to sleep through the beautiful, dreamy summer evening in the magic peace – that beloved, ideal night of the poet. Walking briskly, we reached the foot of the Bjelasnica Mountain, boasting of our speed and wiping large beads of sweat from our brows. After a short rest and a bite at the edge of the forest, we started to climb …

Without a word we progressed hesitantly through the forest, entranced by the magic, deep silence, listening to the whisperings of the sweet-smelling flowers and motionless trees. Following our noses, we struggled upward through the thick forest; we looked at each other despairingly when we were surrounded by hellish darkness, which seemed like the laughter of ugly monsters. A light, faint shudder went through our weary limbs, and we continued to march upward in silence, lumbering over fallen trunks and scattered branches. Heavens, how many times the thought went through my mind that I would be hurled into some bottomless precipice.

We could go no further. We ate our frugal supper. We built a fire – the best sight I ever saw. No poet ever described it well enough. Oh, if you could have seen what beautiful and ever-changing scenes were made by the lively red fire and black … hellish darkness, the whispering of the tall, black fir trees, and this hideous Night, the protector of hell and its sons; it seemed to me like the whisperings of bedeviled giants and nymphs, as if we were hearing the song of the four sirens and the sad Aeolian harp or divine Orpheus.

My companions fell asleep around the fire. I could not. I was sleepy, I dozed, but how could one sleep in this empire of brooding illusions. A little storm – the wild winds howled sadly through the silent giant trees. My friends woke up – with regret – my heartache, my sorrow, my life – my visions and my illusions. We started to sing a sad song, and my own heart whispered and trembled more strongly than my bedevilled monsters.

My companions burrowed into the leaves, and I sang, dreamed and prayed to my secret; oh, what sweet and painful moments in the beautiful time before the dawn, sweeter than sleep, more beautiful and ideal than any European poet has described it – this heavenly flash and blood-red-coral sun could only be described by a son of the glorious and imaginative east. Look at it and you will see it.

After a happy and pleasant halt of Mr Stenik's we continued our journey ...

Gavro had more opportunity to practise his lyricism in the letters he exchanged with Vukosava Cabrinovic, the sister of his friend and fellow conspirator Nedeljko Cabrinovic. Vukosava kept their correspondence with her for nearly 30 years after the assassination.

Vukosava married a doctor and became a dentist. At the start of the second world war they were living and working in a town in Croatia when a young man whom they had earlier treated came to warn them that he had overheard a group of Utasa fascists plotting to come to their home and kill them straightaway. They fled, leaving most of their possessions behind, and although the Princip letters were buried first they were never retrieved.

A surviving relative, Ranka Cabrinovic, told me that Vukosava could not have children because of a 'bad intervention' when she was young. I wondered whether this intervention had been a termination, but that was pure speculation. She later took on the raising of her sister's four children, after her sister's early death. Ranka said Vukosava was like a peacock, meaning, I think, that she was bright and vivacious and, as the photograph she gave me proves, very beautiful, so drew young men to her.

The writer Rebecca West met her when she was older, in the late 1930s, and said she 'possessed the usual foundation of Slav beauty, lovely head bones. Her skin was bright, her eyes answered for her before her lips had time, and she had one of those liquid and speeding voices that will never age ...'

They were 'very good friends', Vukosava and Gavro, according to Ranka, and that was all. But one contemporary of Gavro's gave evidence at the trial that he had been told by Gavro of the 'intimate correspondence' he had shared with Vukosava. The contemporary, Dobrosav Jevdjevic, said Gavro had told him that Vukosava was 'an upright girl.'

Dedijer reprinted just one of the letters that Gavro had written, which was apparently recreated by Vukosava from memory for an earlier writer. Dedijer thinks the letter was written on the eve of the assassination, but I think it is more likely it was written sooner, before Vukosava left Sarajevo to study and after Gavro had left Sarajevo, as he did in 1911. It certainly sounds as if he thinks he is writing with instruction for a young girl. The letter is a clear expression of romantic interest. What memory is it, for instance, of their departure that might cause the rose to blush? The letter also hints at her unhappiness, perhaps to do with domestic life with her tyrannical father and wayward brother Nedjo. Or perhaps her sadness is at the departure of Gavro, and she really did love him after all ...

> I feel a deep, sincere pain reading your letter, as if I were looking at the grief of a girl abandoned by everyone and forgotten. Do not suffer and do not let bloodshot eyes reveal your sorrow. Think and work. One needs a lot of strength in order to live, and action creates this. Physical labour also strengthens the character and firmness of will. Be individualistic, never altruistic. My life is also full of bitterness and gall, my wreath has more thorns than others. I go from nothingness to nothingness, from day to day, and in me there is less and less of myself. Do read, you must read; this is the best way to forget the tragic side of reality. How beautiful Wilde's The Happy Prince is ... Is the rose I gave you on our departure still alive? I know that it withered a long time ago, but perhaps the memory is enough to make it blush. I would like so much to be with you again in the first warm days of autumn somewhere under the leafy branches, and to hear you reciting to me:

> In the black knot of the pine tree
> The cricket chirps away
> With the stifling trochee and the strident black iambus
> It is noon. The sun's dithyramb is dispersed like the becalmed sea

Gavro was sick for two months during this period in Sarajevo. The nature of the sickness is undisclosed. He claimed to Pappenheim he had always had good health but there was evidence that he had tuber-culosis in his system before 1914 and he told a contemporary he had coughed blood – which could be a symptom of the disease. Ill health was a common thread among the young men. It can't be coincidence. They were poor and ate badly and probably did not generally take care of themselves too well. They lived with intensity, in the shadow of death, and this must have created its own debilitating strains.

Missing his studies, getting some low grades for his work, then par-ticipating in student demonstrations, led Gavro to be expelled from Sarajevo High School. He did not tell his family, not even his brother, and decided to slip away to Belgrade. He made the 300-kilometre journey on foot and said he kissed the soil when he crossed the border into Serbia. Because of his sudden, unexplained departure, his brother refused to help him when he wrote asking for money. He had no money to leave, he said, and no money to stay. He survived on credit and the kindness of friends, such as Nedjo who said he had often given Gavro money when he was starving.

Dedijer said some of the Bosnian students in Belgrade slept in dustbins or dog kennels or took shelter in monasteries where, with a letter of introduction from a sympathetic professor, they could get some food, while being assured of a theological debate.

A roommate of Gavro's described him, typically, spending his time reading. Times were hard and they occasionally had to sell books to buy bread, though Gavro would always keep back his favourites. They would go out for late night walks in the park to pass the time and Gavro would recite Serbian poetry.

In spite of all the interruptions to his studies, they were evidently still important to him. The Serbian Minister for Education at the time of the assassination, Ljuba Jovanovic, would later describe how Gavro had earlier visited his department two or three times to ask the Minister directly for permission to sit his exams:

He remains in my memory: slight, broadish in the shoulders, with a broad though somewhat pinched countenance. He spoke naturally and without nervousness. I advised and encouraged him – as I did many other youths who came to Belgrade from Austria-Hungary almost like emigrants – to pursue his studies and finish his schooling, because the better his equipment the greater use would he be to the nation, and in general the better he would serve his own ideals.

I allowed him to sit for his examination on both occasions … the last time I saw him we parted in quite an amusing way. He came to see whether my permission for his examination was ready, and whether it had been sent to the Lycee. It often happened that young strangers like him came and pestered me about details of this kind, and I was annoyed and flew out at him and began to give him a piece of my mind.

The wretched Princip first looked at me in amazement and then immediately turned hastily to the door, stammering, 'I am sorry. I did not know …' and made for the exit. I turned and made to reassure him in more kindly fashion, but he was in a hurry to be off as soon as possible. Who could then have foreseen what this same agitated young student would do …?

Perhaps resuming his studies enabled Gavro to make peace with his brother so that some money now appeared. He was soon back in the Green Wreath cafés again, playing billiards. He failed his exams and sent a postcard to a friend: I flunked, Gavro.

With the general mobilization for the Balkan war, Gavro and his friends wanted to join the Komite, the Serbian regular army of volunteers, led by Major Vojin Tankosic. Gavro went directly to his headquarters but was rejected because he was too small. He went with friends to try again, at the border town of Prokulpje where Tankosic was basing his units. Gavro wrote to a friend in Sarajevo, a leading young Bosnian. 'Look up on the map where Prokulpje is. We are now here and where we shall go further I do not know. ("For freedom and fatherland"). Regards from yours Gavro.'

A student who had travelled from Belgrade with Gavro added a note of his own: 'If we do not see each other, please accept this as our last greetings. Where we go I do not know, and if we survive we shall know where we have been. If you are pious, pray to God for us, but if you are not, ask the young ladies to pray for us.'

Gavro's war was ended before it began. He was seen by Major Tankosic and with a wave of his hand, instantly dismissed. 'You are too small and too weak.' At his trial Gavro would say he was rejected because he had been ill. He returned to Belgrade and then to Hadzici.

He went back to Belgrade again and moved between the two places, back and forth, over the next year or so, studying and spending time at his brother's home.

In 1912, before leaving Sarajevo, Gavro had visited the cemetery of St Mark's, where the young students had found and marked and tended the grave of a fallen martyr. Gavro visited that grave many times, but just before he had left for Belgrade he swore an oath to avenge the martyr. His name was Bogdan Zerajic and his self-sacrifice was the inspiration for the assassination.

3

The Legends of Kosovo

Unless he was being deliberately provocative, or someone in his own government was purposely trying to set him up, and both are possible, the Heir Apparent was demonstrating extraordinary ignorance when he chose 28 June 1914 as the very day to parade his imperial presence on the streets of Sarajevo.

He ought to have known what an inflammatory act that would be. Making such a visit was to invite trouble at any time, but all the more so on that particular day; someone should have told him that those awkward, rebellious young Serb students looked to history for their inspiration. The Serbian story was, in part at least, one of proud and dogged resistance to imperial oppression. Many of the young men revered their martyrs and were romantically absorbed in the folklore and legends of the past, in which the date of 28 June featured prominently.

In origin, this was St Vitus Day, known to the Serbs as Vidovdan, a traditional saint's day observed by straightforward religious rituals and feasts. Vidd was a pagan deity before he was a faith-based saint, of Finnish-Ugric beginnings. But in time, in Serbia, the name took on a much more potent significance.

Because of its strategic position, located on the boundary between east and west, at the so-called crossroads of Europe with a commanding charge of trade routes in either direction, the Balkans region was constantly being encroached upon from beyond and bothered by its neighbours. Internal strife was commonplace too, of course, perhaps unsurprisingly given the insecurity of its position.

Indeed it was inner conflict that had failed the Serbians at their greatest moment, six centuries earlier in the mid-1300s, when a sudden expansion of its own territories had promised to establish for Serbia an empire of its own. Then the ruler had died and, with no one leader emerging in his place, the fledgling empire had immediately cracked and descended into civil war.

For a brief moment, the Serbians had been ready to advance towards Constantinople. Now the Turkish-Ottoman empire, choosing its moment with care, pushed forward winning a significant battle beside the river Marica in what is now Bulgaria. By 1389 the Serbian armies, led by Prince Lazar, were ready to make a last attempt to repel the Turkish forces of Sultan Murad and this last, decisive battle took place on 28 June at Kosovo Polje – the field of blackbirds – in the south of the region, in what is now Kosovo.

The battle became enshrined and handed down in the proud tradition of Serbian epic poems, variously called folk poetry or heroic poetry and performed sometimes in song-form as ballads or sometimes spoken as oral narratives. The central story of this cycle of poems told how Prince Lazar held a feast on the eve of the fight at which he toasted the courage of all his commanders, except Milos Obilic who he said would act like Judas and betray him in the next day's battle and go to join Sultan Murad. At this Obilic bowed before the prince and said (according to the poem, in translation):

> Let me die if I should lie to you!
> I have never been unfaithful to my Tsar –
> Never have I been and never shall I be –
> And I am sworn to die for you at Kosovo
> For you and for the Christian faith.

Obilic then described what he planned to do:

> And when on Vitus-day tomorrow morning
> We make our dawn attack upon the Blackbirds' Field
> We'll see right there at bloody Kosovo
> Who is loyal to you and who is not!
> I swear to you in God Almighty's Name
> That I shall go down at dawn to Kosovo
> And slaughter like a pig the Turkish Sultan
> Put my foot upon his throat.

Turkish historical accounts suggested that Obilic feigned death on the battlefield and then stabbed the Sultan as he passed. But in Serbian folklore he crept into the Sultan's tent, before the battle, and ripped the Sultan's chest open with his dagger before being set upon and killed – a heroic act of martyrdom and self-sacrifice, as well as devotional loyalty to the Serbian Prince Lazar.

> While Milos, Lady, lost his noble life
> Fighting near the river Sitnitsa
> Where many dying Turks lie all around.
> But Milos killed the Turkish Sultan, Murad,
> And slaughtered many Turkish soldiers with him.
> May God Almighty Bless the one who bore him!
> He leaves immortal fame to all the Serbs
> To be forever told in song and story
> As long as Kosovo and human kind endure.

There was not much else to celebrate, since the battle ended in humiliating defeat that marked the end of Serbian independence and the beginning of five centuries of subjugation to Turkish rule. No wonder the myth-making extended to the anticipation that avengers of Kosovo would awaken or come forward.

In fact, as others have pointed out, the poems or songs were not simply created in spite of the defeat but seemed to celebrate it and speak of the sense of tragedy that was ingrained in the Serbian psyche. In the years to come the rendering of the songs became both a reminder of the old wounds and a call to arms, a weapon of the rebellion. They were too, of course, bound to arouse chauvinistic feelings of deep patriotism in the Serb people who heard them.

There were other martyrs from the same Kosovo sequence, commemorated in their own verses, such as Stefan Music, who fought and killed three pashas, but when he met the fourth that warrior smote him, and there he died beside his servant Vaistana.

Then there was the Prince himself, Lazar, who came to embody the idea of noble defeat, having made his choice, before the battles, to sacrifice an earthly kingdom for a heavenly kingdom, and so lead his men to sure defeat for the greater valour of eternity:

'O, Dearest God, what shall I do, and how?
Shall I choose the earth? Shall I choose
The skies? And if I choose the kingdom,
If I choose an earthly kingdom now,
Earthly kingdoms are such passing things –
A heavenly kingdom, raging in the dark, endures eternally.'
And Lazar chose heaven not the earth.

Prince Lazar was killed and beheaded on the battlefield so he too was immortalized in the ballad, The Miracle of Lazar's Head:

When they cut off Lazar's head upon the Blackbirds' Field
Not a single Serb was there to see it
But it happened that a Turkish boy saw,
A slave, the son of one who had been made
Herself a slave, a Serbian mother
Thus the boy spoke having seen it all:
'O have pity, brothers; O have pity, Turks.
Here before us lies a sovereign's noble head!
In God's name it would be a sin
If it were pecked at by the eagles and the crows
Or trampled on by horses and by heroes.'
He took the head of holy Lazar then
And covered it and put it in a sack
And carried it until he found a spring
And put the head into the waters there
For forty years the head lay in that spring.

The poems were devised in their original Serbo-Croat in ten-syllable lines, which created a distinctive rhythm that translators sometimes struggled to recreate.

They were first collected and written down in the early nineteenth century by an academic and fighter, Vuk Karadzic, who is described as travelling around the region 'crippled by a mysterious withered leg that required the use of both a wooden attachment and a crutch'. The four-volume collection *Serbian Folk Poems* was published in 1862, ironically, in the Austrian capital, Vienna.

Karadzic recorded the songs from the men who performed them, known as guslars as they accompanied their singing with the playing of the gusle, a one- or two-stringed instrument, the strings made of entwined horsehair, loosely resembling a banjo but played with a bow, so that the harsh sound of the instrument fused with and was intended to punctuate or enhance the story being sung.

In his novel, *The Bridge on the Drina*, Ivo Andric created an evocative portrait of a Montenegrin guslar performing to a group of Serb labourers, tired after a long day's work:

Suddenly, after he had more or less attuned his voice to the gusle, the Montenegrin threw his head back proudly and violently so that his Adam's apple stood out in his scrawny neck and his sharp profile was outlined in the firelight, and sang in a strangled and constrained voice: A-a-a-a-a-a-a- and then all at once in a clear and ringing tone:

> The Serbian Tsar Stefan
> Drank wine in fertile Prizren,
> By him sat the old patriarchs,
> Four of them....

The peasants pressed closer and closer around the singer but without making the slightest noise; their very breathing could be heard. They half closed their eyes, carried away with wonder ... The Montenegrin developed his melody more and more rapidly, even more beautiful and bolder, while the wet and sleepless workmen, carried away and insensible to all else, followed the tale as if it were their own more beautiful and more glorious destiny!

The legend of Kosovo infected the religious symbolism of Vidovdan too, so that the Christian calendars would have that date ringed in red and the priests would tell the peasants that on 28 June the rivers would run red, coloured with the blood of the fallen on the field of the blackbirds.

In 1914 one young man was standing in a court of inquiry, explaining how he felt when he heard what day the Archduke had chosen: '... this fact fired me with zeal to carry out the attempt. Our folklore tradition tells how the hero Milos Obilic was accused before Vidovdan that he was a traitor, and how he answered: "On Vidovdan we shall see who is and who is not a traitor." And Obilic became the first assassin who went into the enemy camp and murdered Sultan Murad.'

This was Nedeljko Cabrinovic, informally known as Nedjo, who was 19 years old when he threw a bomb at the Archduke's car in the hope of killing him – he missed – and then tried to commit suicide, failing also at that. When he was asked to identify himself on his arrest he said, 'I am a Serbian hero.' Both Nedjo and his father had been accused of being spies for the Austrians. Like Obilic, Nedjo was driven to show his loyalty and his readiness for self-sacrifice on 28 June.

His was a city family, a contrast with the rural or small-town backgrounds of many of the other plotters. Nedjo's father had progressed under Austrian rule, owning one of the first coffee-grinding machines in Sarajevo, which he operated from his family home on the main street, which had at this time been named for the Austrian emperor Franz Josef. He had roasted and sold coffee too and run the house like a social centre, always cooking for the family and their extended network of friends.

The father, Vaso, had been born in 1864 so that he had seen the end of Turkish rule and the coming of the Austrians. There had been uprisings and a gradual erosion of the Ottomans' authority in Serbia during the 1800s, so that Serbia was by now self-governing. Neighbouring Bosnia, however, was still under Turkish control and Sarajevo an important outpost of the declining Ottoman empire.

Over the centuries a substantial part of the community had converted to Islam and created their own Bosnian Muslim elite which exploited and taxed the Serb peasantry, arousing an endless cycle of rebellion and dissent. The final peasant uprising began in 1875 and gradually spread beyond Bosnia & Hercegovina to involve Serbian and Russian forces also aligned against Turkey.

It was only with the Congress of Berlin in 1878 that the imperial powers of Europe attempted to impose some stability and created the Treaty which gave control of Bosnia & Hercegovina to the Habsburgs, the ruling dynasty of the Austro-Hungarian empire. It was an uneasy solution and fermented yet further discontent among the Serbs, who felt betrayed at losing territory that by rights, they believed, belonged to them; there was also dismay among Bosnia's sizeable Catholic community and of course among the Muslims who had lost their ruling power in Bosnia.

Sarajevo itself had been shaped by Ottoman rule, a city of a hundred mosques, it was said, though it had also historically enjoyed a healthy cultural mix with different quarters for Muslims, Jews and Christians both Catholic and Orthodox. More importantly it had developed an inherent resistance to authority which had given it the atmosphere of a free city in which, according to Rebecca West, 'The Slavs lived as they liked'. Mutinous and insubordinate, she called Sarajevo.

In her epic 1930–40s study of the Balkans, *Black Lamb and Grey Falcon*, West created a portrait of Sarajevo that is still partly true today. I missed the air of luxury she found in the rich colours of the predominantly Turkish style of dress; the reds, golds, blues and greens that contributed to what West described as the 'tranquil sensuality' and romance of Sarajevo – qualities we struggle to associate with our modern view of Islam as monochrome and puritan. But here were the same mosques, the same latticed windows and walled gardens and open-fronted shops in the bazaar that, for West, gave the city its air of pleasure. The Austrians could no more contain the life of the city than the Turks had. They faced house-to-house fighting when they marched into Sarajevo in the summer of 1878.

A military bulletin described how, 'from every house, from every window, from every door, our troops were fired upon, in many instances by women ... indescribable scenes of fanaticism are reported ... our losses unfortunately are considerable.' The Austrians eventually established their authority there with a range of increasingly oppressive measures. They caused fury in Belgrade in 1908 when they formally 'annexed' Bosnia & Hercegovina to the Habsburg empire. There was dismay, among all Serbs, in 1911, when their own government was forced by political expediency into a humiliating acceptance of the annexation.

At least the Austrians, for some, had brought a new mood of opportunity and prosperity to Sarajevo. Nedjo's father had used the proceeds of the coffee business to open a kafana – café – nearby which seemed like a natural extension of the social life of the house. He dressed to show off his success and enjoyed wearing fancy suits, selected from the ever-expanding collection in his wardrobe. He was a big man who cut an imposing and sometimes severe figure and appears to have been a little terrifying, sometimes violent towards his family.

He fathered ten children but three died at birth or in infancy, so that Nedjo was the oldest among seven surviving children, including his beautiful next born sister Vukosava and his youngest brother Dusan.

In the 1930s Vukosava told Rebecca West about her stern Bosnian father; how there had never been a gentle word in the house and how he would refuse his children anything they ever asked for, as a duty, for fear they would become spoilt and self-indulgent. He sounded small-minded and vindictive too, Vukosava describing how he loved to be photographed when things were going well, surrounded by his children, putting the photographs on display at home. But then when he quarrelled with any of the children he would go around the house cutting their pictures out of the groups.

'But he would never destroy them; perhaps he was too much of a peasant, with primitive ideas of magic, and to burn the images of his children or to throw them into a wastepaper basket would have seemed too much like killing them. He kept them in a box, and then when he took us back in favour he would paste them back into the group, so that some of our photographs presented a most extraordinary appearance.'

Later, when she was grown and married, Vukosava's husband was horrified to be told by her father that he should box Vukosava's ears because she was late meeting him for lunch at a café. 'It was extraordinary how it had never occurred to him that family life might be conducted agreeably.'

4

June 1914 – the Angry Anarchist

It was to this dysfunctional household that Nedjo returned in the early days of June, when he too arrived back in Sarajevo along with Gavro and their third fellow conspirator, Trifko Grabez, after the guns and bombs had been smuggled out of Belgrade.

Nedjo had been away from Sarajevo for most of the last 12 months and called in briefly to visit his grandmother before walking home to 69 Franz Josef Street, where his father decided he must immediately register his son's return with the police. He went straight to the station and on that part of the form asking for recent addresses, Nedjo's father wrote, a little testily perhaps, 'all around the world'.

In the next three weeks Nedjo would meet several times with Gavro as they walked through the town. But the pair had fallen out during the smuggling of the weapons and Nedjo was now firmly 'outside the loop', even though he had been one of the initial instigators of the plot, and Gavro would tell him very little about what was going on, especially in relation to the weapons. Nedjo had no idea if the weapons had even arrived, or if they had, where they were.

Both Gavro and Trifko Grabez told their friend and fellow conspirator Danilo Ilic that they thought Nedjo was a very naive young man and not fit for an assassination. Gavro later said to Pappenheim that Nedjo had first wanted to be the lone assassin, as Pappenheim recorded in his notes: 'but he was a typesetter, not of sufficient intelligence. Also not sufficiently nationalistic because previously anarchist.' This suggests some academic snobbery on the part of Gavro – he was the high-minded nationalist student, and Nedjo the simple anarchist printer. A reversal, almost, of the class snobbery it would be suggested that Gavro had experienced as a peasant boy mixing with the urban sophisticates in Nedjo's family.

Nedjo was equally unaware that other conspirators were being brought in and eventually concluded there would be no assassination and carried on believing this almost up to the last minute. He took a job at a local print works and travelled around Sarajevo and beyond, several times visiting the spa town of Ilidza which was being prepared for the arrival of the Archduke, who was due to stay there. During his visit to the spa, with his mother, just over a week before the assassination, he was told the baths were closed because of the Archduke's imminent arrival.

Despite being kept in the dark, and knowing next to nothing of the details of the conspiracy, Nedjo continued to talk too much. Loose talk. He told various people at home about his recent travels, describing to the family servant Marija Talanga how he had spent seven days journeying with two friends from Belgrade to Sarajevo. He also spoke in similar terms to his sister and to his friend Tomo Vucinovic. Gavro would have been furious, had he known.

Whenever he met with Gavro and tried to talk about the assassination, Gavro would tell him to shut up. He met with Ilic too and they talked about the assassination, but Nedjo was not told the weapons had arrived nor that there was now a second trio of assassins. He still believed there would be no assassination right up until the Friday before, when he saw Gavro who finally disclosed the plot to him.

They agreed to meet the following day, Saturday, 27 June and Gavro told Nedjo to come and see him at the offices of Ilic's journal, *Zvono*. When Nedjo went there the place was empty; he spent some time looking around for Gavro, not finding him at the Serbian Reading Room or elsewhere. Nedjo went to his work at the printing plant and Gavro called there and said they would meet that evening at the social hall in the town.

Ilic and Gavro must have planned together where everyone would stand, as Gavro took Nedjo on to Appel Quay, by the Teachers' School, and pointed out where he wanted him to stand, outside the Austro-Hungarian Bank, putting him second in line for the approaching imperial procession, with the others after him. Nedjo did not know who the others were, and still believed Ilic would be one of the assassins.

Gavro told Nedjo to meet him the next morning, Sunday, 28 June, the morning of the planned assassination, at 8am in the pastry shop,

Vlajnic's on Cumurija Street, just a hundred yards or so from Appel Quay. Only then would he be given a bomb, but not a pistol. Ilic said he never intended to give him any weapons at all, after hearing from both Gavro and Grabez that Nedjo was a naive fellow and not fit to participate in an assassination.

Some of Nedjo's friends were called to give evidence at the trial and gave illuminating descriptions of Nedjo's character and the time they spent with him in the days before the assassination. Here was Milos Pura, a 19-year-old tailor, who had known Nedjo since elementary school. They had been social democrats together in the same organization until Nedjo was expelled and boycotted. After his boycott, Pura and other 'comrades' were not even allowed to talk to Nedjo in public. If they met, Pura would simply say 'hello' and move on, but then Nedjo had been expelled from Sarajevo altogether and they had not seen each other at all for many months. He was allowed back into the organization on his return, and had again been expelled, just a month before the assassination, but was at least no longer being boycotted.

In these last days in Sarajevo, Pura and Nedjo would meet regularly, usually on the quay where they would stand and chat. The conversations were rarely about politics. Normally they would both be with girls so it would be how are you?, fine. Nedjo told them he was working in the printing plant and earning good money so life was 'easy'. They had fun when they got together and would sing.

According to Nedjo himself, whenever he met Pura and his friends they would beg him to sing them some songs and they would want to go elsewhere as you were not allowed to sing in the city. One day they had gone out to Jekovac, by the old fort on the outskirts of the city, up in the hills, where Nedjo had talked and sung.

No doubt they were Serb songs, expressions of patriotism towards the Serb people. Because he had travelled so widely by comparison with many of the other young men, Nedjo would tell them about Serbia and the freedom you could find there and how beautiful that was; and the army, brave and ready, the soldiers always talking about an attack on Bosnia, which of course, in Serbia, they regarded as their land. It did not properly belong to Austria.

Jovo Karic was only 17 and always being told off by Nedjo for being too immature. Karic knew all about Nedjo's disagreements and expulsions and had been working in the printing plant a month earlier when Nedjo called there looking for work, after his journey from Belgrade. He had boasted about the high wages he had been earning in Belgrade – 26 dinars! – and how cheap and free the life was there. In Belgrade you were not prevented from singing.

It was Karic's misfortune to be working for the socialist journal that had attacked Nedjo in print when he was last in Sarajevo, accusing him of being a spy or agent for the Austrians. The journal, *Glas Sloboda*, had held a fund-raising party in a supporter's garden on the Sunday before the assassination. Nedjo, bold as ever, had turned up there and got into an argument with Karic, asking how he could work for such a journal. They met again with their girls on Appel Quay on Friday, 26 June. Nedjo asked Karic why he was angry and Karic said he wasn't angry. Perhaps Nedjo was the angry one. He said he'd had a row with his father and was leaving town and asked to borrow a crown, which he repaid the following evening after receiving his wages.

The young men would gather on Appel Quay even when it was raining, as it was one Sunday two or three weeks before the assassination when 19-year-old Kosta Kostic was strolling there and met Nedjo for the first time in a year. They too had known each other since elementary school. How are you! Where have you been!. Nedjo had been in Serbia and all over, he explained, and Kostic wanted to hear all about it, but Nedjo had his dog with him, who was running here, there and everywhere nipping at people's trousers. Sorry, I'm going to take the dog home. Nedjo had to go, but they met on several other occasions, usually with their mutual friends Jovo Karic, Milos Pura and Tomo Vucinovic, all of them with their girls, and Nedjo too, high spirited and joking, leading them like a conductor as they sang.

When I met her in Sarajevo in the autumn of 2006, Nedjo's niece, Ranka Cabrinovic, the daughter of his youngest brother Dusan, expressed her disapproval of the idea that her uncle had been a 'charmer of ladies'. That wasn't him at all, she said, he was a very serious person.

This must have been how Ranka wanted to think of him because, in truth, according to the accounts of his contemporaries, Nedjo was obviously highly politicized but also passionate, irreverent and fun. He used to joke in the printing plant about the Serb party in the

Sabor having a party journal called *Truth*. The irony of it! He was
a character and no wonder then that women liked him, his appeal
perhaps enhanced by the sadness that sometimes seems to have envel-
oped him, in his difficulties with his family, especially his father.

Nedjo had been pleasantly surprised at the open welcome he had
received from his family, even his father, on his return to Sarajevo. He
had not expected that and felt uncomfortable, a little guilty maybe, at
being embraced by them in that way. After a while he began to feel at
ease in his family home and felt good about it. This must have been
the first time in a long while, years even, that he had been getting on
with his parents. He didn't even mind that Gavro kept brushing him
away with a wave of his hand: Shut up!

It was bound not to last and eventually his father began to complain
about Nedjo staying out in the evenings until nine or ten o'clock.
The quarrels became more and more regular and were soon occurring
daily. Nedjo was being scolded by his quick-tempered father and was
ready to leave. He even considered suicide so must have begun to feel
quite desperate about it.

The 'servile loyalty' with which, in Nedjo's words, Bosnia was getting ready to greet the Heir Apparent only made everything worse.
He got dressed up on Thursday, 25 June, the day of the arrival of the
imperial party, to make one last visit to the spa town of Ilidza, where
the royal couple would stay. He hoped to get a glimpse of the man
whom he wished to blow up.

That morning's edition of the pro-Catholic, pro-Austrian newspaper, *Hrvatski Dnevnik* (Croatian Daily) reported that 'a very, very
high official' (the Governor Oskar Potiorek) had been in Ilidza the
day before and seen all the flags that were flying there in readiness.
He had seen the Austrian and Hungarian flags and also the Kallayevist
flag, which was the name, apparently, for the red-yellow colours of
the Sabor government. But then the very, very high official had seen
the Croatian and Serbian flags too. 'Down with them!' the governor
had cried out in his native German, 'I know no Croats and no Serbs; I
know only Bosnians, Austrians and Hungarians! Down with them!'

So by the time Nedjo arrived the Serbian and Croatian flags had
been removed and Nedjo was not the only one who felt the grievous
insult. Vaso too cited this at the trial as one reason for his participation
in the assassination. According to one source, Nedjo saw a detective

watching him in Ilidza and feared he would be stopped or arrested so he did not stay long and went home without seeing the royals. He was right, he had been spotted and the detective recognized him but, when he phoned through his report it was dismissed by the detective's superior, who perhaps associated the name of Cabrinovic with Nedjo's seemingly loyal father.

According to Nedjo's niece Ranka, the father was no great Austrian loyalist either, but knew which side was buttering his bread and was prepared to behave accordingly. He had a lot to lose, said Ranka – his family, his business – and he was wise enough to keep quiet, not so stupid as to be an outspoken opponent. He was always trying to tell Nedjo to keep quiet too – these young revolutionary hot-heads were explosive. That evening, back in Sarajevo, the same argument about the flags was played out inside the Cabrinovic home. For Nedjo this must have been a further blurring of the boundaries between the personal and the political as he got ready to carry out the assassination.

The Lord Mayor of Sarajevo had issued a proclamation that everyone in the city should decorate their homes. Vaso Cabrinovic, Nedjo's father, wanted to fly the Austrian and the Serbian flags, side by side, but he could not find the flagpoles. Both Nedjo's parents got involved in the search, scouring the entire house and still unable to find the poles. Nedjo knew where they were all along, but had no wish to see the Austrian flag flying outside his house so kept quiet until his father began to curse his mother for not finding the poles. Perhaps Nedjo feared his father would become violent. He told himself that raising the Austrian flag would at least make him seem less suspicious. Nedjo then disclosed to his father that the flagpoles were in the closet. At last, the flags were flown.

Still Nedjo could not resist complaining to his father for hoisting the imperial as well as the Serbian flag. His father told him that he lived under the emperor and esteemed him and was leading a better life because of him. If the house did not suit Nedjo, his father told him, he should look for a better one.

This must have been played out at some volume as the servants heard at least some of it, Marija Talanga later reporting that Nedjo had shouted at his father, 'Franz Ferdinand will not be the emperor, you will see! Next year King Petar [of Serbia] will reign here!' Finally,

Nedjo went out, as he explained, to escape his father's strength and his shouting.

That weekend, Nedjo pared down his life in anticipation of his death on Sunday. He gave away the few things he owned, giving his mother his pocket-knife and watch, which she accepted, even though she was angry with him for the incident with the flagpoles. He gave his grandmother twenty crowns out of his last wage packet from the printing plant: 'I gave her money because I love her and I had promised her I would help her. On her side she always gave me money when I had none.' She said five forints would be enough for her, but as one forint was worth two crowns he gave her double her request.

He spent a few crowns on the 1914 equivalent of Inter-flora, buying a bouquet of flowers for delivery to a young woman, Jela Uljarevic, who must have been close to his heart, although it was not possible to find any further information about her. Perhaps she had been the girl, or one of the girls, who promenaded with him on Appel Quay.

He changed a further five forints and gave five of his last ten crowns to his sister Jovanka and told her he was going away on a trip and they would never see each other again. She left him and Nedjo stood alone, crying. He must have been feeling exceptionally sentimental as he said he felt sorry for his family, all of them, even his father.

When he spoke of this at the trial the prosecutor said, 'I could show you a letter from your father in which he complains about you.' Nedjo replied, 'I have not been satisfied with him either and the raising he gave me brought me to this. But again I feel sorry for him.'

The family tensions seem also to have strengthened Nedjo's resolve. He wrote to a friend, 'Tomorrow is Vidovdan and we shall discover who is faithful and who is unfaithful. Do you remember the great oath of Milos Obilic?' Nedjo obviously did remember the oath, as he was paraphrasing it in his note: We'll see right there at bloody Kosovo, Who is loyal to you and who is not!

So far as I can establish, when Nedjo left the family home the next morning on his way to the assassination it was the last time he would ever see them. The defendants were kept in isolation in prison before their trial and were not allowed visitors. There was no open gallery for family or other interested parties at the trial. There were only a few specially invited spectators. After the trial, and until his death, Nedeljko Cabrinovic only had two visitors that I am aware of and they were not members of his family. Anyway, his family had their own problems, arising from his actions, in the aftermath.

As Nedjo left for the rendezvous of conspirators at the pastry shop that morning, his dog followed him from the house for some distance until Nedjo saw him. The dog would not go back on his own, so Nedjo had to retrace his steps to his home on Franz Josef Street, one last time, and leave the dog behind a firmly closed door.

5

Infested Suits

Meeting Nedjo's niece Ranka, in the autumn of 2006, it seemed like she must be one of the last Serbs left in Sarajevo. She had evidently survived through the years, including the siege, by living quietly and discreetly and not broadcasting her notorious Serbian surname. No doubt it helped that her Muslim neighbours had little interest in Serb history and cared less about the assassination itself.

Ranka was keen to emphasize the status her family had enjoyed at that time and its social superiority to others, such as Gavrilo Princip, Nedjo's best friend who had been born and brought up in the backwoods of Bosnia and had seemed to Nedjo's family like a poor farm boy, according to Ranka. Gavro's infatuation with the beautiful Vukosava, in Ranka's eyes, was doomed to failure as she was in a different class to him and, according to Ranka, liked Gavro only as a friend and nothing more.

Nedjo Cabrinovic had lived some of the time as a child with relatives in Trebinje, in southern Bosnia, where he had also attended the Merchants' School. Perhaps this had been some kind of exchange, as Nedjo's father had also taken care of the relatives' children and paid for their schooling in Sarajevo.

In 1907, when he was still only 12 and at school in Trebinje, Nedjo had received a letter from his sister Vukosava, in which she complained that their father was 'mistreating' the children and his own wife at home. Nedjo wrote to his mother saying he had wept on reading Vukosava's letter: 'Let him be ashamed of what he did … let his bones be disturbed in his grave … my dear mother do not be angry and do not cry … if I were there I would sue him in the law court at once … I want to come there at once…'.

As it was, he seems to have remained in Trebinje, where he failed his end of year exams after an unspecified illness. He said the curriculum there was different from his earlier schooling in Sarajevo. Nedjo's father summoned him back to Sarajevo, refusing to pay further for his schooling. As Nedjo put it, his father was angry and mistreated him so he ran away from home for a while and was all on his own, trying to learn a trade. He returned home but his relationship with his father worsened.

He tried being a locksmith but ran home when a bullying journeyman put a piece of red-hot metal on his neck. His father then arranged a job as a sheet metal worker before, at the age of 14, Nedjo began an apprenticeship at a printing plant, the Serbian Press in Sarajevo. He stayed there for two years and learned typesetting but he always resented being forced to leave school and was alienated from his father.

Nedjo became interested in politics and at just 14 was elected to become founding president of the newly formed Printers' Apprentice Guild. He began reading about socialism and revolution and was caught by his father reading a Russian revolutionary novel at night. His father hit him and removed the light bulb. Nedjo began advising his friends on the literature they ought be reading, including the Communist Manifesto, and made speeches to the apprentices extolling the virtues of worker solidarity.

By all accounts, Nedjo could be hot-headed and impulsive, a young firebrand by the sound of it. He was slapped, for some unexplained reason, by an older colleague at the printers and walked out on the job, provoking his father to eject him from the family home. He went and stayed for a month in Zagreb, with a friend of his father's, and then returned home, only to land himself in more trouble with his father when he refused to apologize to a housemaid he had argued with; his father went to the police and had him jailed for three days.

After his release he found a new printing plant to employ him, and where he must have become involved in agitation as, after six months, a strike broke out and the police called at the family home to accuse him of threatening to burn down the printer's premises. He again left Sarajevo and this time travelled further afield seeking jobs at socialist printing presses, struggling for money at times, having to walk long distances because he couldn't afford to take transport, and selling his possessions to repay loans he had borrowed to pay for food and lodging.

He finally ended up in Belgrade and took a printing job with a group of anarchists. He said he argued with them at first, refuting their theories as best he could, as a socialist worker. 'One day I was no longer able to resist because I myself felt the same anarchist ideas as they.'

He was especially influenced by the anarchosyndicalists who believed in the labour movement and unions as a force for social change. Nedjo began attending lectures and debates every evening that started early and often went on to the small hours. He became ill and wanted to go home, so travelled back to Sarajevo where, on arrival, his mother discovered his collection of anarchist literature and tried to burn it all. He salvaged some and distributed what was left among his friends.

Nedjo was ill and did not work for two months in Sarajevo. He was only just 17 and perhaps his health was affected by the poverty and the consequent poor nutrition he had experienced on his travels; then too, there was his intense lifestyle, with its late night meetings, the obsessive reading and the agitating for change. Not to mention the emotional drain of the conflict with his father which had driven him away in the first place and, as he must have known, was always waiting for him back in Sarajevo.

During his illness he became involved with one of the numerous new radical Serb youth groups, broadly known as Mlada Bosna – Young Bosnians – springing up throughout the region. When he was well enough he returned to work, printing a political journal, until he quit to take part in a typographers' strike that began in the summer of 1912.

It was around this time that Nedjo first met Gavro, six months his senior, but also, perhaps like Nedjo, a sickly sort of character, rarely in the best of health. They took to reading together and made notes and underlinings in the books they shared. In *News from Nowhere* by William Morris, a book about revolution, Nedjo was said to have written the inscription: 'I have just finished reading this book at a time when I was both individually and socially in the darkest mood as compared with the optimism of this book.'

As Ranka Cabrinovic told me, Nedjo sometimes brought his new friend home to eat, and that must have been where Gavro Princip first saw and fell for Nedjo's sister, Vukosava, who was three or four years younger so was still a child, in her early teens at most, when they met.

She later told how he found her reading an Arabian Nights type novel which he took from her and replaced with some stories by Oscar Wilde and some Serbian literature. Vukosava described him as 'a reserved boy, sometimes witty, almost sarcastic with deep eyes, handsome teeth and a very high forehead'.

Perhaps Ranka is right when she says that Vukosava was too far up the social scale to be interested in Gavro. But it certainly seems that some tenderness and intimacy grew up between them, over the two years leading up to the assassination. They exchanged many letters, which were later lost, but were subsequently recreated, in part, by Vukosava.

After he quit work, Nedjo's father once more made him leave home and he lodged for a while with a strike leader, trying to influence the course of the strike from his own anarchist position, and working hard to prevent the strike being broken. Finally he was jailed for three days, accused of threatening to burn down some presses that were still working. When he refused to disclose the name and whereabouts of the strike leader he was punished by being banned from Sarajevo for five years, and exiled to Trebinje.

He was escorted out of town by a police officer, after being given a lecture by an Austrian official. 'I was sorry at that moment I had no weapon with me,' Nedjo told the trial in 1914, 'I was prepared to drive all six bullets into him. A personal motive drove me to vengeance after I was banished from Sarajevo. I was suffering because a foreigner, who came to my country, banished me from my native town.'

Perhaps, in Nedjo's mind, the Austrian authorities and his father were becoming entwined. It would be a simplistic explanation of course – the two oppressive faces of paternity, one political, one personal – but it seems plausible that something of the sort was going on.

Instead of Trebinje, he went to Belgrade. Gavro had also gone there to study and the two young men frequented the group of cafés used by the Bosnian Serbs in the city, popular with students and other expatriates who were both working and unemployed and with the guerrilla volunteers, the Komite, who had signed up to participate in the Balkan wars.

Gavro was studying at this time and Nedjo relying on day work. Like most of the other men in the cafés they had little money. These were not elegant 'café society' establishments but 'lower class' cafés, as one man described them, where the customers could sit cheaply and long over a coffee or a small meal. Some had outside seating; inside it was gaslight and shadows.

The cafés were mainly based around the Green Wreath market area, and Gavro and Nedjo and the other young men mostly had lodgings in the apartment blocks nearby. Some were sleeping on floors, occasionally even outdoors if they had no money for rent and no friends to call upon. Some of the cafés, such as the Green Wreath itself, had rooms of their own, over the premises, for lodging. Others nearby included the Green Acorn, the Golden Sturgeon, the Café Moruna and the Café Amerika. Komite officers would often hold court at the cafés and conduct business from them. They too were poor. One man remembered such an officer, Milan Ciganovic, being thrown out of the Green Wreath café by the owner because his suit was infested with lice.

It was intriguing that, though they may have been poor and mostly from rural backgrounds, the Young Bosnians rejected the Turkish-style peasant garb of their elders, with their loose tunics, wide sash belts and traditional fez headwear. The Young Bosnians dressed smartly in three-piece suits, starch-collared shirts and ties and city hats. In one surviving group photograph of an unidentified gang of Young Bosnians from the radical stronghold of Tuzla they pose like gangsters, almost before gangsters had been invented in their iconic Hollywood form, with wide-brimmed hats, dark suits and cigarettes dangling from their lips.

They were striking a pose, no doubt about it. In spite of their social-ism and revolutionary fervour and apparent lack of concern with life's mundane details and domesticities, they were posturing and image conscious.

I only wonder how many changes of suit and shirt they each pos-sessed. There is no mention anywhere of anyone, not Gavro, Nedjo or any of them, ever packing a suitcase for their long pedestrian journeys, back and forth across the region. I suspect they did not have expansive wardrobes, had limited opportunities for dry cleaning their suits and shirts or washing their own bodies, and even more limited access to the modern tools of personal hygiene, such as deodorants. No wonder Ciganovic's suit was infested with lice and, if it does not seem too trivial or impolite to mention – and the point does not occur in any of the histories I've read – those Young Bosnians, some of them at least, were probably a little reeky.

The students would sit in huddles at tables, dreaming of assassinations, plotting the revolution and often exercising the finer points of their political differences. Gavro, for instance, was a radical nationalist, while Nedjo, of course, was an anarchist socialist.

Someone described a group of them passing around a photograph of the Heir Apparent one afternoon. 'The pumpkin is ripe!' one said. Another said, 'We showed the Turks and the Bulgarians and now we will show those Austrians too ...'

Serbia fought first the Turks and then the Bulgarians during the Balkan wars of 1912 and 1913 and it was in these battles that the irregular Komite units played a decisive rôle. Many of the students volunteered and went to war after the sparest training and with ragtag uniforms and supplies.

One visitor from Sarajevo described the mood of aggressive solidarity in Belgrade and how on moaning to a city clerk that he wanted to go home to Bosnia he was told by the clerk, if you leave us at a time like this, when people are needed most, you should be tied to a stone and thrown down a well.

The clerk said he would find the Bosnian a role with the guerrillas so he agreed to stay and was taken to the Green Wreath café where he was told the guerrillas ate and lived, and then ushered into the presence of the Komite leader Vojin Tankosic, who said, 'are you ready to join the guerrillas?' The man was, so he was packed off to a nearby village for training, receiving only some peasant clothes, no uniform and just enough money for tobacco, though the food, he said, was good enough.

After a short stay in Belgrade, Nedjo heard that his father had successfully appealed against his son's expulsion from Sarajevo. Nedjo had no money to get home, so wrote to his father asking for enough to return. Then he met a man in the Green Acorn who agreed to take him to an organization that would give him some money if Nedjo was willing to pay the man a half-litre of native brandy by way of commission.

Nedjo accepted the fee and in August 1912 was taken to the Belgrade headquarters of Narodna Odbrana (National Defence) which had been mobilizing troops in readiness to fight Austria, following the annexation, until the 1911 climbdown when it too had been forced to accept the annexation and demob the troops. It was now ostensibly an organization for the promotion of Serb culture, while also running a network of agents, keeping itself informed of Austrian activities.

Nedjo told the military official he met that he was after some money to make the trip home to Sarajevo. He was told to go away and come back later and when he did he was given 15 dinars. The official saw the French literary novel Nedjo was reading and, pulling the book from Nedjo's pocket, said what's this? It was a book by Guy de Maupassant. This isn't for you, said the activist. In replacement Nedjo was given some Narodna Odbrana publications: Statutes of the National Defence and Popular Heroic Songs.

'I don't know how to thank you for your kindness,' said Nedjo. 'Always remain a good Serb,' said the official. Suddenly, Nedjo noted, the Serb nationalists did not seem like chauvinists any more but were his friends.

Instead of using the money for the journey, Nedjo bought yet more books by Zola, Tolstoy, Kropotkin and others, that reflected his socialist leanings. And more or less the next day he received some travel money from his father and some further money from the typographers' union, so he packed his books into a trunk and used the money to post that home instead, then walked to Sarajevo.

Back in his native city Nedjo finally qualified as a journeyman typographer and perhaps relied on that new-found status to begin a war of words in print with the social democrats in Sarajevo, whose organization he belonged to, writing an article in a local journal criticizing their undemocratic ways. They responded with a personal attack on him in their own paper, accusing him of being a spy and an agent of the Serbian government and also publishing, for the first time, rumours that had been circulating in the city suggesting his father was a spy for the Austrian police.

Every which way he turned, Nedjo's life was bound by conflict. The social democrats expelled him and ordered him boycotted by his former colleagues. His father banned him from writing to Vukosava, who was away at teacher training college in Croatia. The father said they were a pair of anarchists, but clearly blamed the bad influence of his son. Nedjo felt he couldn't stay, he said, as it would be too shameful and he might do something bad. The idea of a dramatic gesture was clearly forming in his mind. He had something to prove and was moving increasingly towards the Serb nationalist cause.

He went to Trieste in Slovene for a few months and was studying and mixing with socialists there while working at a printing press. The owner was apparently cleaning his Browning revolver one day when Nedjo saw him and asked if he could have the gun. The owner gave it to him. Nedjo must have felt bolder, with that gun in his possession. He offered his services to one of the Young Bosnian leaders and wrote complaining when nothing happened. He told fellow workers at the Trieste printers that they would hear something great in connection with him. When he left Trieste he told the print works' owner who had donated the weapon, I am going now, but you will hear about me.

He headed for Belgrade, visiting his sister Vukosava in college in Croatia on the way. He was still writing to his younger sister, Jovanka. 'You asked me if I am still a socialist,' he wrote in one letter to her, 'I am but a little more intelligently, a little differently. You asked me if I am hungry. For the moment I am not, but I have been hungry many times. On our saint's day you ate steak and I had only dry bread.'

There was discontent in Bosnia with student demonstrations on the streets and growing awareness among the Austrian authorities that all manner of plots and possible assassinations were being hatched. In May 1913, the Austrian governor General Oskar Potiorek introduced emergency measures, banning assemblies and organizing and taking charge of the schools, some of which were closed. The courts were suspended and Serbian newspapers were confiscated at the border. The Austrian press suggested there could be an attack on Serbia, who was already distracted by the second Balkan war, against the Bulgarians.

Nedjo hated this prospect. 'Serbia would be empty and then they (Austria) could invade her with 100,000 men. I felt I had great nationalism in me and when that Balkan war began there developed in me a great desire to go to Serbia.'

By the time he arrived back in Belgrade in late 1913 the war with Bulgaria was all but over and there was little money and great hardship for many in Belgrade. Nedjo did not find work for some time until he eventually got a poorly paid job at the state press.

He must have struggled even to eat, as he later said how he suffered there, how frightful it was, but still he did not want to write home because he was still not on good terms with his father who had by now even forbidden his sisters to write to him.

He became desperate and though he received a small raise at work his need was still great and so finally he wrote home – but there was no reply. So he felt that he was dead to them, his parents, and, being by his own admission a pretty sentimental person he was caught up daily in ever more desperate thoughts.

He must have let his sister Vukosava know his plight as she pawned a gold cross to send some money for him and his friend Gavro.

Nedjo went to the Green Acorn and the Golden Sturgeon and talked in revolutionary terms with the people he met there, who were mostly returning Komite. He was still an anarchist and they were mostly radical nationalists, but like them he believed in the unification of all Serbs in one pan-Slavic state. They all believed Austria must be forced out of Bosnia & Hercegovina.

One morning in late March/early April 1914, Nedjo received a letter delivered to him at the Golden Sturgeon café. He did not know who had sent it, but the stamp bore a portrait of Franz Josef the Austrian emperor, a clue to its likely origins in Bosnia. Inside the envelope was a clipping from a newspaper. It was just a small clipping and only one word 'greeting', had been added to it. The text read, 'from Sarajevo it is announced that the Archduke Heir Apparent with his wife will come to Sarajevo and participate in manoeuvres.'

Nedjo put the clipping in his pocket and forgot about it, for a few hours.

6

Death of a Hero

When the grave of Bogdan Zerajic was opened, around 1920, it was noted that the skull was missing from the coffin. It was soon discovered, in the Museum of Criminology in Sarajevo, where it had formerly been exhibited, and reunited with the rest of the corpse.

At the time of his death a decade earlier, in 1910, the Austrians were apparently influenced by the Italian criminologist Cesare Lombroso who theorized that criminals could be recognized by inherited defects in their appearance, or physiognomy. In particular, they were thought by Lombroso to be recognizable by their large jaws, high cheekbones, handle-shaped ears, hawked noses and fleshy lips.

Zerajic's skull had evidently been removed in pursuit of this early attempt at eugenics – he was widely described at the time as a lunatic or a lone anarchist – but then found some practical application on the desk of the Sarajevo chief of detectives, Viktor Ivasjuk, who had used it as an inkpot, and as an instrument of psychological torture, threatening Young Bosnians he was interrogating, 'if you do not admit everything I shall make inkpots out of your heads, as I did with Zerajic.'

This does not seem to have done much to diminish, and very probably enhanced, the lionizing of Zerajic that took place following his death.

He was a little older than most of the 1914 plotters, born in 1887, one of nine children in a poor peasant family. He had to abandon law studies at Zagreb University because he could not support himself then spent some time in Serbia, working as a primary teacher, and becoming politicized, reading Russian socialist works, especially those of Prince Kropotkin, one of the original exponents of anarchism and revolution.

Zerajic was among the hundreds of young rebels who flocked to join the Komite after the Austrian annexation of Bosnia in 1908, when Serbia suspected it was about to be invaded. 'We must liberate ourselves or die,' said Zerajic. He despaired at news of the Serbian government's acceptance of the annexation and was disappointed that the Bosnian Serbs did not rise up, as they had in the 1870s.

The docility of the older Bosnian Serbs was a popular theme among the young. 'The whole of our society is snoring ungracefully. Only the poets and revolutionaries are awake,' wrote Ivo Andric, a Young Bosnian and much later a Nobel Prize-winning author.

Zerajic became an active Young Bosnian, agitating for change, and borrowed a pistol which he wrote about to a colleague as 'a little thing' that would not be wasted. The colleague was Vladimir Gacinovic, who acted as the conscience and the chronicler of Young Bosnia, and wrote a series of essays about Zerajic, after his death, which helped to create the legend of his martyrdom. They were friends and so Gacinovic knew all about Zerajic's plan to assassinate the Austrian emperor Franz Josef (the uncle of the Heir Apparent, Franz Ferdinand), when Josef made a state visit to Bosnia in 1910 to celebrate the annexation.

Gacinovic accompanied Zerajic to the railway station when he set off on his mission to assassinate. 'He grabbed me in his arms, as if he were seeing me for the last time. He was silent, and when the bell rang for the departure of the train, he told me his last words, the message to all young ones and to all his friends, "Youth must prepare for sacrifices! Tell them." He departed, quiet, noble and unobserved.'

In one of his essays, 'To Those Who Are Coming', Gacinovic made a clear call to arms: 'We the youngest have to make a new history; into our frozen society we have to bring sunshine, we have to awaken the dead and cheer up the resigned ... having a belief stronger than life and a love that is capable of lifting people out of the grave, we shall win.'

Zerajic shadowed the emperor for much of his visit and got so close he could have touched him, at the Mostar railway station. But for some reason, never explained, he could not take out his gun and shoot him and be a hero. Another friend who heard this story at first hand from Zerajic, in a café, wanted to cry out loud in his disappointment, 'Such men are not among us.' Instead he kept repeating, 'they do not exist, they do not exist, they do not exist …' The friend wondered later if he had re-awakened Zerajic.

At the end of his state visit the emperor told the Bosnian governor, General Varesanin, 'I assure you this voyage has made me 20 years younger.' The Austrians set up a puppet parliament, the Sabor, in Sarajevo and it was opened by General Varesanin on 15 June 1910.

Varesanin returned home in his carriage along Appel Quay, beside the Miljacka river where Princip would stand waiting for the Heir Apparent four years later. As his carriage turned onto the bridge Zerajic was there waiting for him (he had earlier been refused entry to the Sabor itself) and stepped forward and fired five bullets, all of which missed the governor. Zerajic used the last bullet to shoot himself in the head.

He was found there by the governor who stopped the coach and walked back to find his would-be assassin, 'lying across the bridge in his death agony, thick blood flowing from his mouth'. It was noted that Zerajic was wearing a hand-made badge on his jacket, a red cardboard circle 10 centimetres wide, with a black border, and a picture of a man carrying a scythe, open-mouthed, hair flying. It was copied from the cover of Kropotkin's book *The History of the French Revolution*.

For Bosnians who were ready to collaborate with the Austrians, there was, as one of the new Sabor politicians put it, 'disgust for Bogdan Zerajic's base act'. The general sent a note to the Heir Apparent, who had offered condolences for his narrow escape: 'Deeply moved by most gracious sympathy. Beg graciously to receive most submissive and most respectful thanks. Population regardless of religion indignant about accursed anarchist crime.' Even the Archduke cannot have been fooled by that. He knew the Austrians were becoming a common enemy in Bosnia.

Among the young students there was initial confusion that something different and unforeseen had happened. Soon their attitude hardened and changed. They understood that Zerajic had made a self-sacrifice. He had become a martyr – a Kosovan avenger, in spirit if not in deed. The young men took to removing their caps in respect as they passed the spot where he had died, this in itself an act of defiance in the Austrian Sarajevo. They built up his sacrifice with apocryphal details. His last words, it was said, had been, 'I leave my revenge to Serbdom.' As part of the myth-making, the students came to believe that General Varesanin had gone up to Zerajic as he lay dying and kicked him saying, 'you scum'. This phrase, it was said, never died in the feelings of Young Bosnians, hurting as the worst wound.

The Austrians tried to suppress his martyrdom by burying Zerajic in secret, among the suicides and vagrants, as Dedijer put it, in St Mark's cemetery. His grave was soon found and properly marked with a cross and flowers by the Young Bosnians. Nedjo Cabrinovic carved Zerajic's name into the cross and Gavro Princip helped put the plot in order and removed – stole – flowers from other graves to decorate it.

Eventually, in the years to come, they would all end up together, in the same memorial beneath the Vidovdan chapel.

Gacinovic wrote a pamphlet, 'The Death of a Hero', which glorified his fallen friend: 'The Serb revolutionary, if he wants to win must be an artist and a conspirator, must have talent for strength and suffering, must be a martyr and a plotter, a man of Western manners and a haiduk who will shout and wage war for the unfortunate and the downtrodden … Young Serbs, you who are rising from the ruins and foulness of today, will you produce such men? It seems as though this sums up the whole Serbia problem, political, moral and cultural.'

While Gacinovic complained of the acquiescence of older Bosnian Serbs, he might well have agreed with Gavro when he told Pappenheim that, 'our old generation was mostly conservative, but in the whole existed the wish for national liberation. The older generation was of a different opinion to the young as to how to bring it about. In 1878 many Serb leaders and generals prayed for liberation from the Turks. The older generation wanted to secure liberty from Austria in a legal way.

'We do not believe in such liberty.'

While the students increasingly went further in their readiness to take action, they were not entirely alone. There had been street demonstrations leading to police brutality and deaths during a general strike of workers in 1906. Grievances were widespread, with long hours expected by employers and payment haphazard. In a sizeable civil service only a quarter were native Bosnians and most of those were from the favoured Catholic Croat community. Schooling was still a novelty for most and less than a fifth of all children were able to attend. There were few schools in the province – less than one for every 6,000 people.

In 1910 there was a further uprising among the kmets which brought only a limited concession, in the shape of a long agreement to end the feudal system, freeing the peasants from their financial burdens. One expert calculated that, according to the proposed concession, the last peasants would not be free until the year 2025. The kmets referred to their landlords as kmetoders – people who skin the kmets. Some of those landlords were bourgeois Serbs.

Most of the students came from peasant backgrounds and they were gradually united in their hatred of the Austrians. 'I wonder if you can understand how mighty hatred can be?' Rebecca West, the writer, was asked by a Bosnian Serb in Sarajevo, in the 1930s. 'I think you English do not, for you have long been so fortunate that nobody else's hatred could touch you …'

Many have likened the beliefs of the Young Bosnians to a religious creed, in the passion and rigidity of their fervour. There was no one single Young Bosnia organization with a hierarchy or overall leadership or unified and structured direction. Rather Young Bosnia was a collective name for the group of secret societies formed on a sometimes casual basis by students, often open to just a handful of people, and often operating as both a literary or theoretical forum for debate and discussion as well as a cell for plotting future direct action. The secret societies were an inevitable response to repressive measures taken by the Austrians when they took charge of the province, banning both the organization of and participation in student groups.

Only one youth society was allowed in Sarajevo and that was run by a Jesuit priest, Father Anton Puntigam, who was also part of the inner circle of the Archduke and his wife, sometimes acting as their confessor. Puntigam gave sermons criticizing socialists as atheists and enemies of the emperor and the state. He did, however, once invite two anarchists for coffee in his rooms to discuss their ideology with him. One was Nedjo Cabrinovic.

While he was not a leader of Young Bosnia, because there was no leader, Vladimir Gacinovic was clearly the guiding spirit of the movement. He railed against the past generation: 'Our fathers, our dictators are real tyrants who want to drag us along with them and want to dictate to us how we should lead our own lives.'

Gacinovic travelled to study in Lausanne, Switzerland and got to know Russian revolutionaries who were living there. He formed a particular association with Leon Trotsky and met with him in Serbia and later in Paris.

It seems that Gacinovic was keen to impress Trotsky with the codes of abstinence and asceticism observed by the Young Bosnians. They were fundamentalist in their adherence to strict behaviour in pursuit of their non-religious religion, as Gacinovic described to Trotsky: In our organization there is a rule of obligatory abstinence from love-making and drinking, and you must believe me when I tell you that all of us remain true to this rule.

Gavro indicated his chasteness to Pappenheim, explaining how he never kissed the girl he fell for at school. It seems certain he died a virgin as did Bogdan Zerajic, according to Dedijer. Gavro never drank, until the eve of the assassination, and then only to disguise himself in plain sight, masquerading as a hail fellow, instead of the puritan he really was, the martyr he hoped to become.

By the standards of the day it seems that although they were over-whelmingly male, the Young Bosnians respected and sought equality for women, especially Gacinovic, who met a number of female Russian revolutionaries and evidently saw them as contrasting favourably with some Serbian women who were leading their 'catastrophic way of life in cafés full of cynicism'. Of course, that was not true of Jovanka, the wife of Veljko Cubrilovic who had presented herself at military headquarters in Belgrade in 1908 as a volunteer assassin – only to be laughed at and patronized for her trouble.

The Young Bosnians took a strict view of morality, disapproving of the decadence and corruption brought by the Austrians, such as brothels for the soldiers, which had polluted Sarajevo, apparently for the first time in the city's history. Dedijer quotes a student being told by Gavro that, 'syphilis and clericalism are an unhappy inheritance from the Middle Ages which the present civilization does not know how to cure.' What a potent combination – debauchery and the political influence of the Church. Obviously, Gavro had no patience with either.

Sometimes, it seemed, the Orthodox Church had little time even for itself. One cleric from Hercegovina, Bishop Ducic, was once told by the Bishop of London that he must be very fortunate in his people, as the Bishop of London had heard they were very devoted. 'Yes,' said Ducic, 'in Serbia we do not trust too much to God. We prayed God five centuries to free us from the Turks, and finally took guns and did it ourselves.'

Not everyone was an atheist, like Princip, but for many the Church and the nation of Serbs were equally important and served a mutual purpose on the road to liberation and independence, where self-sacrifice was a noble and worthwhile end.

While the Austrians, much as the Turks had done, sought to divide and rule, favouring one community over another – especially the Catholics – the students sought the solidarity of collaboration between Serbs, Croats and Muslims. They held to a vision of a unified south Slav state which would benefit all, even if the dominant Bosnian Serbs regarded Belgrade, Serbia as the natural capital city of such a federation. It even had a name – Yugoslavia.

There were joint Serbo-Croat societies, one involving Ivo Andric boasting a secret badge depicting the two flags of Serbs and Croats. When Princip joined this group he soon encountered criticism from the Serb nationalists who said that Princip and others in this joint group could not be real Serbs. 'This caused a deep breach and hatred between us,' he wrote in a letter.

Andric described the deep-rooted religious divisions of Bosnian society in 'Story from 1920':

Anyone who spends one night in Sarajevo sleepless on his bed, can hear the strange voices of the Sarajevo night. Heavy but steady strikes the clock on the Catholic Cathedral: it is 2am. More than one minute will pass (exactly seventy-five seconds, I counted) and only then will the Serbian Eastern Orthodox Church announce itself. It strikes its 2am. A while after, with hoarse faraway voice the Sahat Tower near Beg's Mosque declares itself. It strikes eleven times, the eleven ghostly Turkish hours, according to some strange alien part of the world. The Jews have no clock of their own which strikes the hours, but only the good God would know what is their time, according to Sephardic and Askenazic calculations. And thus even during the night, when everybody is asleep, in this counting of the hours in the dead part of the night, the difference which divides these sleeping beings has been emphasized, beings who will, when they rise, rejoice and mourn, entertain and fast, according to their four different hostile calendars, and who will send all their wishes and prayers up to one heaven in four different church languages. And this difference, sometimes openly and visibly, sometimes invisibly and basely, approaches hatred, often identifying with it.

There were also links with groups and societies in other south Slav provinces of the Austro-Hungarian empire, such as Croatia, Dalmatia and Slovenia. Out of these associations with their cross-pollination and their common aim of driving out the Habsburgs, new plots, inspired by Zerajic, inevitably formed. There was widespread unrest throughout 1912, spreading out from Zagreb where students began protesting after a new governor, Count Slavko Cuvaj, was appointed by the Hungarians, in spite of an election voting local parties into power.

Several students were wounded by police sabres when they tried to hold a banned protest. Students started a sit-in at the university, while others combined with workers to stone the police. A second wave of protests and demonstrations began across the region and there were widespread student strikes. Gavro was among students who led the demonstration in Sarajevo and according to one account was wounded by a sabre. A general strike was called and Dedijer cites a contemporary diarist recording how Gavro went from class to class threatening boys with a knuckleduster to force them to join the strikers.

One of the other organizers of the Sarajevo protests was a Croat student, Luka Jukic, who later complained to colleagues, 'this schoolboys' movement is not enough. It is too innocent. Other means must be applied and Cuvaj should be removed at all costs and I am prepared to do it, either with poison … or with bombs and revolvers.'

Others had the same idea but Jukic was determined to press ahead and obtained weapons in Belgrade. He was another poet-revolutionary and wrote some verses which he called 'My Motto': I feel sorry for myself, But I have no other choice, For freedom and people, I will sacrifice everything!

He twice set out to shoot Cuvaj and returned without doing anything. There were arguments with his colleagues and he was called a coward and a braggart. Someone spat at him to show their contempt and he said he was giving up and going home. Instead, he took his chance the next day and shot at Cuvaj on a street corner in Zagreb.

He missed but instead shot and killed Cuvaj's secretary. Jukic ran off and was chased for twenty minutes through the streets of Zagreb by officers with drawn sabres. He turned and fired three times, wounding two officers and killing a third. He shot at a passer-by who finally arrested him.

It seemed that dozens of students had known what Jukic was planning, and they began celebrating his attempt even before it became widely known to the authorities. There were many arrests. Some pamphlets were seized which proclaimed the creation of a new south Slav republic called Yugoslavia.

Jukic was 25 but when he stood trial later in 1912 he shared the dock with a dozen others, aged from 15 to 18. One 15-year-old said Jukic had told him they should kill Cuvaj because it was not a crime but a good deed when a tyrant was killed. At his conviction a girl in the public gallery threw Jukic a rose and he turned and shouted, down with tyranny!

Jukic was sentenced to hang but, realizing they would only be creating a new martyr, the authorities commuted his sentence to life imprisonment. According to Dedijer he was released in 1918 and lived out his life in his home village in Bosnia, where he died in poverty in 1929, leaving his wife and children nothing but a few poems.

A second student, Ivan Planiscak, tried to kill Governor Cuvaj, climbing a telegraph pole to shoot at him through a first-floor window. He missed too, and then committed suicide. Governor Cuvaj decided to stand down.

A third attempt on Cuvaj originated in the United States where, like the Irish republicans, the Serbs and Croats had organized support groups. A young Croat man travelled from Wisconsin to Zagreb and set out to shoot the former governor. By now Cuvaj's movements were being kept secret and the American Croat could not find him. Hearing in a letter that he was becoming a laughing stock back home for his failure he decided to shoot someone else instead and targeted the new governor of Croatia, Baron Ivo Skerletz, shooting at him as he came out of a Catholic church service. This time the bullet struck, though only wounding the governor in the arm. As he was sentenced to 16 years the American Croat said, 'I am convinced after me will come others.'

In Dalmatia another would-be assassin was arrested with a loaded gun on the eve of his attempt against the governor of the province. Yet another student was arrested after a tip-off that he had obtained a gun and was planning to go and shoot the Heir Apparent in Vienna. He told the police, 'Franz Ferdinand is the enemy of the unification of the South Slavs and I wish to eliminate this rubbish which is hampering our national aspiration.'

Gavro himself later admitted that he first thought of assassinating a Habsburg after the student demonstrations of 1912. He had attended secret meetings in Sarajevo at the home of two Muslim boys and they had discussed various targets before agreeing to draw lots to decide who would carry out the deed. One student went to Belgrade to get some weapons but came back empty-handed, complaining that Jukic was getting all the attention.

One young Muslim wanted to shoot the emperor and wanted to do it himself since he was an orphan and would not be mourned. He later went to Belgrade and joined the Komite to learn how to shoot. Nothing further happened.

It was hard to plan a terror campaign when many of the participants were disappearing off to join the Komite, so the first Balkan war acted as a brake on activities for some months until the spring of 1913 when tensions suddenly increased between Serbia and Austria and the new governor of Bosnia & Hercegovina, General Oskar Potiorek, introduced the state of emergency. The constitution was suspended and military rule established.

During the increased police surveillance of students, some members of Gavro's group were arrested and, acting on a tip-off, the police raided another student's home where they found a revolver and a list of members of the secret society. Gavro was questioned and the group's plans neutered.

It was during this period that Gavro drifted back and forth between Belgrade, Sarajevo and his brother's home in Hadzici. As he later told Pappenheim he was often in the company of Danilo Ilic, his roommate at the home of Ilic's mother in Sarajevo. They were best friends, though Gavro said that he was the stronger of the two, able to influence Ilic, even though he was five years older and already a teacher. They discussed making an attempt on Potiorek and resolved to do it between them.

Ilic had already obtained a revolver, but then apparently it was stolen or taken from him, perhaps to prevent him carrying out the assassination. He went to Switzerland – probably not to look at the possibilities of studying pedagogy, as he would claim in court at the trial, but to meet some of the Russian revolutionaries there and to talk plots with Vladimir Gacinovic. On one account, Gacinovic told him, 'that the heads of some of the leading dignitaries of the Empire must fall', but at the same time it seems that Ilic and Gavro pulled back from the idea of trying to assassinate Potiorek.

Ilic went to join the Komite at the outbreak of the second Balkan war. He spent some time as an ambulance driver but returned to Sarajevo in the autumn of 1913, evidently suffering again with poor health, in an unspecified stomach complaint.

Gavro told Pappenheim that Ilic became ill and was in the hospital feeling a little light-headed. They spoke of their pan-Slavist ideas and agreed that they must first create an organization in Bosnia and Croatia and then, when all was ready, they should make an assassination attempt. So the plan was given up for the time being, with Gavro concluding that he should study further in Belgrade, in the library, as he was not yet ripe and independent enough to think about it.

Ilic would say in court that he agreed with Gavro in assassination as a means of protest against bad government and that he too wanted a south Slav state. Ilic chose his words carefully in court, while Gavro said quite openly that if he could he would destroy Austria completely.

Gavro described himself as a Yugoslav nationalist who wanted the unification of the south Slavs in a state free of Austria. He believed in the use of terror to achieve that aim and wanted to destroy from above to do away with those who obstruct and do evil, who stand in the way of unification. He was also motivated by revenge for all the torments which Austria had imposed on the people.

While these two were in Sarajevo planning a revolution, Nedjo Cabrinovic was in Trieste, borrowing a gun and making his own plans. In early 1914, Vladimir Gacinovic left Switzerland and travelled to France, to the southern city of Toulouse where some kind of secret meeting or conference took place at the Hotel St Gerome, attended by some Young Bosnians and a Muslim, Mehmed Mehmedbasic, who would become one of the Sarajevo assassins in six months' time. Mehmedbasic was a trained carpenter from the Hercegovina town of

Stolac. He was the son of a feudal landlord who had fallen on hard times. Mehmedbasic had allowed his father's last servile kmets to buy their freedom, in order to raise the money for his trip to France.

This Toulouse meeting is where the story begins to get murky and uncertain. Some historians – in particular Albertini who published a three-volume, 2,000-page account *The Origins of War* – see this meeting as the opening move in the plotting that led directly to the assassination of the Heir Apparent. Dedijer seems to think it was just one more plot, amid a hatful of similar, sometimes overlapping conspiracies. On some accounts it was there that a plan to kill the Heir Apparent was first hatched. But at that stage no one even knew the Archduke was coming to Sarajevo.

Albertini had some contact with Mehmedbasic during his lengthy researches. According to him, although other targets including the Heir Apparent were discussed, Gacinovic spoke at the meeting of the urgent need to kill General Potiorek and Mehmedbasic was assigned to the task, and told he must kill Potiorek with a poisoned dagger. He was given a small phial of poison and a knife and left Toulouse to travel back to Sarajevo by train. During the journey he suddenly realized that gendarmes were searching the carriages and, fearing they were looking for him, he went to the lavatory and threw away the dagger and the poison. Only then did he discover the police were merely looking for a petty thief.

A friend of Mehmedbasic's told Dedijer that he returned home to Stolac where he obtained a revolver and went to Sarajevo, still intending to kill Potiorek. But by now the visit of the Archduke had been announced and the assassination plan was underway, so when Mehmedbasic met Danilo Ilic he was told to go home and wait to be summoned, to take part in this new conspiracy, which Ilic was organizing.

According to Albertini, Ilic wrote inviting Mehmedbasic to meet him in Mostar where he told him there was going to be an attempt on the Heir Apparent and guns and bombs would be provided, and this would now take precedence over the assassination of the governor.

Mehmedbasic said he had promised Gacinovic he would kill Potiorek and didn't want to change targets without Gacinovic's approval. Mehmedbasic and Ilic wrote a joint letter to Gacinovic and got a brief reply: 'Forward Lions'.

At his trial Ilic gave yet another version of events, in which Mehmedbasic had written inviting him to Mostar: 'Rather, he looked me up and he gave me the idea for the assassination before Princip did.' Mehmedbasic was the only one of the 28 June plotters who escaped and never faced trial. It seems likely that, during the trial, Ilic was simply trying to blame his absent co-conspirator. The tactic didn't work. He was not believed.

7

June 1914 – Martyrs in the Making

Gavro had been short of money the whole time since arriving in Sarajevo with 50 Serbian dinars in his pocket, borrowing 20 crowns from Ilic and still engaged by his seemingly constant struggle to make ends meet, while spending the little he did have mostly on books.

It was only in the last week before the assassination that he was finally able to earn some money, taking a job at Prosvjeta, the Serbian cultural institution and reading room on Appel Quay, for a few crowns, copying minutes of Prosvjeta committees. He was lucky, it appears, to be living rent free at Ilic's mother's home on Oprkanj Street, albeit later sleeping with a small arsenal under his bed. He told Pappenheim that, just as he had in Belgrade, he read constantly in Sarajevo and studied quietly. He had a 'nice' library because he was always buying books. Books, for him, signified life. In prison, afterwards, he would be denied books and this, he would say, was his greatest suffering, being deprived of the opportunity to read.

During the days before the assassination he read much about the Russian Revolution, about the fightings, in articles by Kropotkin and others. The idea of assassination as a means of revolution had taken hold of him now. Any earlier constraints had vanished. Gavro was told by Ilic that the second group was ready, though he did not disclose their names. Because he trusted Ilic and believed he was reliable he did not doubt that he would also find trustworthy companions.

Gavro discussed with Ilic how they would collect the weapons from Misko Jovanovic in Tuzla. Because he had been afraid to bring them directly into Sarajevo, Gavro had left them back in Tuzla, on the last leg of the smuggling journey, with a businessman who was a sympathizer but had seemed so nervous that Gavro was afraid he might denounce them. Someone had to collect them and because he had already been there Gavro said it would be safer if Ilic collected them instead.

On Sunday, 14 June, precisely two weeks before the assassination, Ilic took the train to Tuzla to collect the weapons. Gavro had told him to take a box of Stefanija cigarettes – the secret sign he had agreed with Jovanovic – and to be careful in case they had been betrayed.

The night before, in Tuzla, there had been an exercise of the Serbian Sokol that Misko Jovanovic had attended, while his wife and her friend Mara Sainova went to the cinema, which was owned by Misko. The Sokol was a pan-Slavic organization for sport and fitness which also celebrated traditional culture through song and dance and drama. It had spread out across the region from its origins in Czechoslovakia and was rightly regarded with suspicion by the Austrian authorities in Bosnia & Hercegovina, where it was often supported and maintained as a defiant expression of Serb nationalism.

When he returned from the exercise Misko heard that his friends Veljko and Jovanka Cubrilovic had arrived in the town from their home in Priboj and were staying at the inn. They had come for the following day's Orthodox feast in celebration of the saint's day for emperor Konstantine and his wife, empress Helen. Misko waited for the end of the evening performance at the cinema, at about ten o'clock and then walked over to the inn with his wife and Mara. Later that night Mara's husband was due to arrive on the train from Mostar, to take her home.

They found Veljko and Jovanka together with another couple from Priboj. They sat together awhile, until the train was due and Veljko said to Misko, I'll come with you to the station.

The two walked alone, behind the others who were with them and Misko said to Veljko, those students left things with me and said that they would come but they are not here yet. He was obviously anxious about having the weapons in his home. Veljko had also been involved in the smuggling – it had been he who passed Gavro on to Misko – and tried to reassure him: if they said they would come, then they will come. Then Veljko asked him, do you know why? Misko said he didn't know and Veljko said, be silent, poor fellow, it's better that you don't know.

Veljko then said, 'Do you see how he despises us? Just now, when the Heir Apparent is coming …' At that moment Misko's wife inter-rupted them and the two men went quiet. Misko concluded that Veljko was talking about the Bosnian governor, Oskar Potiorek and how much he despised the Serbs. By now they were at the station and there were too many people and police around to continue the conversation.

Mara Sainova's husband appeared on the platform beside the arriv-ing train from Mostar. They all went back and Veljko and his wife went to the inn, agreeing to join Misko and his family and friends for lunch at his apartment the next day.

That morning, early, Misko's wife came to tell him there was a young man at the door to see him. Let him in, said Misko. Ilic ap-peared, showing the box of Stefanija cigarettes. Misko asked how he planned to carry the weapons back to Sarajevo, because six bombs and four revolvers could not be carried in his pockets. Ilic asked Misko to pack the weapons into a box. Ilic did not want to take them now, but asked Misko to find a man to bring them to the first station after Tuzla where he would collect them.

Misko had only two servants and one of those had aged parents and a sick sister and was looking after them all on 60 crowns. Misko could not bear the thought of this servant being arrested and the other one was not available either. He would run the errand himself. He told the trial he had to go to Doboj anyway, which was further along that route, on Monday to get some lumber ready for transport. He admit-ted the lumber had been there four years but said he had been several times to try to conclude the business.

Ilic left and Misko found an empty black sugar box and put the weapons inside. He wrapped the box in paper and tied it with rope. When Veljko arrived for lunch Misko whispered, 'Veljko, someone came after those things.' Veljko said, 'yes, that's okay.' He took some books with him when he left after lunch. Misko went to the three o'clock cinema showing.

The following morning, he left early to take the box to Ilic. He claimed at the trial he carried the box himself. The trial prosecutor seemed suspicious at Misko's claim and perhaps suspected he let his servant or someone else carry the box instead. Misko had gone on the train to Doboj with Mara Sainova and her husband, who were going through to Mostar. Mara had been interviewed and said she did not recall seeing Misko carry a box, though she in fact had carried a sugar box. When Misko had attempted to take it from her she had said, don't you dare.

Misko answered the prosecutor that this must have been a genuine sweet box as his wife had given her friend some sweets she had prepared from strawberries.

If someone else had carried the box this was a brave deceit by Misko, an act of self-sacrifice, as this evidence would help get him hanged, alongside his friend and god-relative, Veljko Cubrilovic, and the man with the box of Stefanija cigarettes, Danilo Ilic. Those three would be the only direct participants to be hanged.

On his account, Misko kept waiting for Ilic to appear on the train. He went through the first station, no sign of him, and through the second and third. Nothing. He wondered if Ilic had fallen asleep and missed their meeting. He left the train at Doboj hoping to find him there, but still there was no sign. He wasn't sure what to do now, so he went into the second-class waiting room and left the box there. It was a cold day and Misko was wearing his pelerine, a cape, which he took off and threw over the box to cover it. He went outside and looked around, leaving the six bombs and the four guns in the box unguarded in the waiting room. Ilic was nowhere to be seen.

Misko decided to take the box into town and leave it at the tailor's workshop of his friend Vuko Jaksic. There was only an apprentice there and so Misko left the box, hung his pelerine on a hook and went out to conduct his lumber business. When he returned Jaksic was there and they sat and chatted about affairs in Tuzla until it was time for the next train. Misko told Jaksic not to lock the workshop if he went for lunch because a man was coming to collect the box.

Finally, when Misko reached the station, the train came and Ilic was on it. The two men walked to the tailor's which was both empty and unlocked. Ilic collected the box. Misko telegraphed his wife to tell her he would be home later in the afternoon and went for lunch.

Two weeks later, Misko heard about the assassination and immediately thought of those weapons. As he waited to be arrested he must have known that, in some way, his comfortable life was over. He was asked in court why he didn't do anything to prevent it.

He began by telling a story of an earlier sacrifice he had made when he was by the river Sprec and a young boy, the son of a landowner, began to drown. Misko was among a group of 20 on the bank and all the others were laughing so Misko jumped in to save him and the boy grabbed him around the neck so that Misko was lucky not to choke and drown himself.

'Now, gentlemen,' he told the court, 'I have a wife and child which she carried for seven months under the heart, and why should my family suffer? Then I thought that those two peasants also had families, and Veljko is my god-relative, and I absolutely could not do that, I could not prevent it. Maybe I could have said, "don't do it man, think about what you're doing!" … I was in a difficult position. I could not. I did not have reason to make so many people unhappy.'

His own lawyer – an Austrian lawyer, of course, in an Austrian court – admonished him: 'You remember your child, the wife of Cubrilovic etc, that's all very well, but one should also remember that the late Archduke also had children. Didn't you think of that?'

Ilic took a convoluted journey home with the sugar box to avoid the police. He got off the train at a station a few kilometres outside Sarajevo and took a local train which was heading towards the spa town, Ilidza, getting off at a neighbouring station, Mariendvor, inside Sarajevo. He took a streetcar to the Catholic cathedral and then carried the box home. He unpacked the box and put the weapons into a Gladstone bag which he then hid under the fold-down bed in which Gavro was sleeping, where it would now remain for the next 12 days.

8

Flame Am I

Gavrilo Princip registered his arrival in Belgrade with the police on 13 March 1914. This was to be his last visit to the Serbian capital. When he left ten weeks later on 28 May he would be on his way back to Sarajevo with guns and bombs hidden around his waist to carry out the assassination and, when that deed was done, would live out the rest of his life in prison, in chains, in solitary confinement, going nowhere except in his dreams, which he described to the psychiatrist Pappenheim.

He had also made his final visit home to Grahovo, stopping there on his way through from Sarajevo, a journey paid for by his businessman brother, Jovo. He stayed there in Grahovo for a couple of weeks. It had been a harsh winter and the snow was as high as the house, Gavro's mother Nana later told an interviewer, describing the last time she had seen her middle son. He was, she said, even more brooding and quiet than usual though she remembered he spent much of his time in the company of his cousin Vladeta Bilbija, who had been involved in some of the plotting back in Sarajevo and continued the onward journey with Gavro when he left for Belgrade.

Gavro and his cousin took rooms together on Carigradska Street near the Green Wreath market, along with several other Young Bosnians. Gavro read a great deal during these last days in Belgrade. He read political literature and Serbian poetry and was said to have memorized and recited favourite verses, including some lines from the German poet, Nietzsche:

> I know whence I arrive
> Unsatisfied like the flame
> I glow and writhe

Everything that I embrace becomes light,
Everything that I leave becomes coal,
Flame am I, surely

Among the roommates at Carigradska Street was an old friend, Trifko Grabez, who was, you might say, a true son of Milos Obilic, having been born on St Vitus Day, 28 June 1895. In the spring of 1914 he was still only 18, and living and studying in Belgrade but homesick for Bosnia, having been expelled from there 14 months earlier.

Grabez, from the town of Pale near Sarajevo, had studied first in Sarajevo and then at the gymnasium in Tuzla. After some time he had switched courses, withdrawing as a regular student and enrolling as a private student instead. He must have been a trying student as a professor who had been teaching him, on hearing this, laughed and sarcastically said, thank god! Grabez promptly assaulted the professor with a slap and was sentenced to 14 days in jail. The school had already been admonished by the education authorities in Tuzla for not expelling him when he could not pay the tuition fees. Now, finally, he was not only forced to leave school but barred altogether from Tuzla and expelled from Bosnia.

Like all the others in Belgrade he frequented the cafés, though he found them expensive places in which to eat, and sat there plotting the revenge on Austria that he so much wanted.

Grabez's father was a priest and he too was a believer but, he said later, 'we were bound to conclude that Austria had to pay handsomely for her wrongdoing.' He wanted unification as Yugoslavia and he wanted political freedom. When Grabez was asked at his trial what he meant by political freedom he replied, cutely, that he did not know as he was not familiar with it.

Other young men in the cafés were newly returned from the front lines of the second Balkan war, some of them aimless and lost after the end of their adventures. Here for instance was Djuro Sarac who would sit around in the cafés regaling any willing audience with tales of his exploits as a soldier. Sarac was a student of theology and had been studying to become a priest until he decided instead to fight for Serbia, showing such prowess that he had risen to become the personal bodyguard to Major Vojin Tankosic, the Komite commander.

Sarac and Gavro were old friends from Sarajevo. Sarac, who was four years older, had been studying there at the time of the annexation back in 1908 and had been sent to prison for two months after being reported to the authorities for saying that Austria's annexation of Bosnia & Hercegovina was 'sheer theft of somebody else's property'. This was the life of the cafés in Belgrade in the spring of 1914, when revolution and assassination were in the air. The young men would see each other daily, no doubt having the same sorts of conversations, reading the same newspapers, holding the same sorts of beliefs, struggling with poverty and waiting for something to happen.

Nedjo Cabrinovic still had that news clipping in his pocket at noon when he went to the Green Wreath café and lunched alone and then talked for a while with another man who he suspected might be an Austrian spy. Spies were everywhere and it was easy to fall under suspicion, as Nedjo himself had discovered.

The two men discussed Nedjo's desire to kill another man, a fellow Serb whom Nedjo considered a traitor for his work with the Austrians. The other man said, if you are thinking of assassination it is better that you kill the Heir Apparent. This jogged Nedjo's memory and he pulled the clipping from his pocket and said, just today I got this communication. Then the door opened and in walked Gavro, so Nedjo put the clipping away and they must have changed the conversation. Gavro had warned Nedjo before that the other man might be a spy: 'Watch out,' Gavro had told Nedjo, 'he often speaks about assassination. Maybe he is paid to spread the idea.'

Gavro left the café but when Nedjo went from there to the Green Acorn to have a coffee and read the paper he found Gavro already there, dancing, apparently, with a couple of other Bosnians. When the dance had finished he showed Gavro the cutting and Gavro read it and returned it without comment. Nedjo put it away, not seriously thinking of an assassination and never imagining the receipt of the clipping would come to define his life. If he had thought recently of assassination he would have liked to throw a bomb in the Sabor, the hated puppet parliament in Sarajevo, and assassinated what he called an 'assembly bootlicker'.

That evening, back in the Green Wreath, Nedjo was just finishing supper when Gavro came in and suggested they go out for a walk to discuss the news clipping. Nedjo realized at once that Gavro was thinking about an assassination. In fact Gavro had seen the reports himself in other newspapers, about the Heir Apparent's planned visit, and had already been giving it some thought.

They went to a nearby park, close to the modern day Palace Hotel, and sat down on a bench where Gavro suggested that the two of them carry out an assassination of the Heir Apparent. After a short hesitation, Nedjo agreed. They gave each other their word of honour and shook hands.

9

The Footloose Heir

And the Archduke's wife, Nedjo was asked at his trial, did you plan to kill her too? Oh no, said Nedjo, they agreed to make every effort to spare her. They condemned Luccheni's assassination and considered it a common crime.

Luccheni, an Italian anarchist, had assassinated Elisabeth, wife of the Austrian emperor Franz Josef, in 1898, stabbing her with a file, as she walked to board a ship for a trip across Lake Geneva. He had pretended to stumble and fall, reaching out to her for support and stabbing her as he did so; the wound so small it was not even noticed for many minutes, so that the empress carried on walking and boarded the boat before collapsing.

The emperor's misfortunes seemed boundless, as he too must have felt, on the day he had to acknowledge his cousin the Archduke Franz Ferdinand as the Heir Apparent to the Austro-Hungarian empire. The emperor did not like his cousin and cared less for the 'common' wife he had married. He had not attended their marriage. Nor would he attend their funeral either.

Franz Josef was born in 1830 and had presided over the declining authority and prestige of the Austrian empire, which had fallen out with Russia, been usurped in power by the ascendant German empire and finally forced into a dual monarchy with its former charge, Hungary.

Josef had one daughter, who died as a child, and only one natural heir, his son Rudolf, who was found dead with his mistress Marie Vetsera at a hunting lodge in Mayerling, Austria in 1889. It was said to have been a murder-suicide pact, with Rudolf first shooting his lover and then himself. He was said to have been affected by depression and by the effects of syphilis, but there were suspicions too that he also might have been murdered.

While the incident became an object of fascination for conspiracy theorists, the imperial inheritance technically passed to Karl Ludwig, the emperor's brother (and the father of Franz Ferdinand). It might have gone to the emperor's older brother, Maximilian, but he had renounced his right to the throne on becoming Emperor of Mexico many years earlier, a post he had held for three years before being executed by a Mexican revolutionary firing squad.

Karl Ludwig was almost as old as the emperor and so his oldest son, Franz Ferdinand, seemed bound to accede. When Karl Ludwig died of typhoid in 1896, after foolishly drinking the heavily polluted waters of the River Jordan in a gesture of faith during a visit to the Holy Land, Franz Ferdinand ought to have been proclaimed as the Heir. The emperor's initial silence on the matter made many suspect that he did not want to be succeeded by Ferdinand and, like many courtiers and ministers, favoured Ferdinand's younger brother Otto instead.

Some time earlier, either in 1894 or 1895, Ferdinand had met and secretly fallen in love with a lady-in-waiting at the family home of his friend Archduchess Isabella. While the Archduchess eagerly supposed that Ferdinand's succession of return visits were discreet expressions of interest in her eldest daughter, they were in fact for her lady-in-waiting, Countess Sophie Chotek. Sophie was born of noble stock herself, from a Czech family, but not noble enough for royalty, and an unacceptably low match for the Archduke. He pursued her anyway, in secret, and it was said the Archduchess only discovered the liaison when a maid brought her a gold watch the Archduke had left lying around, attached to a chain with trinkets including a locket. When the Archduchess opened the locket she saw Sophie's portrait inside. Sophie, born in 1868, was five years younger than Ferdinand.

The emperor was said to feel betrayed by the relationship and even more when he discovered that his grumpy nephew was determined to marry Sophie – Sopherl as he called her – and become emperor. In the end, he was forced into a humiliating acceptance of a morganatic marriage, a device enabling the higher ranks to marry the lower ranks, while allowing the higher ranks to keep their titles and privileges. In Ferdinand and Sophie's case she could never be Archduchess and their children could not accede to the throne. She was given the meaningless title of Princess instead. The Archduke swore the 'oath of renunciation' on 28 June 1900. St Vitus Day. 'Life begins from count upwards' the nobility would say. But between the counts and countesses and the Archduke lay an impassable ocean of royal blood.

Franz Ferdinand, like many a footloose Heir Apparent before and since (including more than one Prince of Wales) struggled to find a role and spent many years idly travelling around the world. His one great passion was hunting, a passion he shared with the emperor but which they approached with significantly different styles. The emperor hunted with subtlety in pursuit of his prey, while the Archduke favoured quantity over quality and would mow down as many creatures as he could. His family home at Artstetten in Austria contains a museum of artefacts about his life and death and includes a framed sheet – his Schuss List – logging the tally of his hunting throughout his life which he bureaucratically recorded, with sub columns for different types of animal.

The grand total of kills amounts to 272,439 which is not bad for a lifetime's work and, perhaps, in the early 1900s did not seem as obscene as it does now. Of course, many of those came home with him as trophies.

In addition to Artstetten, Ferdinand had various other homes including a castle at Konopischt in Bohemia. A Prague official who visited the castle described the scene:

The antlers of a Scandinavian elk, the skins of the black and brown bear, of the African and Asiatic lion, of the leopard and the panther, and the heads of the wild cat and wild boar all present themselves for admiration in the corridors. The foot of a giant elephant, shot by the Archduke in Kalawana in 1893, serves as an ashtray; the foot of another such colossus from Ceylon as a wastepaper basket. In one room, on whose walls hangs a portrait of the Emperor Franz Josef in hunter's clothes are assembled special mementos of memorable shooting days – a white partridge, a white crow and heads of deer and chamois with a single horn for antlers.

A chamois is an Alpine goat. In one photograph the Archduke stands proudly in the foreground in a Tyrolean get-up of socks and knickerbockers and a tall hat with a feather in it, surrounded by a vast army of gamekeepers and beaters who have assisted him. The day's kill is spread out at his feet. It is hard to be precise but, at a conservative estimate there appear to be at least 30 chamois carcasses, a veritable slaughter.

The Archduke apparently liked it when the beaters drove the animals towards him and he could pick them off at will with his big guns. He recorded in his journal that he 'could not describe his joy' at bagging his first tiger on a trip to India in 1893.

The Archduke was not a popular man, outside his family, where his children, two sons and a daughter (a fourth child was stillborn in 1908) seem to have regarded him as kind and gentle and, though firm, not at all overbearing. Outside, at large in the world, he was ill-tempered, intolerant and often quick to judge others while bitter at his own perceived mistreatment and ultra sensitive to sleights.

While he was admirably impatient with English codes of gentility, such as dressing for dinner, white tie and all, in tents in the middle of an Indian safari – 'instead I appeared in a sort of hunting garb ... even if the astonished company laid an English curse on me for it, I don't care ...' – dislike of Hungarians bordered on the pathological: 'Just look at that animal dance! That's one of the first things I shall do away with,' he bellowed, loudly, at a Hungarian regimental dinner, watching a young hussar participate in a traditional dance.

Apparently having the time to spare he filled thousands of pages of journals throughout his life and sometimes had them published, and became upset when people suggested a proper writer must have worked on them. 'People simply believe that every archduke just has to be a nincompoop,' he complained.

His lifelong bugbear, besides Hungarians, was the tyranny of protocol, the endless petty humiliations he and his wife faced in royal society because he had married beneath him. She could not sit at the top tables at dinners and could not share the royal box at the theatre. The Archduke nearly caused an international incident in 1910, trying to insist on her accompanying him to the funeral of King Edward in London. Propriety simply would not allow for her presence, not even, as he suggested, if she attended 'incognito'.

Had they but known it, the Archduke and his young assassin had more in common than they realized. The Archduke had not supported the annexation of Bosnia and had actually proposed and supported the idea of a south Slav kingdom, albeit of course, under the Austrian flag, which Gavro would never have accepted. In the Archduke's plan the Dual Monarchy of Austria and Hungary would have been replaced by a three-way Monarchy, so-called Trialism, in which the south Slav kingdom would have risen in equal importance, albeit favouring the Catholic Croats. Still, in some ways Ferdinand and Princip were thinking along similar lines.

Then there was the tricky issue of class and status that had polluted the Archduke's marriage and affected Gavro's idealized love for the unattainable girl, Vukosava, the sister of Nedjo Cabrinovic, the sophisticated urban young woman unmoved by his peasant appeal.

Most of all, Ferdinand and Princip shared a common sickness, tuberculosis, which was lying in wait for Gavro, the germs already inside him in 1914. The Archduke had contracted the disease in 1895, a year or so after he met Sophie. Luckily for him he could spend a year recuperating, travelling to warm, dry climates such as north Africa and the south of France where his lungs were able to clear. Even so, it was not until 1898 that he was finally told he was no longer in danger, and was fit for military service.

Looking for a role to play, he took an interest in the Austrian army and sought a position where he could have influence. Instead of a title he was given an odd, unspecific function attached to military supreme command as an inspecting general. While he advised and influenced the emperor on strategic matters he had no real authority until 1913 when he was finally appointed Inspector General of the Army by the emperor.

It seemed a natural move to make that autumn, when he told the chief of staff, General Conrad (Franz Conrad von Hotzendorf, to give him his full name) that he proposed to visit the troops in Bosnia. He had been advised as far back as 1911 that the situation in Bosnia was 'extremely difficult', the memorandum elaborating that both provinces, Bosnia & Hercegovina, were 'politically unconsolidated, culturally and economically underdeveloped, rent by political dissension and wide open to foreign subversive influences'.

Oskar Potiorek had been sent in, at the age of 57, to be a strong provincial governor but he too suffered the same character weaknesses as the Archduke, being described as arrogant, over self-confident and remote. So remote in fact, that when the Archduke had first suggested he might visit, the governor urged him to do it, saying that his presence in their midst could not fail to encourage sentiments of loyalty to the Crown amongst all sections of the community.

By late 1913 it was apparent that Serbian successes in the Balkan wars had made the Serbs ever more defiant, and that Potiorek's emergency measures had only made matters worse. Even the usually loyal Catholic Croats were turning against the Austrians.

Pamphlets circulating in Bosnia depicted the royal couple as 'the Este dog and the filthy Bohemian sow'. Sophie, the leaflets said, was a 'monstrous Bohemian whore' who had to be killed off.

During her travels in the south Slav states, in the 1930s, Rebecca West formed a harsh impression of the 'unlovely' Archduke with his 'slow working and clumsy mind' and his excluded wife. She characterized Ferdinand as a put-upon creature and said that had he been a different kind of man he might have evoked a sympathy that would have consoled him and his wife for their hardships: 'but all his ways were repellent.' Sophie, said West, had 'an anaphrodisiac and pinched yet heavy face ... in a day when women were bred to look like tablebirds she took this convention of amplitude and expressed it with the rigidity of a drill sergeant. We know that she impressed those who knew her as absorbed in snobbish ambitions and petty resentments, and that she had as her chief ingratiating attribute a talent for mimicry, which is often the sport of an unloving and derisive soul.'

The visit would give Potiorek a chance to show off the readiness of his 15th and 16th army corps. The Archduke wanted his wife, the 'Duchess of Hohenberg', to accompany him too and, in a military rather than a civil context, it would be easier for her to be accorded full royal honours, and not be sat at the lower table, so to speak. She also, apparently, was keen to go. Some said she was afraid for her husband and wanted to protect him. Others said it was a chance for her to present herself as the wife of the Heir Apparent, particularly as it seemed that his accession might come sooner, rather than later, as the emperor's health was declining.

Ferdinand had already written a 10,000-word 'accession programme', his blueprint for becoming emperor, much of it devoted to the 'stubborn Magyars' (the Hungarians) and 'the position of Her Highness the Duchess of Hohenberg'.

He had written his own accession proclamation, in which he proclaimed himself as follows:

Manifesto – to our people! We, Franz II, by the Grace of God, Emperor of Austria, Apostolic King of Hungary, King of Bohemia, Dalmatia, Croatia, Slavonia, Galicia, Lodomeria, Rama, Bosnia and Hercegovina, Kumania, King of Illyria, Jerusalem etc, Archduke of Austria-Este, Grandduke of Tuscany and Cracow, Duke of Lorraine, Salzburg, Styria, Carinthia and Bukowina, Prince of Siebenburgen, Margrave of Moravia, Duke of Upper and Lower Silesia, Modena, Parma, Piacenza, Quastalla, Auschwitz, Zator, Tetschen, Friaul, Ragusa, Zara etc, Count of Habsburg, Tyrol, Kyburg, Gorizia and Gradiska, Prince of Trient and Brixen, Margrave of Upper and Lower Lausitz and Istria, Count of Hohenems, Feldkirch, Bregenz, Samenberg etc, Lord of Trieste, Cattaro and the Windisch Mark etc etc.

It having pleased Almighty God to call from this life my august ancestor His Majesty Emperor and King Franz Josef I after more than six decades of beneficent rule …

We hereby solemnly proclaim before all peoples of the Monarchy Our accession to the throne, having been called upon by virtue of the Pragmatic Sanction to place the crown upon Our head …

We desire to treat with equal love all the people of the Monarchy, all classes and all officially recognized religious faiths. High or low, poor or rich, all shall be held the same before Our throne …

It goes without saying, of course, that this extraordinary tribute to the Archduke's own importance would never be delivered. Nor indeed would the next emperor retain those titles for very long. It was the end of the cycle.

The visit was announced in the press in the middle of March 1914 and read in a newspaper in Sarajevo by a Young Bosnian poet, Jovan Varagic. He discussed it with friends and they agreed it should be mailed to their comrades in Belgrade. They chose Nedjo Cabrinovic because, in his usual careless, boastful fashion, he had told a friend he'd acquired a pistol and that was now common knowledge among the Young Bosnians in Sarajevo. They were not to know he had left the gun behind when he set out for Belgrade. Another man, Mihajlo

Pusara, took the cutting with him when he went to his job as a clerk at the Sarajevo City Hall. It was pasted on a piece of paper and placed in an envelope with the one-word addition, greetings. Pusara posted it from Zenica, so that it would not be detected by the Sarajevo police censors.

10

Are You Ready? I Am

After they had shaken hands and given each other their word of honour to carry out the assassination of the Heir Apparent together, Nedjo and Gavro then discussed where they might obtain the necessary means. Nedjo knew there were people in Belgrade who could help, but they didn't exactly know whom to ask. Gavro said they might at least manage to buy one revolver. They thought perhaps they could enquire at the offices of Narodna Odbrana, the national defence organization, but Gavro complained he had already been there to ask one official for a stipendium to support him during his studies, and had been refused. There was another possible Narodna official to approach, but he was Nedjo's manager in his typesetting job and Nedjo hated him, so that was no good either. And anyway, both those officials were out of town.

They parted with Gavro agreeing to take on the task of finding the weapons. According to Nedjo they met at the cafés every day and every day it would be the same, 'hello', 'hello', 'anything new?', 'nothing'. Gavro had said he would look everywhere for the means and Nedjo did not know what was involved but began to believe nothing would come of it, that there would be no assassination.

As was his usual way, Gavro continued to spend his days immersed in socialist and revolutionary literature, always reading, always keeping up with current events from the newspapers. He was buried in a newspaper one day while sitting with friends when suddenly he exclaimed, 'the Russian emperor has just been killed!' Then, after a pause, 'I am joking, I just wanted to see what kind of revolutionaries you are and how you would react.'

One student who was not so fond of Gavro said that he stood out among the young men in Belgrade because he liked to pretend there was no one better than him, especially in his knowledge of literature, and he used to say he was the best of them. While this student knew his place and stayed in his own circle, Gavro had boasted of his access to higher circles, and described a dinner at the home of a university professor, who was also a Narodna Odbrana official, along with some other senior activists. Gavro was 'bragging about the good food and that they had watermelon …'

The student did not like Nedjo either: 'He was unattractive to me.' This man, Dobrosav Jevdjevic, later wrote his own account of the assassination in which he wrote sourly about a number of people, including the unfounded claim that Ilic had acted like a coward on the scaffold. Gavro, had he been around to read it, would no doubt have taken issue with Jevdjevic's account. When he gave evidence as a witness at the trial, Gavro stood to object, denying there had ever been a dinner at the home of the professor, and saying he and Jevdjevic had been in conflict in the past.

While Gavro sat around reading, Nedjo, by contrast, was working hard during these last weeks in Belgrade, taking on overtime which extended his day from seven in the morning until ten in the evening, so that he could pay off his debts. He hoped to go to Kosovo, he said, to celebrate St Vitus Day.

Nedjo had continued to carry around the news clipping and one day, he told the trial, he had met Milan Ciganovic, a popular, prominent guerrilla, the one with the lice-infested suit, who was now a low-ranking clerk on the Serbian State Railway.

Afterwards, when the Serbian government was being accused by Austria of direct involvement in the plot, the Austrians would be citing Ciganovic as a government official in the Serbian Ministry of Public Works, and the minister of that department would look long and hard for the culprit, before finally unearthing Ciganovic in some small clerical post in the railways' division. The minister would joke to his fellow ministers: 'There, you see! It is true enough what they say, if any mother has lost her son, let her go and look for him in the railway administration.'

When Nedjo showed Ciganovic the clipping the meaning was obviously clear. Ciganovic said, that's fine, but only if there are people. Nedjo said there were people, but not the means and Ciganovic said he could get the means.

According to Nedjo he did not disclose this encounter to Gavro for some days. But Gavro told a different story at the trial, suggesting perhaps that both Nedjo and Gavro were keeping each other in the dark about their activities.

According to Gavro he immediately thought of approaching Ciganovic for weapons. He had known him for a while but did not feel he knew him well enough to speak directly about an assassination so he asked friends to act as go-betweens instead.

Ciganovic was then 28 years old, a Serb from the Bosnian villages, like Gavro, and a heroic figure among the Komite, having been awarded a gold medal for bravery in battle. He was a close colleague of Major Tankosic, the Komite leader. Some historians have said that Gavro and Ciganovic had shared lodgings for a while. At his trial, Gavro said he thought of Ciganovic because he had once been at his home, before the 1913 war, and had seen the collection of bombs – about 12 in all – he had brought back from the first Balkan war.

Gavro had formed close friendships in Belgrade with two other Young Bosnians, Djuro Sarac, the trainee priest turned guerrilla fighter who had been imprisoned back in Sarajevo for likening the annexation to a theft, and Djulaga Bukovac, a Muslim boy the same age as Gavro, who had been expelled from school in Sarajevo after taking part in the demonstrations there. He had been involved in some of the earlier conspiracies and only recently wounded as a fighter during the second Balkan war.

It was these two who made the introduction to Ciganovic. Gavro explained what he hoped to do and asked Ciganovic to provide the bombs, saying he would find the revolvers himself. Ciganovic was quiet for a while and finally said, 'we'll see.' He added that he would have to discuss it with someone else first – a gentleman.

That was Major Tankosic, who must have given his approval, because, at their next meeting, Ciganovic told Gavro he could have the bombs and, because Gavro was poor, he would see about supplying some revolvers too. Ciganovic warned Gavro that success with the bombs was not certain, because they only exploded after several seconds.

It seems that one reason for the delay in providing the weapons was the serious illness of the Austrian emperor, Franz Josef, now 84, who had been stricken in mid-April with a severe attack of bronchitis.

Regular medical bulletins had been published and a train put on standby to carry the Heir Apparent to Vienna if Josef came close to death.

'Nothing doing,' Ciganovic was said to have told the plotters at one stage, 'the old emperor is ill and the Heir Apparent will not go to Bosnia.' In May, when it was signalled that the emperor's health had improved, Gavro once again asked Ciganovic.

Meanwhile, Nedjo and Gavro had agreed a third person was needed to complete their terrorist cell and Gavro suggested his friend and roommate from Carigradska Street, Trifko Grabez, who readily agreed on being asked. Grabez knew he was capable of it; that he would do it, no matter what. After all, he said, it was the duty of Bosnians to 'welcome' the Heir Apparent.

When he had taken an exam around Easter, Grabez went home for a few weeks and read the newspapers in Sarajevo where it was being suggested that the manoeuvres Ferdinand would attend were the prelude to an Austrian attack on Serbia. When he read that, Grabez definitely decided that the Heir Apparent had to be destroyed.

He was back in Belgrade by the second or third week of May and saw Gavro and found out that he too was still committed. Grabez knew Nedjo, but had never spoken to him about the plot. Gavro told him anyway that Nedjo's mind was made up.

They were sitting out front at the Café Moruna when they saw Ciganovic who told them that the major wanted to meet one of them and see for himself who would receive the weapons.

Grabez wanted Nedjo to meet Tankosic. Nedjo wanted to go too but, as he put it, because he was always laughing at the most serious moments and didn't have strong features it was decided that Grabez should go instead, as he looked solemn. Gavro, apparently, would not go because he had not forgotten the insult he had suffered when Major Tankosic had dismissed him as a guerrilla fighter because he was too small and weak.

Grabez was taken by Ciganovic to meet the major in his rooms.

'Are you one of them? Are you ready?'

'I am.'

'Are you determined?'

'I am.'

'Do you know how to shoot a revolver?'

'No.'

'Do you know how to handle one?'

'No.'

Tankosic produced a gun and handed it to Ciganovic. 'Here is a revolver. Teach them to shoot on the firing range.'

Ciganovic took Gavro and Grabez to Belgrade's Topcider park – a Turkish name, meaning valley of the cannons – where they went into the forest and shot at trees. Gavro was the better shot, but then he had already trained with Brownings at Prokulpje on the Drina frontier.

In one account of this episode both Djuro Sarac and another man, Milan Mojic, accompanied Ciganovic when he took Gavro and Grabez to the park for shooting practice, which went on over six days. They used an old oak tree shaped like a man's body as a target. Gavro hit the tree six times in ten shots from 200 metres and then scored a perfect eight out of eight over 60 metres. They tried running and firing and Gavro hit twice at 200 metres and three times at 60 metres. A guard eventually came and told them they were not allowed to shoot in the woods so they left.

Perhaps because he was busy at work, Nedjo was never taught to shoot. He and Gavro went to a camp to see which of them was the better shot and he also practised on the firing range of the Belgrade Gun Club. But he never had a gun on 28 June, only a bomb, and no one taught him how to use that either.

These young men were operating in a secret and largely undocumented world, in an age before electronics and electronic surveillance and forensic science where they left only the barest trail of themselves as they moved around. They did not always tell the truth and often lied to protect others and none of them ever knew the whole picture so that the story itself, the true story based on hard, reliable facts, becomes obfuscated and hard to follow. There is one account, and then another, and then another, and sometimes then another, so that, by this time, it is difficult to divine the truth from the half-truth and the lies.

Were the young men acting alone, and self-motivated, or were they part of a larger conspiracy, in league with or directed by shady, unseen forces?

One historian, himself a former Young Bosnian, while researching in the 1960s, nearly 50 years after these events, found in a Serbian

archive an unpublished account of the life of Djuro Sarac which suggested that he had founded his own secret organization in order to
carry out the assassination.

He had named the organization Smrt ili Zivot – Death or Life
– and it had a central committee of seven members, known as the
duhovi – spirits – of the Avengers of Kosovo. This Council of Spirits
would hear the oaths of allegiance of new members, and their sworn
pledge not to reveal the existence of the organization to anyone, neither father nor mother, nor sister nor brother, nor wife nor girlfriend
nor any other living soul. New members had to write a letter to the
council, giving their word of honour that they would kill themselves,
if required, after carrying out the tasks of Smrt ili Zivot.

The rules stated that only Bosnian Serbs could join and they must
be honest and abstemious with alcohol. Sarac was the leader and Milan
Ciganovic was on the council, along with the subsequent author of
the Sarac biography, Dusan Slavic.

The Council of Spirits met in another of Belgrade's parks,
Kosutnjak, which then shared its forests with Topcider, the more
central park. Kosutnjak had symbolic significance as it was the scene
of the death of another Serbian martyr, Prince Mihailo Obrenovic,
who had been murdered in 1868 in the middle of his preparations for
a Serbian uprising against the Turks and the Austrians. It was popular
myth among the Serbs that the Austrians had conspired in his murder
– another motive for any would-be avengers.

At these meetings, it was said, the Council of Spirits drew up a
shortlist, rather a long list in fact, of 19 possible assassins, which
included a shoemaker from Mostar and the trio, Princip, Cabrinovic
and Grabez. In this version of events Gavro and Nedjo were sworn in
as members of Smrt ili Zivot at midnight in the cellar of a house in
Kraljica Natalija Street.

The ex-Young Bosnian historian who found the papers that told
this story gave it credence because he personally had seen the author
Slavic around the Green Wreath cafés with the other conspirators.

Apparently this group had first considered sending an emissary to
obtain arms from Macedonia, where Komite units were still engaged
in skirmishes with their Bulgarian counterparts. The Council of Spirits
thought perhaps the Komite might have some bombs to spare, but
then rejected the idea because of the risks involved – the bombs might

be too old and malfunctioning and approaching the Komite opened the possibility that the Serbian government might discover the plot.

It was decided, according to the Sarac memoir, that Ciganovic should approach Tankosic instead, having extracted from him a promise not to disclose the plot. Ciganovic was accompanied by the memoir writer Slavic, who listened as Tankosic told them, 'if a similar request came from anyone else I would reject it outright, but I cannot do this to you. And I want to tell you why. Up to now, for similar purposes, I have given many weapons, and not only has nothing been done but even the firing of the weapons has not been heard. This time the whole plot seems serious and I am ready to give not only the weapons but myself also for this cause.'

At the end of this speech Ciganovic and Slavic, as one, roared, 'long live, Vojveda!' Vojveda would be an affectionate variation of Tankosic's forename, Vojin, or Vojislav, in full.

Tankosic was a small, frail figure and, in private, he could be quiet and gentle. He came from a Bosnian village not far from Gavro's home in Grahovo and his mother was a peasant woman who told fortunes. Because of the life her son had chosen she was often consulted by army officers who wanted to know their future. Tankosic was an influential Komite leader, running the training school, and drawing Young Bosnians to him by his example. At first sight he appeared timid, but like many a small, quiet man, before and since, he could be cruel and barbaric, and not always just in battle.

In one story about his fierce nature he had ordered a group of young recruits in Belgrade to jump into the Sava river from the railway bridge – a drop of around 45 feet – 'just to see whether you are going to obey my orders'.

Tankosic could be disorganized and short of funds, often using bills of exchange as a substitute for the hard cash he lacked. He incurred debts and one of his debtors complained to Tankosic's powerful friend, Prince Djordje, the son of the Serbian king. The prince summoned Tankosic and started to rebuke him for behaving dishonestly. Tankosic was angry and said he would not put up with criticisms from the prince about his private life. When the prince continued, Tankosic 'boxed his ears and cuffed him'. Perhaps because of their earlier friendship, the prince never punished him.

After the burst of 'long live Vojveda!', Tankosic then handed them a revolver, with no trademark on it, which he said had been a gift during a visit to a French arms factory, while he was supervising the purchase of weapons for the Serbian army.

You can see how this sequence of events at key moments touches and matches the details given by Gavro and Nedjo. Gavro *had* asked Sarac for help in approaching Ciganovic and Ciganovic *had* gone to Tankosic.

Were Gavro and Nedjo simply hiding the role of this secret organization, or was it a fanciful invention, perhaps created to suggest its alleged participants were more closely involved in the assassination than they actually were? Maybe it was tall tales, made taller in the telling, afterwards, in the Green Wreath cafés.

Certainly, as I understand it, none of the pistols given to the assassins were made in France and all had trademarks. They were Belgian-made Brownings, and, according to Austrian investigators at the time, had been distributed through a weapons' supplier called Firma Doucet in Belgrade. They had been delivered to Firma Doucet on 3 December 1913. All four had five-digit serial numbers beginning 19 and two of them had numbers in sequence. The four serial numbers fell within a range of 50 numbers.

Even today, as you will read later, there is an unsolved mystery about those guns and a desire to keep the serial numbers secret.

The bombs were made in Serbia at the Kragujevac arsenal. They were small, but heavy rectangles, not neatly finished but roughly assembled, looking as if they had been handmade and hammered into shape. They had a cap at the top which had to be unscrewed to reveal the detonator beneath, before they could be primed. They could only be primed with a sharp knock or tap, by hitting them against a wall or a post, for example. They would then explode after approximately 12 seconds. You were advised to count to ten and then throw, in the hope that they would explode as they hit their target, but that of course ran the risk that they might explode in your hand and maim or kill you.

Altogether, Tankosic supplied four pistols and six bombs. The involvement of Tankosic gave rise to the other famous conspiracy theory that surrounds the assassination – that it was organized and directed by the notorious Serbian secret society, Ujedinjenje ili Smrt, Union or Death, better known as The Black Hand. Historians have constructed entire theories of the assassination, with eyewitnesses and documentary evidence to support them, based on the premise that it was initiated and prepared by Major Tankosic's closest army friend and ally, The Black Hand's senior figure, Colonel Dragutin Dimitrijevic.

Dimitrijevic had long ago been nicknamed Apis, though here, almost immediately, history goes in two directions, wherein it is either Apis the bull (a sacred symbol of ancient Egypt) on account of his physical prowess, or Apis the bee (a name for a particular bee species) because he was always so restless as a student.

In 1914 he was 'Colonel Apis', a veteran at 37 years old, unmarried and with no children of his own, but a renowned military figure in Serbia. He was formally the head of the Intelligence Service of the Serbian General Staff but his legend was based primarily on his role in the 1903 killings of the Serbian King Alexander Obrenovic and his wife Queen Draga. The king had been an unpopular, despotic leader and had made a tactical error in marrying one of his mother's ladies-in-waiting, Draga, who was described by one court visitor as 'overblown, over made-up, plump, stupid and middle class'. She had been nepotistic, gaining favours and positions for relatives, and had interfered in state business. She had also pretended to be pregnant after their marriage – the inevitable discovery of the sham harmful to her husband's reputation. The king, who was seven years younger than his wife, had himself come to power in a *coup d'état* ten years earlier, abolishing the constitution and promoting the cult of his wife, much as Franz Ferdinand would have liked to do, given absolute authority, naming villages and schools after her.

Under their rule the army was under-paid and under-fed and when in early 1903 anti-royalist demonstrations began on the streets, some soldiers disobeyed instructions to stop the rioters, and joined them instead.

A group of young officers, including Tankosic, with Apis as one of their leaders, then only in his mid-twenties, had decided to kill the royal pair and some of their courtiers and instal in their place the head of a rival Serbian royal dynasty, Petar Karadjordjevic who had been in exile in Russia. The officers first thought of sending the king and queen into exile, but the recent assassinations of the Italian King Umberto and the American President McKinley made the more violent solution seem practical and in keeping with the ways of the wider world.

They considered poison, and practised successfully on a cat before dismissing the idea. They then considered a fatal attack at a royal ball, and planned it as a careful military operation which went wrong in numerous ways, most notably that the king and queen didn't actually attend the ball.

Finally, in June 1903, a group of officers dynamited their way through the palace doors and spent two hours searching for the royal couple before they were found cowering in a concealed wardrobe in the royal bedroom. The queen was wearing only a petticoat, white silk stays and one yellow stocking. She tried to shield the king with her body but they were both shot repeatedly and cut with sabres before being thrown out of the window to cries of 'the tyrant is no more!'. The queen's brothers and some other officials were also killed.

Apis had been shot while fighting with a palace guard before the murders and reportedly lay wounded with a pistol in his hand, ready to kill himself if the plot was stopped. He recovered but the bullets remained in his body, as living trophies. He was hailed in the Serbian parliament as 'the saviour of the fatherland'.

The growing influence of the military in Serbia was reflected across both eastern and western Europe in the period leading up to the outbreak of the first world war in August 1914, just over a month after the assassination. Forces were being mobilized or readied by France, Britain, Germany, Russia and Austria long before the hostilities began, amid growing instability and the realization that war was inevitable.

While Narodna Odbrana, the national defence organization, had been formed to play a military and espionage role after the Austrian annexation of Bosnia & Hercegovina in 1908, recruiting and training Komite, spies and saboteurs for the perceived struggle ahead, it could not continue in its quasi-official role once the Serbian government had been obliged to accept the annexation.

But even as Narodna was being rebranded as a cultural institution, there was a widespread sense of betrayal, especially among the army, and among some politicians and academics who did not want to kow-tow to the Austrians but wanted, in a sense, to stand and fight.

Those who had taken part in the 1903 killings were now regarded as the regicide veterans, and it was inevitable that they would take the lead if any new patriotic secret society for terrorism, or direct action, was to be formed. Apis was chief among them, by all accounts a powerful and charismatic figure.

One contemporary remembered him as someone who exercised exceptional influence on those around him, in particular on his associates and on junior officers who were all his inferiors in qualities of mind and character. He was:

… gifted and cultured, honourable, a convincing speaker, a sincere patriot, personally courageous, filled with ambition, energy and the capacity for work … He had the characteristics which cast a spell on men. His arguments were always striking and convincing. He could represent the most intractable matters as mere trifles, the most hazardous enterprises as innocent and harmless. Withal he was in every respect a remarkable organizer. He kept all the threads in his own hand and even his most intimate friends only knew what was their own immediate concern.

But at the same time he was extraordinarily conceited and thoroughly affected. Ambitious as he was, he had a taste for working in secret, but he liked it to be known that he was doing secret work and that he kept all the threads in his own hand. He was incapable of distinguishing what was possible from what was not and perceiving the limits of responsibility and power. He had no clear conception of civil and political life and its requirements. He saw only his own aims and pursued them ruthlessly and without scruple. He loved adventure and danger and secret meetings and mysterious activities. How far his private ambition reached it is hard to say …

It was for him to plan, organize and command, for others to obey and carry out his orders without questioning.

Another Serbian historian who knew him said he did not correspond to the image that existed in the general public about him.

He was neither temperamental nor high-handed; he was what one called 'a good friend'. But not only that. Through conversations with his friends I learned to know him better. He worked hard for the advancement of his followers; he was always pushing them ahead.

For himself personally he did not move a finger. Although he was a soldier with ambitions, he was indifferent to his career. He never spoke about his own personal merits and success; he was not boastful nor a big talker. When he would recall the *coup d'état* of 1903 he would tell everything except his own role. He was one of those leaders who accomplishes more than they speak. As all fanatics, he esteemed more the success of a cause than the lives of men.

He sent his own nephew into the Komite and the boy was killed as soon as he crossed the Turkish border. Friends for Apis were at the same time very dear and very cheap. His friendship had a dangerous quality; but this made his personality very attractive. When he wanted to draw his friends into a conspiracy or into some other adventure he behaved like a seducer.

With Apis at the centre, there were talks about a new secret society from 1909, following the Austrian ultimatum in March, when it demanded Serbia demobilize its forces and be a good neighbour, in accepting the Austrian annexation of Bosnia & Hercegovina.

Capitulation came on 31 March when the Serbian government responded to the ultimatum and announced that it would relinquish its opposition and end its protests over the annexation. 'In accordance with this statement and with confidence in the peave-loving intentions of Austria-Hungary, Serbia will reduce her army to the level of the spring of 1908, as far as its organization, location and effectives are concerned. She will disarm and disband the volunteers and their companies and will not permit the formation of irregular units on her territory.'

The resentment at this retreat was nowhere greater than among the military elite so that Ujedinjenje ili Smrt was being talked about and planned for two years before it was founded in May 1911. Though it is worth noting that a group of officers who had also been involved in the 1903 regicide did not support Apis but remained loyal to the government and supported its position on the annexation. Those officers became known as The White Hand.

For The Black Hand, however, a printing press had already been

Gavrilo Princip as a young man, in an undated photograph taken before 1914.
(Muzej Sarajeva)

The heir apparent to the Austrian Empire, Archduke Franz Ferdinand, and his wife Sophie Chotek, Duchess of Hohenberg, in 1908.
(AKG Images)

The imperial couple with their three children in 1909.
(Getty Images)

The Archduke (centre) killed over 250,000 animals during his lifetime of hunting.
(Schloss Artstetten)

An anarchist in the making:
Nedjo Cabrinovic as a boy
with his sister, Rosa, and their
father, Vaso.

Above right Nedjo's beautiful
sister Vukosava Cabrinovic, who
received romantic letters from
Gavrilo Princip.

The teacher-gentleman Veljko
Cubrilovic with his wife Jovanka
and their newborn daughter
Nada outside their home in
Priboj in 1914.

A Komite unit from the Serbian irregular army, *circa* 1912.

Gavrilo Princip in 1914.
(Muzej Sarajeva)

Nedjo Cabrinovic who attempted
assassination with a bomb.
(Muzej Sarajeva)

Trifko Grabez, who joined Princip on the mystic journey to Sarajevo. (Muzej Sarajeva)

Above right Danilo Ilic, one of three young men who were hanged for their role in the plot. (Muzej Sarajeva)

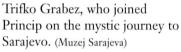

Cvjetko Popovic, the youngest of the plotters, aged just 16. (Muzej Sarajeva)

Vaso Cubrilovic, a would-be assassin, unbeknown to his brother Veljko. (Muzej Sarajeva)

Veljko Cubrilovic, after his arrest, not long before he was hanged. (Muzej Sarajeva)

Misko Jovanovic, the Tuzla businessman who helped the plotters, and was hanged. (Muzej Sarajeva)

Lazar Djukic, one of the leading young Bosnian plotters. (Muzej Sarajeva)

Ivo Kranjcevic, who hid some of the guns at home and brought ruin to his family. (Muzej Sarajeva)

Below left Mitar Kerovic, the head of the 'peasant' family who helped the smugglers and died in prison. (Muzej Saraeva)

Below right Nedjo Kerovic, the son of Mitar who also died in prison. (Muzej Saraeva)

(from the left) Trifko Grabez, Djuro Sarac and Gavrilo Princip in a Belgrade park in May, 1914.
(Muzej Sarajeva)

The Semiz wine shop where Princip met with friends on the eve of the assassination.
(Muzej Sarajeva)

obtained from Berlin so that the society would have its own journal, its own propaganda. The paper was called *Pijemont* and it was soon being cited as a mouthpiece of the Serbian army, in addition to having been financed by the Serbian King Petar, who owed his title to Apis, and his son Prince Alexander.

It was even said that Prince Alexander had asked to become head of The Black Hand. Alexander was the younger brother of the natural heir to the Serbian throne, Prince Djordje, whose ears had been boxed by Tankosic. Djordje had been passionately involved in the annexation protests, participating in a burning of the Habsburg flag and having a stand-up row in the street with an Austrian military attaché. He was too quick-tempered and when he kicked his butler in the stomach and the butler died he was forced to stand aside and let Alexander become the Serbian Heir Apparent.

Pijemont was the region of Italy where the Risorgimento had been initiated in the last century. Indeed, the Risorgimento had itself begun as a newspaper, with the aim of unifying Italy. So, The Black Hand was established to further the unification of the south Slav states and create a 'Greater Serbia'. It was the same nationalist idea shared by many of the Young Bosnians, but there was more chauvinism involved for the members of The Black Hand – they wanted the region united under Serbia.

The first issue of *Pijemont* complained about the complacency of conventional politics and parties who 'have shown in practice their immorality, their lack of patriotism and understanding of culture'. The paper's position was clear: Austria was the aggressor and war with this 'infamous opponent' was inevitable, no matter what the Serbian government said.

Secret or secretive societies and organizations everywhere – the IRA, the KKK, the Mafia, the Masons, the Jesuits, the covens of Satanists, the Bloods and Crips street gangs – create their rituals, oaths and means of terrorizing their own membership into remaining loyal. They seem to share an enthusiasm for theatrical display which perhaps is intended to concentrate the mind, instil fear and remain in the memory.

The forerunner for many of these groups was the Italian Carbonari, charcoal burners by translation, a secret society of political agitators in the early 19th century who paved the way for the Risorgimento and also favoured a little drama in their ceremonies. The Black Hand created their own seal in the image of the Carbonari – a clenched fist holding an unfurled flag depicting a skull and crossbones and beside them a dagger, a bomb and a bottle of poison. Around this fearsome motif was printed the name, Ujedinjenje ili Smrt.

The inner workings and values of the organization were set out in its detailed constitution and by-laws. Article 1, aims. Article 35, oath of allegiance. Initiations – supposedly around 300 in the early months – took place in a darkened room illuminated by a single candle. In the centre was a table shrouded with a black cloth on which were set a dagger, a revolver and a crucifix. One man described how he was admitted to the room by a member and listened while the aims of the society were explained. Then a door opened silently and into the darkened room lit by the single candle came a man dressed in a long black domino cloak with a hood on his head and his face covered by a mask. The hooded man never spoke but stood still, waiting. The newcomer repeated the oath:

I, Oskar Tartalja, swear by the sun that warms me, by the earth that nourishes me, before God, by the blood of my ancestors, on my honour and on my life, that I will from this moment till my death be faithful to the laws of this organization, that I will always be ready to make any sacrifice for it. I swear before God on my honour and my life that I will take all the secrets of the organization with me into my grave. May God confound me and my comrades in this organization judge me if, intentionally or unintentionally, I break or fail to observe this oath of allegiance.

When the oath was finished the man was hugged by the member who had brought him into the room, but the hooded man merely shook hands with him and walked out. The light was switched on and the member had to sit and listen while the entire constitution and by-laws were read to him. Then he signed his name to a printed text of the oath.

Members were advised in article 30 that in joining The Black Hand each individual 'loses his personality; he can expect no glory, no personal benefits, material or moral. Any member, therefore, who attempts to misuse the organization for his personal, class or petty interests will be punished. If the organization suffers any damage or loss because of him, he will be punished by death.'

The 11 members of the central committee were only known by number and were divided into isolated cells. The different groups were only allowed to contact each other through the advertisement columns of the Belgrade newspaper, *Trgovinski Glasnik*, with the specified wording (Article 19): 'One seeks a link with a rich person for the purpose of a big deal.'

It seems clear, at least, that there were overlaps and links between the membership and leadership of Narodna Odbrana and The Black Hand, and the Young Bosnians. Those organizations, of course, shared broadly common aims. There is good evidence that at least one man, Vladimir Gacinovic, the friend of Trotsky, was involved in all three organizations. He appeared on a membership list as member 217, in group 203. Some accounts give The Black Hand a role in the assassination efforts of both the martyr Bogdan Zerajic and Lazar Jukic who stalked the poor governor in Zagreb.

In *The Origins of War*, the three-volume study of the Great War's causes, the author Luigi Albertini cites two sources, Cedo Popovic and Oskar Tartalja, as saying that all the main conspirators in the 28 June plot were members of The Black Hand, notably Ilic and Princip. Other historians repeat the point, perhaps because it suits their purpose, but have nothing to add by way of proof. The problem is that there is no real evidence to back this up. Lists of members have been produced but these names are not on them. None of the conspirators ever admitted to being in The Black Hand and while they might have been bound to deny it even if it were true, in court, Vaso Cubrilovic, the young conspirator who lived on afterwards, always insisted none of them were members, long after it ceased to matter whether they were or not.

Did Gavro and Nedjo turn to Ciganovic, who almost certainly was a Black Hand member, to obtain weapons because he was in that organization or because he was known to them as a prominent member of the Komite who already had bombs? Did The Black Hand approach Gavro and Nedjo with the idea to assassinate the Heir Apparent, or was the idea their own, prompted by the news reports of his forthcoming visit to Bosnia, something, arguably, they had been working up to throughout their brief adult lives?

What did The Black Hand hope to achieve by the assassination, if they ordered and directed it? Did they intend to start a great war in which millions would die, or were those military figures too blinkered to realize what would happen, just as those young students could not foresee the terrible impact of their action? In this version of events The Black Hand acted to strike a blow for Serbia and thwart the weak government that had betrayed them in accepting the annexation.

Much of the subsequent strength of opinion about the involvement of The Black Hand was formed in the aftermath of the so-called Salonika Trials in 1917 when Apis and a group of other military/Black Hand figures stood trial for an alleged attempt to kill Alexander, who was by now ruling Serbia as the Prince Regent, following the abdication of his father, King Petar.

Serbian plotting and subterfuge grew ever murkier, with Prince Djordje apparently trying to reclaim his right to the throne and Alexander trying to have him poisoned, before finally having him locked up in solitary confinement for two decades. Serbians were said to have started talking about Colonel Apis as the real Heir Apparent and Alexander began to fear Apis's authority and lack of humility.

Alexander, according to one source, was offended that Apis was not the type of man who wished to bow. Apis said he was not a lackey and would not take off Alexander's jackboots. He was dismissed as Chief of Military Intelligence and his power base began to erode, many of his associates, including Tankosic in 1915, dying on the battlefields of the great war. He gathered around him those old Young Bosnians and Black Handers who had survived. Alexander became increasingly convinced that Apis, the killer of kings, was planning to kill him too.

Apis and his group were arrested at the end of 1916 and put on trial the following spring. It was a kind of show trial because the charges, that he had led an attempt on the life of the Prince Regent, were not really the crime for which he was being tried. The charges were made up, there had been no attempt at assassination. Instead, by now it suited Serbia to offer up a sacrifice for the 28 June assassination. Apis appears to have had some kind of breakdown, or been broken during interrogation and put his name to a full confession that he had organized the assassination of Ferdinand. He sent pleading letters – 'shameless', according to Dedijer – to the old king and his son, Alexander.

Of eleven defendants at the Salonika trial all were found guilty and nine including Apis were sentenced to death, though two were commuted to twenty years in prison. Apis and two others were led to a ditch outside Salonika in the early hours of 26 June 1916 and made to stand for two hours while all the charges against them were read. Then they were shot by the waiting firing squad of 15 soldiers. 'Long live Serbia! Long live Yugoslavia!' cried Apis.

What seems more plausible, and to fit with the events as known, is the account given by Apis a year after the assassination when he said that he too had feared the Austrian military manoeuvres were the pretext for an attack on Serbia, which was then riven with political difficulties and internal divisions. Austria could have overrun Serbia with one or two cavalry divisions, and the Archduke would have been their leader.

Hence when Tankosic came one day into the office and told me, there are some Young Bosnians asking to go to Bosnia, am I to say yes? I unreflectingly at once replied let them go. Tankosic then added that these youths had come to an agreement with other Bosnian comrades that they were going to make some attempt on the Archduke Francis Ferdinand. I thought such an attempt would be impossible and that probably nothing would come of it. I imagined that the Archduke Francis Ferdinand would be well guarded and that nothing could happen to him. At best there might be an incident which would be a warning to him and those around him and would make them understand it was dangerous to attack Serbia.

However, after a certain time when I thought the matter over, I tried to call the youths back after they had crossed the frontier and at all events to prevent the outrage. My attempt was made through the Comitaji Djuro Sarac. It was too late. The perpetrators, both those from Serbia and those in Sarajevo, would not give up their purpose.

The sequence of events around the alleged attempt to stop the assassination is no less puzzling than the entire story of The Black Hand, and touches on the sudden, mysterious change of heart of Danilo Ilic, in Sarajevo, days before the Archduke was due.

Ilic knew of the plot and was involved from around mid-April of 1914, when Gavro wrote to him from Belgrade to say that it was going ahead and that they were obtaining weapons in Belgrade, writing in code, in some allegorical form, at the same time asking Ilic to find a second group of three, a cell, or kruzhok as they were also called, to join Gavro, Nedjo and Grabez. All that now remained was to finally receive the weapons from Ciganovic and transport them into Sarajevo.

Gavro and Grabez received their weapons separately and not with Nedjo who said he had settled his debts and bought some clothes and was all ready to begin his trip to Kosovo when he saw Ciganovic at the Green Acorn and Ciganovic said, sabaile, which was a Turkish expression meaning the day has dawned. He showed Nedjo a pack of cartridges. He then handed over six boxes of cartridges, a Browning pistol and two bombs.

Nedjo went to the typographers' union to collect his typographer's book, which was his job record, and was ready to go.

As Nedjo later described it, Ciganovic told him that the three aspiring assassins would 'pass through a channel' on their journey to Sarajevo. According to Slavic, in his Sarac memoir, Nedjo was slow on the uptake and when he was told of an underground 'kanal' he literally thought it would be a tunnel beneath the earth.

Gavro and Grabez met Ciganovic outside the Café Moruna the day before the journey began and it was here that they received the rest of the weapons. Ciganovic first brought the bombs and 130 dinars which they complained was not enough. The money had been obtained as a loan, with one of Tankosic's notorious promissory notes. Ciganovic brought them a further 20 dinars which they added to their pot of money, which included the additional 40 dinars Nedjo had put by from his wages. Gavro told the trial that they could not get any more money of their own because they could not telegraph home.

In the Slavic memoir version of events, Djuro Sarac and others in the Death or Life society organized a collection among the wealthy Bosnian & Hercegovinan merchants of Belgrade to raise funds for the group, while telling the merchants the money was needed to build a school in Bosnia. They even gave the deception credibility by making a special charity seal and faking a letter from a board of school governors. They raised a thousand dinars, it was said, but there is no evidence the trio spent this sum or had access to it. By all accounts they were as broke as ever. So much so that Gavro pawned his coat before they left, raising eight dinars.

Ciganovic went off and came back with the guns and cartridges. He also wrote his initials, M.C., on a card and put it in an envelope for them to hand to the first contact they would meet on the journey, the frontier guards' officer at Sabac, Captain Rade Popovic. Ciganovic told them to head for Tuzla and said that if they could not easily get the weapons into Sarajevo from there they should turn to Misko Jovanovic who lived in Tuzla. He was a good Serb and would not reject them if they turned to him.

Grabez had studied a map and plotted a route through the 300 kilometres from Belgrade to Sarajevo that avoided the known barracks and guard posts. Ciganovic had warned them to avoid the gendarmes and the police at all costs. In particular he told them to avoid the local civil administrations where they could be arrested and sent back. They must ensure that the Serbian minister of the interior never got to hear about them. Gavro had made the journey several times himself and did not feel he needed anyone's help in getting there safely. He only wanted to ask the best place to make a discreet border crossing. He then told Ciganovic he would kill himself after the assassination, and Ciganovic said that was good.

That evening there was a farewell supper with friends from the Council of Spirits.

The trio met at one of the cafés for the last time the following morning, with the guns and ammunition in their pockets and the bombs tied around their waists. It was a beautiful morning, as Nedjo described it, and they came to terms, agreeing between them what had to be done, prepared for the journey ahead. Gavro told the other two they must not talk to anyone during the journey about where they were going and what they were carrying. All three pledged their words of honour to keep to this rule.

They set off down to the shores of the river Sava, which flowed north-westwards from the Danube in the heart of Belgrade. Two men came with them to the jetty, Djuro Sarac and Milan Mojic, the same two who had accompanied Ciganovic when Gavro and Grabez went for shooting practice at Topcider park. Those two now ensured the trio boarded the steamer that would take them 50 kilometres west to their first stop at the town of Sabac.

Farewell, Belgrade.

11

A Mystic Journey

Gavrilo Princip later described the smuggling of the weapons from Belgrade into Sarajevo as a mystic journey. When he was asked to explain what he meant he refused, typically you may think, perhaps not wanting to give himself away, dismissing the remark as being of no importance. But from the little he would eventually say, about how he felt and how he dreamed after he had completed the journey and arrived in Sarajevo, in the days before the assassination, he must have sensed both the literal weight and the metaphysical burden of those weapons, the expectation, the responsibility and the great personal test that lay waiting for him as he advanced towards his destiny.

Travelling regularly by night, losing sleep, facing physical and emotional exhaustion, living with the stress of the fear of discovery, walking many hours in the rain, stumbling blindly over waterlogged fields, becoming more and more ingrained with the mud of the Serbian and Bosnian land, being received with warmth and hospitality at every step by peasants and sympathizers, bathed in their good wishes but mindful too, perhaps, that his mere presence was condemning the men and their families to future hardship and in some cases death, it would not be surprising if the whole episode had taken on a greater meaning and significance. Nor would it be surprising if, in these conditions, deprived of sleep and food, he had come close to a kind of madness, so that the journey assumed a surreal quality and aroused in him a mystery and wonder, inspiring such thoughts as the poetic idea that 'Bosnia is a tear in the eye of Serbia', as he would tell Veljko and the peasants during their conversations between his fitful sleep at the Kerovic zadruga in the hills above Priboj.

Right from the start, on 28 May 1914, day one of the journey, on board the steamboat from Belgrade to Sabac, there were problems with Nedjo. Perhaps it was his naturally garrulous, open demeanour, but he seemed to have immediately forgotten the pact he had entered into at the café, and appeared to want to draw attention to himself and let everyone know what he was up to.

He began talking to a gendarme on the boat apparently trying to engage him in conversation, while Gavro and Grabez looked on, as you may imagine, with the guns in their pockets and the bombs around their waists, in some alarm, dismay and annoyance. Perhaps, for Nedjo, it was like an amusing game of risk, a little like chicken, darting into the road in front a lorry. Luckily for the conspirators, the gendarme did not pick up the conversation, thus missing his chance to detect and prevent one of the most notorious crimes of the twentieth century.

Coming ashore at Sabac they set off to find their first contact, the frontier guards' officer, Captain First Class Rade Popovic, whose name was on the envelope given to them by Ciganovic. Popovic was not in his office, but they met another local official who wanted to tell them about the problem of army deserters. 'Every day 50 of them come across the border,' he complained, 'we don't know what to do with them.' These were Bosnian deserters, of various ethnic origins, from the Austrian army.

The three men were told to look for Popovic at the Amerika café, and sure enough they found him there playing cards with friends. They approached Popovic but he asked them to wait until he had finished playing his hand. He then went and sat with them in a quiet corner where they introduced themselves and asked for a few words with him. He asked where they had come from; they told him Belgrade and he said he had been in Belgrade the day before and they suspected that while he was there he may have been told to expect them. Popovic was on special assignment as a border guard reporting to the military intelligence department led by Colonel Apis.

They asked him where they might cross the border into Bosnia and he suggested the village of Klenak but this was evidently a public frontier point and Gavro told him they had reasons not to go that way, they were travelling secretly and needed a more discreet location. Popovic shrugged his shoulders. He didn't know anywhere else but advised them to take the train to Loznica and see his colleague, Captain Prvanovic.

They asked Popovic, as Ciganovic had recommended, to give them half-price passes for the railways, which could be issued to revenue officers. He asked them if they wanted the passes issued in their own names or false names and Gavro said false names so Popovic looked down a list of officers and picked three names at random and wrote out the passes. Then he wrote a note for his colleague in Loznica, Captain Joca Prvanovic: 'see to it that you accept these people and conduct them to you know where' which he handed to Gavro.

It was too late by now to take the train so the three of them spent the night at a hotel in Sabac where they hid the guns and bombs and ammunition inside a stove. At 7am the next morning, 29 May, they retrieved the arms and once again secreted them around their bodies before setting off to the railway station, where they handed in the passes and paid for the discounted tickets.

After the short journey to Loznica they soon found Captain Prvanovic at his office and gave him the note from Captain First Class Popovic. They told Prvanovic they were Bosnian students, but did not give him their names nor did they disclose the purpose of the journey. When he asked where they were going they were not specific but merely told him they wanted to go to Bosnia and he said they could easily get across, so they again explained that they had to enter Bosnia without being observed, because if they were spotted the gendarmes might arrest them. He didn't know the way either but said he would call his revenue officers who worked along the border and ask them if it was possible. He tried to call the revenue men, sergeants who were based in a series of watchtowers, looking out for smugglers and any Austrian military activity. He was using his telephone but either couldn't reach them or couldn't make a connection. He told the trio to come back to his office the next day and said he would summon the revenue officers to join them so that they could find the best way to make a safe crossing.

The three young men went to the market and then, having a day off from their travels, went to the nearby spa town of Koviljaca which, like Loznica, was on the shores of the Drina river, the bent Drina, as the Serbs call it, which follows the western boundary of Serbia at its border with Bosnia & Hercegovina. The Drina is a potent symbol in Serb culture of both the divisions that have plagued it and the continuous turns of history. On the eastern side, Serbia and on the western side embattled Serbs and bitter enemies, both invasive such as Turkey and Austria and endemic, such a Bosniaks and Croats. Battles have been waged to and fro across the Drina and many bodies of all ethnic types have been cast or fallen into its waters.

It was best immortalized in the 1945 historical novel of Ivo Andric, *The Bridge on the Drina*:

Here, where the Drina flows with the whole force of its green and foaming waters from the apparently closed mass of the dark steep mountains, stands a great clean-cut stone bridge with eleven wide sweeping arches. From this bridge spreads fanlike the whole rolling valley with the little oriental towns of Višegrad and all its surroundings, with hamlets nestling in the folds of the hills, covered with meadows, pastures and plum-orchards, and criss-crossed with walls and fences and dotted with shaws and occasional clumps of evergreens. Looked at from a distance through the broad arches of the white bridge it seems as if one can see not only the green Drina, but all that fertile and culti-vated countryside and the southern sky above.

A Turkish army had crossed the Drina here in 1804 battling through Loznica and Sabac to defeat Serbian forces. And now, in less than three months this area would be the scene of one of the first battles of the Great War, with the Bosnian governor, Oskar Potiorek – the other man the young assassins would have liked to kill – in overall command of the Austro-Hungarian troops as they tried to overrun Serbia, pushing forward to take control of Sabac before being forced back and defeated over several days of fighting in late August at the Battle of Cer, by the nearby mountain, Mt Cer. This would be the first of the battles involving massed ranks of infantry that character-ized the war, with some 200,000 Austro-Hungarian soldiers facing 180,000 Serbian and allied forces. The death toll was just over 40,000 – 25,000 Austrians and 16,000 Serbs.

In May 1914 Koviljaca Spa was just developing as a resort town but had been known since ancient times for the supposed healing properties of its sulphuric thermal springs. On this late spring day in these calming, restorative surroundings, no doubt the three young men could never have imagined they would be the direct cause of mass slaughter.

They met an old irregular soldier from the Komite who knew them and, seeing the bombs at Nedjo's waist, asked him where he was going. Nedjo appeared ready to tell him and had to be interrupted by Gavro, which set off some hostility between the two of them.

Each of them bought a few postcards, Gavro using his to attempt a diversionary subterfuge, writing to his roommate cousin back in Belgrade, Vladeta Bilbija, with the message that he was on his way to join a monastery to prepare for an examination. Nedjo wrote to his sister Vukosava and both Gavro and Grabez added their own words of greeting. Nedjo wrote five or six cards altogether to male and female friends he had made in Sarajevo, Trieste and elsewhere. On one card he wrote, a good horse and a hero will always find the best way to break through. On yet another he wrote,

> Drina water, noble border
> Between Bosnia and Serbia
> Very soon will that time come
> When I will cross thee
> And set out to dear Bosnia

These were lines of heroic poetry celebrating the first Serbian uprising against the Turks from 110 years earlier, in 1804, the very uprising the Turks had been attempting to crush when they crossed the Drina to Loznica and Sabac. These lines of poetry purported to be the sentiments of George Petrovic, known because of his dark complexion and short fuse as Black George, or Karadjordje who had led the uprising and was, as Nedjo hoped to become, a Serbian hero. Karadjordje had founded the royal dynasty of that name and was the grandfather of King Petar who had been brought out of exile and enthroned in 1903 after the Apis-led murders of the rival royal family.

Gavro must have read these words written by Nedjo as a public declaration of intent. He was so angry after he had looked at Nedjo's postcards that, as Nedjo later told the trial, Gavro did not speak to him again during the trip.

As Nedjo explained it, the other two decided between themselves to push him aside and take his weapons. Grabez told him he would travel alone by a different route without any incriminating weapons and meet up with them in Tuzla. At his own hearing, Gavro denied there was anything more than a 'normal quarrel, friendly' between them, but it was clearly much more than that. He said Nedjo travelled alone because he had a passport, but in fact he travelled from now on with Grabez's passport, as Grabez had given it to him, after noting his passport photograph looked similar to Nedjo. Grabez did not mention any argument and was not asked about it, only saying it was 'inconvenient' for the three of them to continue the trip together.

On the rest of his journey, Nedjo would introduce himself as Trifko Grabez.

The three spent the night together and returned together to see Captain Prvanovic the next morning, 30 May, which was the third day of their journey. They were introduced to the three revenue officers and the captain asked them if they could suggest a safe passage. Two of them could not but the third said he could help them and knew of a peasant who would be able to lead them across the border. This officer was Sergeant Rade Grbic who had worked for several years at the Javoric guardhouse and watchtower which overlooked a small island in the middle of the Drina that was popular with smugglers.

The three young men and the three revenue officers went to an inn where they discussed their plans and considered a separate route for Nedjo. Secrecy was no longer a necessity for him, as he could travel 'legitimately' on Grabez's passport, so he would obviously reach Tuzla ahead of them. Grabez had a good friend from the Tuzla high school in the town, Stevo Botic, so he suggested Nedjo stay there and wait for them and gave Nedjo a letter of introduction to Botic.

Gavro and Grabez left first, with Grbic, who was described as a giant of a man with a big red nose. They sat together in Grbic's horse-drawn cart and stopped at another café on the way to his guardhouse. The two conspirators were now heavily laden, with three bombs each around their waists and two guns, one in each pocket, as well as all the boxes of ammunition. It must have been a relief to remove them at the guardhouse where they stayed for the night while the red-nosed Grbic tried to make arrangements for their onward travel.

It seems that Gavro was keen to practise his shooting as he used the gun in the grounds of the guardhouse and shot a hawk from a tree.

Next morning, on day four, 31 May, they crossed over to the island, which could be reached through shallow water that barely came over their knees and in some places was dry altogether. Isakovic's island was nominally Serbian territory and a peasant, Milan Cula, kept a hut there which was like a halfway house for the smugglers and spies crossing the border, where you could be served simple food and illegal plum brandy, when there were no police around. It was known as Milan's cottage.

Here there was another delay while Grbic tried to find some peasants to help. Gavro and Grabez spent the night with Milan, and again had some target practice, firing out of the windows of his hut.

Finally, the following day, 1 June 1914, the fifth day of the journey, a young man appeared from the nearby Bosnian town of Janja. This was Mico Micic who was 26 years old and had recently given up trying to run his bakery, and rented it out instead so that he could live on the land he owned with his sister and mother and work a little as a farm labourer. What he mainly liked doing was crossing the border to the Serbian town of Ljesnica where you could dance and have a good time. They had kolo dances there, which were traditional south-Slav dances and he had already met two young women, Milica and Ljeposava. He was now writing to both of them.

It was never clear if Micic had been summoned by Grbic or just turned up by coincidence. He was always stopping at Milan's cottage, he said, as he went back and forth across the border for the dances. The brandy was good and cheap there – only three seksers a measure – and though you faced 14 days in jail if you were caught trying to cross the border the sergeant generally turned a blind eye to his comings and goings. It was also a popular backdoor route with Muslims. Micic had served 21 days in prison, some time ago, for killing a man with a bottle and had also been imprisoned in the past after being caught in Serbia.

Entering the cottage he immediately saw Grbic with the two young men. He had just gone for a brandy, he claimed, and knew that Milan would be keeping the brandy in the kitchen, so as not to flaunt it in front of the sergeant, so he went into the kitchen and asked Milan to pour him a glass and then hid it behind his hand as he took a swig.

When he went back into the main room Grbic said, here are two students, they are from Sarajevo and they want to go back there, via Tuzla. He said they wanted to travel secretly because they didn't have passports. Micic said he could probably get a cart but Gavro said that would be too obvious.

Grbic was actually looking for another man, Jakov Milovic, who also lived across the border in a village beyond Janja and sometimes ran messages for Grbic, acting as a courier. Grbic asked Micic if he knew the other man and he did so Micic was sent back to town where he found Milovic in the marketplace.

Milovic was in his mid-40s, a widower with four children. He could not read or write and worked as a farm labourer, but was better known as a smuggler and occasional courier. He was a free man and, unlike many other rural peasants, was not a serf, tied to a bey, or landowner – the Austrians had not endeared themselves to the Bosnian Serbs by allowing this system to perpetuate under their rule.

According to Micic, at the trial, he told Milovic that the sergeant was calling for him, that there were two students who wanted to pass into Bosnia and Milovic would be asked to lead them. Milovic said, in his evidence, that Micic never mentioned Grbic. 'I'm telling you', he told the court, 'that's the truth. Even if you cut me into pieces, I can't say anything different.' Perhaps he was trying to disguise his relationship with Grbic.

By the time of the trial all these men were fighting for their lives and the main conspirators were doing their best to protect them.

Milovic was not about to rush off at this command so said he would come later. Micic returned to the island and told the sergeant that Milovic was on his way. He watched as one of the students unwrapped a box from a rag and put it on the floor. 'These are bombs,' said the sergeant, 'watch out or it will blow up and then we will all be gone.' As Micic sat there, one of them produced a pistol and began firing it out of the window. Gavro and Grabez appeared to enjoy playing with, or even showing off their weapons.

When Milovic arrived the sergeant told him, if you can, bring them over. Micic wanted to leave now and go home but the sergeant told him to wait and cross back with them when it was dark. The sergeant returned to his post, but not before he had warned Micic to keep quiet. 'These young men are preparing something great,' he apparently said, 'just keep your mouth shut.'

In darkness the four men, Milovic, Micic, Gavro and Grabez set off for Bosnia, crossing some small branches of the Drina to reach land.

They passed in a line through the low cornfields, Milovic ahead with Micic twenty paces behind and the students still further back, spread out for caution. Of course, it was strictly forbidden to cross this way, but there were no gendarmes around at this time and anyway, according to Milovic, half of Janja was heated with firewood smuggled from the island by this route.

When they reached the road, Micic left them, without saying goodbye, and carried on into Janja, while the other three kept off the road and began walking across fields and along hillside paths. They stopped for a rest at Milovic's home and then continued. The sky was so clear you could see like daylight, but soon it became darker and started to rain, the rain becoming a storm so that the going became heavy. The students were too tired to continue and took shelter in a deserted stable for a few hours until the rain had passed.

They carried on in the direction of Tuzla, passing the communities of Cengic and Trvono. Milovic was unsure of the way and sought help from a friend, Obren Milosevic, who lived on the route. The students waited out of sight while Milovic approached Obren's house, and though he was not at home when they arrived, the travellers were fortunate that his wife was there and she gave them oatcakes and made them some coffee.

Obren had been out all night too, caught out by the rain as he looked after his oxen. He had wanted the animals to graze in the fields and rest after they had spent the day ploughing his land, with the two Turks, father and son, he had hired. Obren was 38, and he too could not read or write, but he had four children and a little land and also worked as a farm labourer. After the hired Turks had gone he had stayed with the oxen and then been forced to shelter from the storm. He grazed them until noon and then tied them up and went home, where he found his wife making coffee for the visitors. 'Finish the coffee,' he told her, 'and look after the oxen.' Obviously he wanted his wife out of the way. It was by now the sixth day of the journey, 2 June.

They asked Obren to show them the road. According to him he said no and that was when they produced the guns, with their implied threat, and asked for some bags. He said he didn't have any but the students, he claimed, pointed to the saddlebags hanging from a hook on the wall, 'what's that?' and he was obliged to help them by providing bags. Gavro said it was hard to decide to take out the weapons in Obren's home, perhaps because the presence of the guns might incriminate their hosts, but evidently it was necessary.

Obren said that Milovic winked at him when the weapons were being shown and told him to keep quiet and just get some bacon and bread sprinkled with salt for the journey.

As well as the guns they took out what Obren described as djumlets, or cannonballs, which were the bombs. In fact, they took everything out and laid it on Obren's bedspread before wrapping it all up and packing it into the bags. They gave the bombs to Obren to carry and the guns to Milovic. Obren said the six bombs were very heavy.

The students wanted to go directly to Tuzla but that was still many kilometres and several hours' walk away and the peasants with their narrow horizons were not sure how to get there. They suggested, instead, going to Priboj to find Veljko Cubrilovic the schoolteacher, the 'teacher gentleman' as Obren called him, who was known to the peasants from his involvement with the Serb cultural group, Sokol.

Then too they may have known Veljko from his work as an agent of Narodna Odbrana as it seems that both Milovic and Obren had acted sometimes as couriers. Grbic had also mentioned Veljko's name to the students as a useful contact. For Obren, portraying himself at the trial as an illiterate farmhand, he was bound to do the bidding of these two students. After all, as he told the court, they were intelligent people, city people; and city people who wore suits were always officials.

This overland trek through forest paths to Priboj was the most gruelling part of the journey, lasting four hours or more through the night with more storms. Gavro and Grabez had now been awake and on the move for most of the last 21 hours with little food so that even though their loads were reduced they were still caked in mud and facing exhaustion.

They saw some footprints in the soil at one point and all four of them began to fear there were gendarmes nearby, their tiredness perhaps exaggerating their anxiety. The peasants of course were especially vulnerable as they were carrying the arms, while Gavro and Grabez kept 100 or so paces behind them, though they too would have been in danger if they had been caught.

They were climbing now and the poor peasants must have been

worn out as, when they reached the top of the hill by the junction on the road to Priboj, Milovic said, 'Do we have to go further?' 'Okay,' said either Gavro or Grabez, 'go and tell the teacher we are here and you get yourselves home,' so Obren and Milovic unloaded the bags and left the students hiding with their weapons behind a bush while they went in search of Veljko.

12

June 1914 – the Teacher Gentleman

Perhaps it was true that Veljko had been out looking for the two students that morning and already knew they were coming. If this was the case, as Vladimir Dedijer described it in his 1967 book *The Road to Sarajevo*, then Veljko had gone knowingly to his fate. It was certainly a convenience for those who preferred to believe in a carefully planned conspiracy, as opposed to a haphazard plot.

But how would he have known? Who would have told him? Uncharacteristically, writing 50 years after the events he was describing, Dedijer offers no source for this information. The two students were not following a precise itinerary and certainly not a timetable. On his own account, so far as he was concerned, Veljko stumbled across them by chance. There is no doubt, however, that the students, Gavro and Grabez, were on their way to find Veljko.

Then aged 28, Veljko Cubrilovic was a tall young man, old for his years, I would say, who carried himself with distinction, with his starched collars, his small, tidy moustache and his close-cut waves of dark hair.

In the traditional rural community around Priboj, where he lived and worked, there were few professionals, so that despite his relative youth he commanded the reverence and respect of those who knew him. The locals would refer to Veljko as the 'honourable teacher' or 'teacher gentleman'. They in turn would be commonly called 'kmets' or peasants and, schooling being a relatively recent development for the ordinary people of Bosnia & Hercegovina, many could not read or write and often did not even know how old they were.

Back home, at the teachers' cottage beside the single-storey village school was Veljko's fellow teacher, his wife Jovanka and their ten-month-old daughter Nada. Jovanka did not yet know, but on this late spring day in May 1914 she had just become pregnant for the second time.

I met Nada in the autumn of 2006 at her elegant home in Belgrade which appeared full of fine wooden furniture, the walls adorned with works of art. She was vividly old, at 93, but still remarkably intact, mobile and alert, speaking fluently in Serbian then waiting patiently with a warm smile while her daughter Vida translated Nada's memories and the family history she had learned from her own mother, Jovanka. Because she had been so young when he died, Nada had no real memory of her father.

There was one photograph of her with her parents, taken earlier that same year, 1914, in the garden outside the teachers' cottage, Jovanka sitting on a chair holding baby Nada, tilting her forward slightly for the camera. Nada, who must be only a few months old, is wrapped in an oversize, crocheted shawl, Veljko standing behind them wearing a buttoned-up suit over a shirt and tie, gripping the back of the chair. Mother and father both are looking down on Nada, their faces turned from the camera.

That morning, Veljko had been out on his horse, a bay, and had fallen in with the Serbian Orthodox priest Father Jovo Jovanovic, who was riding a white horse and was on his way to take a service in a nearby town. Veljko had set out to buy a lamb in readiness for a forthcoming feast in celebration of Pentecost. It was the Serbian tradition to roast a whole lamb over an open fire of hot coals, turning the meat slowly on a spit, either by hand or sometimes automatically by water wheel.

The priest had wanted Veljko to travel with him but there had been rainstorms overnight and the waters they would have to cross could be running high; too high for Veljko, who told the priest, 'if we get into too much water I wouldn't dare to go on because I am not a very good horseman.' The priest had told him not to worry and Veljko had said they would see at the first crossing.

Before they reached it, just as they were turning off the main road, two peasants appeared in front of them. Veljko recognized Jakov Milovic, who had approached Veljko a couple of years earlier and said, if you ever need anything from Serbia I will bring it. A smuggler, Veljko had thought then. Milovic also knew Veljko through the local Sokol, which Veljko had founded and led in Priboj.

On the road before them now, Milovic took off his hat, out of respect, and called a greeting to the teacher gentleman. Veljko asked where they were going and Milovic said, we were coming to find you. Why? We are not alone, said Milovic, there are two more of us, students, who want to meet you. They are for Tuzla, they want to go to Sarajevo.

Veljko asked what was going on, but Jakov claimed he didn't know. Veljko told the priest he would not go on, did not want to face the high water. As he left alone the priest smiled and said to Veljko, perhaps in a teasing tone, why are you such a coward?

From his hiding place behind the bush, Gavro heard the commotion of the meeting and the priest's departure. Now Milovic led Veljko back down the winding road and called Gavro and Grabez to come out, first one, then the other introducing themselves to Veljko with a greeting. He forgot their names but remembered them when he heard them again at the trial.

Veljko noticed their heavy load almost immediately and wondered what it was. He introduced himself in return and asked what they wanted.

Gavro asked if they could get a cart into Tuzla, 40 kilometres away. Veljko did not have a cart himself but knew a family living up in the hillside village of Tobut who would probably help. He gave Milovic and the other man a few crowns each and, evidently realizing the need for secrecy and discretion, told them to travel back to their homes by separate roads, so that one took the low road and the other the high road, just as Veljko had instructed.

Veljko took the students' bags and put them into his saddlebags. What do you have there, he asked. Gavro did not reply. Veljko wondered what it could be. Books? Then why hide them? If they were valuables they would be packed in a box. That provoked his curiosity and, now that Gravo had avoided answering, his suspicion. He wondered about weapons, especially gunpowder because he knew it was cheaper in Serbia and often smuggled. Gavro looked at him and suddenly the thought struck Veljko, like a lightning bolt. He had read a few days before in the newspaper that the Heir Apparent was coming to Bosnia and he wondered if it was connected. Please tell me, he said to Gavro, are those not weapons for the Heir Apparent, because he is coming?

Well, said Gavro, if you want to know, they are. We are going to carry out an assassination of the Heir and if you know about it you have to keep quiet. If you betray us you and your family will be destroyed.

It was still muddy underfoot and the two young men were wet, dirty, exhausted. This was the seventh day of their epic journey, 3 June 1914.

Veljko saw that the second student, Trifko, was struggling and asked if he wanted to ride on the horse but Trifko declined. Veljko asked him why they needed to carry those weapons. The times, the times, said Trifko.

It was early afternoon by the time they reached Tobut and Veljko told the students to remain out of sight in the bushes nearby while he went ahead. The family of Mitar Kerovic lived together here on their zadruga, a family settlement with Mitar as head of the household and his three grown sons and their families, with ten children between them.

The Kerovices, as Veljko would later say in court, were hard-working peasants and not concerned with politics. Veljko must have been close to the family, acting as 'kum', or godfather to some of the children. It is hard to say, at a century's distance, quite why Veljko took the students into the family's midst. Perhaps, as he later said in court, he felt forced to; perhaps he believed the family would want to help, to play their part in the liberation struggle. Whatever the reason, the consequences for the Kerovices were tragic, just as they were for Veljko.

Veljko first saw Mitar's youngest son, Nedjo, who was idling with the craftsmen in the yard on the edge of the property. Nedjo was the same age as Veljko, at 28, with two small children. He was the only member of the family who could read and write. Veljko saw that he had a bandaged hand, having accidentally hit it with an axe some days earlier. Nedjo had been to a local doctor but needed proper treatment at the hospital. He was still facing a call-up to military service in the Austrian army and it was not unknown for conscripts to deliberately injure themselves to avoid serving. People who did that could suffer harsh punishment, to deter others.

Veljko told Nedjo there were two students standing nearby and asked him to go and tell them to sit down somewhere. The students asked Nedjo for some water but when Veljko saw him carrying out a jug he told Nedjo to invite the students inside instead – making sure the craftsmen didn't see them.

Old Mitar, the 65-year-old head of the family, was chopping wood at the front of the house. He later claimed he had been drinking since midday with the craftsmen and when he was drinking he always went to extremes, as if this explained or excused him helping the students. He said he'd drunk an Oka – a Turkish measure, about 1.25 litres – of some unspecified alcohol, perhaps a variant of wine or brandy.

Veljko told Mitar about the students and asked if he could let them take the cart to Tuzla. Mitar was at first reluctant, but eventually agreed. They went into the house and Veljko said, for God's sake find me some brandy and water, I'm tired and can't go on. By the time Mitar returned with the drink, the students had come in and sat down. Veljko laid the weapons on the bed. He was feeling upset, he later said, and drank one glass of plum brandy after another which must have warmed his body and steadied his nerves.

The table was set and the Kerovic wives produced coffee and some food. The students were wet, muddy and exhausted and Trifko took his socks off before they both lay down for a sleep. Trifko woke up, had something to eat and fell asleep again. He later woke up and vomited. Veljko watched the students as they slept.

Mitar's other two sons Blagoje and Jovo were working in the fields, sowing corn when Jovo's little girl appeared, one of his five children, and said that Veljko was calling for Blagoje, who was 34 and the eldest son. Jovo did not know how old he was. Later, in court, he would say his father Mitar knew his true age and Mitar would be forced to admit that he didn't know how old Jovo was either. Mitar, in fact, did not know the ages of any of his children. Jovo had never been to school and his only literacy was his ability to write his own name. The little girl took Blagoje's place in the field and he went back to the house. A family friend, Cvijan, had also been summoned from the fields and he too appeared.

When he entered the house and saw the students, Blagoje said, God with you, and they replied, in return, God with you, and he asked, how are you? And they replied, fine! Blagoje stood there until Veljko said, 'Blagoje, I brought these two students here because I heard that Nedjo had hurt his hand and has to go to the doctor. Let these two students sit in the cart. They don't have travel permits. Let them sit awhile and let them go this evening. Blagoje shrugged his shoulders. What could he say? His father was sitting there. He was in charge.

There was some ordinary, casual talk about the forthcoming local elections and the political parties involved. Gavro said, Bosnia is a tear in the eye of Serbia.

It was agreed then that Nedjo and Cvijan would take the students in the cart, so that Nedjo could get his hand treated at the hospital and Cvijan could collect a suitcase for his brother, who had recently been expelled from college.

Blagoje saw the bags which had been moved next to the bed and asked what they were. Veljko at first said dismissively, they have some things but then said to Gavro, come on, show him those things. Gavro said, sir, why should I show him? Veljko said, show it, show it, so Gavro stood up and took out a small box, like a carton. It was a bomb, which he demonstrated how to prime and throw, first unscrewing the cap, then knocking it against a post and counting to ten before throwing, like this, said Gavro with an overarm action, over your head.

Gavro showed Nedjo and Cvijan, who would take them in the cart to Tuzla, how they could carry the weapons, hidden in the wide sashes of their traditional waist belts. They would have three bombs and two guns each. The students did not want to take the risk of carrying the guns themselves.

Gavro had been given the name of a contact in Tuzla, Misko Jovanovic, the businessman and patriotic Serb, a friend of Veljko's, known to him from the Sokols and also as an agent of Narodna Odbrana.

Veljko was the only one who knew the location of Misko's home in Tuzla so he drew directions and wrote a note of introduction, though he was not sure his friend would agree to help the students, much less accept the weapons. He warned Cvijan, who would drive the cart, not to go too near to the barracks in the next town, Lopare. Then he too lay down for a rest.

Veljko left for home before the cart departed and spoke outside quietly to Blagoje and Nedjo. By his own account, Veljko said to Blagoje, brother it's bad. What is? We've fallen into a great misfortune. The students are carrying these weapons to carry out an assassination of the Heir Apparent if he comes to Sarajevo.

But in Blagoje's version the conversation had an altogether different, more defiant tone, with Veljko saying the students were going to Sarajevo to shake up the Heir. The students had come from Serbia and were ready to sacrifice their lives for 'us Serbs' and they had to keep quiet about it or they would all lose their heads.

Trifko told Blagoje, you only have to keep quiet, you don't have to be afraid that we will give you away. Silence is blessed, said Trifko. Blagoje was astonished that the two young men were ready to risk their lives. But he was worried too, and said to Veljko, I hope you don't ruin me with those students.

Blagoje's brother Nedjo was troubled as well, but it was his place to defer to Blagoje and their father Mitar as the heads of the household. If they said it was okay who was he to argue? And Veljko too gave his assurance they would come to no harm. Veljko gave Nedjo ten crowns for the use of the cart, which he would use to pay the doctor who treated his hand.

Trifko was still sleeping so they had to wake him up when it was time to leave: come on, let's go, we're ready. The cart left after nine, Nedjo sitting up front with Cvijan taking the reins. The students lay in the back, on the hay resting and sleeping. It was a beautiful night. Trifko warned Cvijan to watch out but he did not reply. Trifko noted that Cvijan simply smiled and stayed silent.

13

Brothers-in-arms

When he finally arrived home at the teachers' cottage that night, Veljko told Jovanka all about the students. If the Austrians had ever known of that conversation they would have arrested Jovanka too, and who knows what would have happened to her. Veljko kept that secret from them. But as Nada, their daughter, later discovered from her mother, Jovanka knew everything. Veljko told her how he had looked at the students while they slept and admired their courage and felt humbled by it, seeing himself as a petty official, making compromises in his life, while those students were real idealists, acting on their beliefs. We all make compromises, Jovanka told him. We are also poor and doing the best we can.

The couple had moved to Priboj to take up their new teaching posts in 1910. The move had been partly prompted by the financial pressures they had faced, living and working in Tuzla where Veljko had family obligations to support his brothers Branko and Vaso and his sister Vida who were still studying. Jovanka would remember the terrible headache Veljko experienced on the first of each month when the bills arrived.

Jovanka's parents had died at an early age, leaving her with five younger siblings to look after. Veljko was one of the oldest among ten children, with responsibilities of his own, especially now that his parents were dead. His father had been a successful merchant and had even travelled as a tourist in Europe, a rare thing in those days, visiting the Paris Exposition of 1889, for which the Eiffel Tower had been constructed. Veljko's father had bought a pair of earrings at the Exposition as a gift for his wife and they would still be in the family, 120 years later. He had raised a cultured, middle-class family, though he could not entirely shield them from financial strain. An aunt had been the first qualified woman doctor in Bosnia & Hercegovina.

Like so many other Serbs in the region, Veljko and Jovanka had been outraged by the Austrian annexation of Bosnia in 1908. Jovanka, who was two years older than Veljko, had travelled to the Serbian capital Belgrade that same year, 1908, when she was 24 and had gone directly to the army headquarters where she had attempted to volunteer to assassinate the Austrian emperor, Franz Josef. The officers there had laughed at her but at least she had left with some dignity, having been given a small role as a courier taking messages.

Jovanka and Veljko had first met at a teachers' conference and had later begun teaching at the same school in Tuzla where their relationship had blossomed, though Jovanka told her daughter Nada that she had fallen in love with Veljko the first time she saw him. Even at his trial, Veljko told the court he had married for love and had been happy in his life at home.

Going to Priboj had improved their financial position and made it easier to continue to support their younger siblings. For the four years they remained there they were part of an idyllic village existence, teaching the village children and sharing the local festivities, observing religious holidays and ceremonies such as weddings, baptisms and funerals.

Back in Tuzla, Veljko had helped to develop a programme for implementing good standards of hygiene in primary schools. In Priboj he produced a written study of the area's topography which he had submitted to the Serbian Academy in Belgrade. He had received in return 50 dinars and a letter of thanks which, as he said, was not much for three months' work. Here in Priboj, under the Austrians, his annual salary was 2,470 crowns. He had been doing some work on an ethnographic study of Serbian folklore and traditions, with a fellow writer, but that would never be finished or published.

Veljko's youngest sibling, the tenth-born Vaso, was a regular holiday visitor to Priboj, sometimes annoying others, sitting in a nearby tree playing his trumpet, sometimes swimming or fishing with local children in the nearby river. Vaso also ran messages for Veljko, through his work with the Sokol or the Narodna Odbrana, travelling on foot over the mountains between Priboj and Tuzla where wolves were often seen.

In early 1914, Vaso had just turned 17 and was studying at the high school in Tuzla where he had joined the Mlada Bosna, the Young Bosnians, a network of secret societies whose student members were busily engaged in resisting the Austrians and seeking increasingly dramatic ways of furthering that cause. The Tuzla school was already well known as a Mlada Bosna stronghold.

When the Habsburg imperial anthem was being played during a service at the school, Vaso got up and walked out of the hall. He was expelled and moved to Sarajevo where he moved in with another sister and enrolled at the town's high school. He was soon once again mixing with the other young activists.

Vaso had no idea Veljko had played any role in smuggling the weapons from Belgrade. Veljko had no idea his brother was about to be asked to join an assassination plot, using those very same weapons. Vaso was still in the early stages of a long life, with its own sadnesses. Veljko's life was coming rapidly to a close.

That weekend, following the students' visit, Mitar Kerovic went to church as usual and then called on the teacher gentleman at his home, where he was invited in for coffee. Those students will take the bombs to Sarajevo, Veljko told him. The Heir Apparent will go there on St Vitus Day and they will throw the bombs at him. My God, said Mitar, they will break up my house. Don't worry about that, said Veljko. He told Mitar not to talk about it, in case a bomb fell on the home of the one who talked.

And if they do kill him, said Veljko, then they will kill themselves and nobody will learn anything about it.

When Mitar left he saw his son Nedjo who started to talk about it. Shut up! Mitar warned him. Don't mention it again.

14

June 1914 – Misfortune Calls

Gavro and Grabez only once climbed down from the cart on their midnight ride to Tuzla, as it passed through the garrison town of Lopare where the two conspirators walked separately, by a circuitous route around the town to avoid the barracks, and rejoined the cart at the far side of the town. In a month, a black flag would be flying at the gendarme barracks to mark the sudden passing of the Heir Apparent. And after that there would be too many deaths to count.

Despite resting in the hay, Gavro and Grabez did not feel in a fit state to enter Tuzla, so they asked the peasant to stop the cart on the outskirts, at about dawn on the eighth and final day of their journey, 4 June 1914. The cart pulled up beside a roadside stream by the farm estate run by the Catholic sisters of mercy, which locals called Josip's or divica, meaning the place of the virgins. Gavro and Grabez gave Cvijan a forint and told the peasants to go ahead and hand over the weapons to Misko Jovanovic and ask him to meet the two students after nine o'clock at the Serb reading room.

The cart continued while Gavro and Grabez did their best to clean themselves up in the river Jala so as not to look too out of place when they reached the town. They walked in and went to a café, Kavana Bosna, and sat at separate tables, each pretending they were alone, until the shops opened at nine o'clock when both young men went out and bought a new pair of trousers.

Grabez turned up at the home of a student friend, Bozidar Tomic. Arriving there he was still, as Tomic immediately noted, all covered in mud. He changed into his new trousers. Tomic saw Gavro as well and said to some other friends, look, he really grew up! The friends were less sure. No, they said, he did not exactly grow up. Still too small and too weak, in other words.

Meanwhile, Nedjo and Cvijan had taken the cart into town, to the inn of Gajo Sekulic who catered especially for peasants and provided space for them to leave their carts. They walked round to the home of Misko Jovanovic where Cvijan rang the doorbell, even though it was barely just seven o'clock in the morning.

Misko Jovanovic was 36 years old and not long since married, with one newborn baby. Veljko Cubrilovic was the child's godfather. Misko had been born and raised in Tuzla, the third largest city in Bosnia & Hercegovina, taking its name from the Turkish word for salt, so called because of the rich salt deposits that lay beneath the earth.

Like Sarajevo, Tuzla would be besieged by Serb nationalists seeking unification in the 1990s. Almost exactly 81 years after these events, on 21 May 1995 Serb artillery would hit a gathering of children and young people in the town centre. The exact details would be disputed, but it would be claimed that one single shell had exploded killing 71 people – the Tuzla massacre.

On the day that misfortune called at his home, 4 June 1914, Misko Jovanovic and his father were among the more prominent, prosperous Serb citizens of the town. Until his wedding the previous August, Misko had been in business with his father but, as a wedding gift, his father had given him a building which he himself had constructed to be used as Tuzla's first cinema. Misko had financed the purchase of the projection equipment with a loan from the Serbian Bank, of which he was a member of the board. He was also president of the local Sokol, a member of the Serbian church community, member of the Episcopal council and a local representative of the Narodna Odbrana.

He had opened the cinema successfully and regularly supervised performances himself, while his wife and her friends and family also attended as guests. He lived in an apartment above the cinema, on the third floor. In between, on the second floor, was the Serbian reading room.

A photograph of Misko taken before his arrest shows a handsome, distinguished-looking man with strong features, smartly dressed with an upturned handlebar moustache. Perhaps because of Misko's status and prosperity, a rare sight among all those students and peasants, the prosecutor at the trial seemed to take a particular delight in making him squirm during his evidence, challenging him, time and time again, on his activities and his beliefs. Perhaps it was the same between the

Austrians and their awkward Serb subjects as it was for many decades to come between the British and their subjects in India and Africa, or in America before and during the civil rights struggle. The masters liked to keep the slaves in their place and woe betide anyone who got out from under them or got too big for their boots. They needed to be taught a lesson, to be taken down a peg or two ...

Ironically, and this too seemed to gall the Austrian prosecutor, Misko, in his capacity as the Sokol president, had sent a note of condolence to Austria at the death of the Heir Apparent whom he had helped to kill:

> The prosecutor asked, what kind of task did the Sokol have?
> Misko explained, to cultivate the physical and spiritual health of its members.
> From the political point of view?
> Excluded.
> In the Tuzla Sokol too?
> Generally in every Sokol.
> Weren't you allowed to concern yourselves with politics?
> If anyone began a political discussion I stopped it.
> Did you have some other kind of honorary office which was connected with Serbia?
> Yes. I was a representative of the Narodna Odbrana.
> What is the Narodna Odbrana?
> I read in the newspapers that it holds lectures, educates the people.
> How was it that you became a member of the Narodna Odbrana?

Misko had joined, finally, in 1912. Early in that year he had met Veljko during a Sokol exercise in Priboj and Veljko had told him he was just back from the town of Sabac where the president of Narodna Odbrana had asked Veljko if he thought Misko would like to join Narodna Odbrana as a representative. Misko had said he would think it over but left Priboj sure he would say no because he already had enough duties to contend with.

In the spring he had travelled to Germany and spent some time in Berlin where he found out about the association Deutschland für's

Ausland – Germany for Foreign Lands – and noted how hard the association worked for its settlers in Bosnia & Hercegovina. He had subscribed to the group's newsletter Deutsche Stunden – German Hours – and when it reached him back home in Tuzla he had read it with increasing feelings of shame that he had turned down Veljko and the chance to work for his own community when there were people hundreds, thousands of kilometres away working so hard for their people. He went to Sabac himself then and saw the Narodna Odbrana president, Boza Milanovic, and said he was now willing to take the role on. He had been given some pamphlets which he had taken away and distributed at Sokols and to peasants he met.

You are a representative of the Narodna Odbrana and you don't know what its aims are?
  I don't know.
  You know your tasks in all organizations except this one?
  I knew it from practice.
  But as a representative of the Narodna Odbrana you had to know the goals?
  It has educational, cultural goals. This is what I was told.
  Did you know they trained guerrilla bands into armed forces and provided them with arms?
  Yes in time of war.
  Is that thought cultural and educational?
  This is in time of war. At such times the most humane institutions work in that way.
  The Red Cross does not arm soldiers. You were a representative at that time, and you did not receive orders to give contributions for that purpose?
  No …
  You said that the Sokol had no political goals and yet you gave the peasants the kind of books which said that the Muslims, Serbs and Croats were one people and must be unified. You worked in the political field when you distributed those brochures. What are your political ideals?

Misko said he had never concerned himself with politics but, by this time, the Austrian authorities had searched his home and found letters he had exchanged with his wife which suggested that he at least considered and maybe even tried to become a guerrilla himself during the first Balkan war.

He said he had simply gone to Belgrade to support his sister who lived there after her husband, an industrialist, and his two brothers had all three signed up to fight. He had gone to console her, he said, he was not fit to fight himself and, anyway, he had read that Serbia was rejecting volunteers as she already had 60,000.

Why then, he was asked, had his wife, then his fiancé, written, 'You don't say what you intend or whether they will send you back in another way for dear Serbia …' and '… you work voluntarily, and if not with a rifle in your hand still you expose yourself to danger.' Misko suggested that perhaps his wife was referring to his work for Serbs and the dangers he had sometimes faced, travelling around the region in bad weather, as once in Srebrenica when he had been driven home through a stormy February night.

If he had not concerned himself with politics why had he written a circular letter to all the Sokols in which he said, 'Dear Brothers, to us, to whom it is not yet given to pawn our lives for freedom.' Was that, the prosecutor asked sarcastically, in the sense of health?

No, said Misko, it was written in enthusiasm and it meant if they were not dying it was their duty to help.

When, asked the prosecutor, did he think the time would come [to die]? Perhaps now? Misko said he didn't know. But the prosecutor was not far off.

Was he a loyal man?

No one could say he was not loyal, said Misko.

How far does your loyalty go, when you prepare revolvers and bombs in Sarajevo for the assassination?

I did not prepare them …

It had been his wife's friend Mara Sainova who was visiting from Mostar who answered the call of the doorbell that morning and found Cvijan and Nedjo there. 'Is Misko at home?' 'Yes.' 'Then let him come out!' 'Yes, when he is dressed.' Misko had been asleep until Mara woke him up and said there were two peasants calling on him so he got out of bed, drew on a gown and went out. God with you.

God with you. After the usual greetings Nedjo Kerovic handed Misko a note, which he opened and read. 'Dear Misko, keep these things, greetings, your Veljko.'

Misko ushered the peasants into his kitchen. 'What kind of things do you bring,' he asked. From their belts, they produced the six bombs and four pistols and laid them on the kitchen table. 'What's this?' Misko asked. These are from Veljko, said the peasants, and they belong to some students who are going to Sarajevo. They will come later. Misko said he didn't know who the students were. Cvijan said they would come to the reading room after nine o'clock.

Misko apologized. Normally, he said, he would invite the peasants in for coffee, but it was too early. Perhaps also, this middle-class man did not want two peasants drinking coffee at his home. The peasants left. Nedjo went to the hospital where the doctor bandaged his wound and told him to come back in three days. He went from the hospital back to the inn where they had left the cart, to wait for Cvijan, who had agreed to go back to the reading room to introduce Gavro and Grabez to Misko.

Not quite sure what to do with the weapons, Misko had first hidden the guns and bombs in a cabinet in his hallway but then he suddenly remembered his wife used the cabinet to store kitchen supplies and often went to it. If she saw the weapons she would be frightened. He took everything up the stairs to the attic, which was shared between the four tenants in the building, where each had their own room. Misko found an old box there and put the weapons inside.

Why didn't you throw out the peasants and the bombs?
   I didn't even think of that.
   Just on the basis of the letter from Veljko Cubrilovic you accepted the bombs and revolvers?
   I didn't know what purpose they would serve.
   Everyone knows for what purpose?
   I know that even the most honourable people carry arms.
   Not bombs. I never saw that honourable people carry bombs. Maybe in Serbia ...

At nine o'clock Misko went down to the second floor and into the Serbian reading room where he saw Cvijan reading a newspaper.

Where are the students? They will come soon. Misko took the paper and started reading it himself. Two young men came in. Cvijan stood up. These are the students, he said, and left.

Cvijan returned to the inn and he went with Nedjo to collect his brother's trunk. His brother had been expelled from school in Tuzla after he had helped himself to 50 crowns that had arrived at the post office for another student with a similar name. Cvijan's brother had gone off to study in Belgrade but had left a trunk in Tuzla to be collected. On the way back to Tobut, Nedjo said to Cvijan, those students are stouthearted fellows because they plan to kill the Heir with bombs and revolvers. Cvijan said nothing. He was too afraid to say or do anything.

When Nedjo reached the zadruga his father, old Mitar, was way up in the mountains working. When he came back after three or four hours, Nedjo started to ask him, do you know why those students carried bombs? Mitar cut him short. 'Shut up, you fool!'

Misko took the two students into a side room so that they could talk privately. Gavro noted, somewhat alarmed, that Misko seemed nervous, his hands shaking. They told him they were students from Belgrade, on their way back to Sarajevo, and Misko told them, those peasants left weapons with me and said to give them to you. Gavro said they were travelling without passports, there were already emergency measures and there might now be even stricter controls because of the forthcoming arrival of the Archduke Ferdinand. He asked if Misko would be prepared to take the weapons into Sarajevo himself as it would be much safer for him. Misko said he was afraid of doing that and not prepared to take the risk.

If you won't do that, said Gavro, please keep them at your place for a few days until we can send a friend to collect them. Misko probably would have liked to refuse this request too but couldn't or wouldn't. He shrugged his shoulders. Okay. They agreed the person who came to collect the weapons should carry something to prove who they were. Misko suggested a box of Stefanija cigarettes as this was the brand he liked to smoke.

Misko claimed that Gavro threatened him. 'Don't play with the idea of betraying us, sir, because I will destroy you and your entire family.' As it happened, that's exactly what Gavro was doing, anyway. He said he threatened Misko because he saw that he was afraid and feared he might not be able to go through with the plan.

Before taking the train to Sarajevo, Gavro and Grabez were re-united with Nedjo Cabrinovic who had by now been in Tuzla waiting for them for three days, staying at the home of Grabez's friend, Stevo Botic.

After being sent to the Serbian equivalent of Coventry by Gavro, stripped of his weapons and abandoned with Grabez's passport in Loznica, Nedjo had returned to the scene of his infamous postcard writing at Koviljaca Spa and then gone on to the town of Mali Zvornik. Captain Prvanovic had given him a note, in an envelope addressed to either Suna or Jakovljevic. The letter said that 'one should lend a hand to our reliable persons who pass through Mali Zvornik'.

Unable to find the revenue director, Suna, Nedjo instead located the other man, Jakovljevic and handed him the letter, which he read before taking Nedjo to the watchtower where he took Nedjo's pass-port (which of course was actually the passport of Trifko Grabez) and gave it to the Serbian border guard to record the details.

While they waited for the passport to be returned they went to a café, where Jakovljevic treated Nedjo to a coffee, then they went back to the watchtower to collect the passport and Jakovljevic called a little Muslim boy to take them across the Drina to Veliki Zvornik.

Zvornik was a border town that straddled both sides of the Drina, on the Bosnian side known as Veliki (Big) Zvornik and on the Serbian side known as Mali (Little) Zvornik. A sizeable Roma community would build up there in the ensuing years, on the Bosnian side, acquir-ing homes and in some cases considerable wealth, until around April 1992 when Bosnian Serb soldiers, men and women, would unite with Serbian forces of the Yugoslav National Army to take over the town and carry out mass killings there, so that witnesses would describe the streets of the Roma community as being covered with mutilated corpses. There were also many victims among the majority Muslim community.

During the build-up of tension in Zvornik, before the killings began, Belgrade radio had been broadcasting inflammatory propaganda, re-porting that Serbs were being herded into concentration camps in the area, and that Serb corpses were floating down the Drina.

Arriving in Big Zvornik, Nedjo again handed his passport over, this time to a gendarme in Austrian employ, and chatted with the gendarme, after introducing himself as Trifko Grabez. As he emerged from the guardpost into the town with Jakovljevic they – by chance, according to Nedjo – met Djordje Dakic, who was the clerk of the local commune and, as it turned out, a relative of Nedjo's.

Before he returned to Little Zvornik, Jakovljevic asked Dakic to find Nedjo a place to stay for the night and to help him with his onward journey. Dakic took Nedjo to a café with rooms where he ordered coffee and supper. The next morning Dakic showed him the railway station but no train was due so Nedjo set off walking until he joined a passing stagecoach that took him into Tuzla, where he went to the home of Grabez's schoolfriend Stevo Botic.

On the last afternoon, as he waited to join Gavro and Grabez on the train to Sarajevo, Nedjo was passing time at an inn and met a detective, Ivo Vila, who was passing through Tuzla with a police colleague on his way home to Sarajevo. Vila had been called to Mostar the day before to arrest two students, Young Bosnians, who had been involved in a demonstration, protesting against the visit to Mostar of a German drama group that was presenting an anti-Polish play. The visit had been so controversial it had even provoked a series of formal duels between Mostar residents and some Austrian army officers. Vila had delivered one of the students to the Tuzla jail and was mooching around the town, passing the time waiting for the Sarajevo train when he noticed a modest but hospitable-looking inn. He went in and sat down with the two Muslim waiters. Then Nedjo appeared from another room, apparently with a woman. Vila often visited Nedjo's father's café in Sarajevo in the course of his work and so knew and was known to Nedjo, who had not been back in Sarajevo, by now, for many months.

Nedjo asked him, how are you? I am here in Tuzla, he added.

What are you doing here? asked the detective.

Nothing, I could begin working in the printing plant, but I don't want to.

The detective asked how he supported himself and Nedjo gestured towards the woman with him, this is my relative and she supports me. Nedjo wanted to know how his parents were and Vila told him he had seen his father just the day before, and seen the other members of his family too, and they were all well. And where have you been? the detective then asked. Nedjo told him he had been in Dalmatia and more recently in Belgrade and the detective enquired, how is life there? Nedjo told him it was not too good: 'Low wages and high cost of living. If you want to get something better you have to spend one and one-half dinars and for something not so good, one dinar.'

Nedjo must have seemed very at home at the inn, as if he belonged there, as the detective asked him, is there anything to eat and Nedjo said there would be soon, so the detective stayed for dinner and left afterwards, without seeing Nedjo again, to catch the train to Sarajevo, meeting a police colleague who joined the train at Doboj. There too on the train was Nedjo and they all sat together from Doboj and Nedjo was very chatty and asked the other officer, how are things with the Sarajevo police, and the other officer began to answer him and started to say things were very good but then Vila kicked him under the table to warn him to keep quiet.

By then, however, the officers had helpfully disclosed to Nedjo that the Heir's visit to Sarajevo was scheduled for 28 June – the first time the conspirators had been given the actual date. From where they were sitting, the officers could see Gavro and Grabez who were sitting in a compartment nearby, no doubt fretting over Nedjo's renewed talks with the police. At one point Vila asked who that fellow was with the 'dark eyes, energetic chin and long hair'. That's Gavrilo Princip, said Nedjo evenly.

While Gavro and Grabez sat quietly on the train and talked to no one, Nedjo met yet another friend, Rajmund Zemva, who immediately recognized Nedjo despite not having seen him for three years. They had been together in the apprentices' union until Nedjo was expelled. Zemva remembered how Nedjo had disagreed with tactics and nursed a secret grudge against the leadership.

They talked for a while about Zemva's brother, who had died, and some mutual friends. Zemva warned Nedjo not to associate with one person, who had been expelled from 'the organization', the union. They got off the train at Doboj during the long stopover and then got back on and lay out on bench seats for a rest until daylight when Zemva found Nedjo sitting in a crowded area and said, why are you jammed up here, there is plenty of room over there, so they went and sat together and finished the journey, Nedjo telling Zemva of his travels and his printing work in Trieste and elsewhere, until they parted on the streets of Sarajevo.

15

The Schoolboy Conspirators

Following the letter he had received from Gavro in Belgrade at Easter, in the guise of an allegory, alerting him to the acquisition of weapons and the need for more conspirators, Danilo Ilic had set about recruiting a second trio who would act alongside Gavro, Nedjo and Grabez.

Gavro thought for a while that Ilic himself would join the assassins, but Ilic was apparently happy to work behind the scenes – at least for the time being. He told the trial he used his savings of 300 crowns, from his days as a teacher, to travel to Mostar, 130 kilometres south-west of Sarajevo and meet Mehmed Mehmedbasic at the Hotel Jelic. Mehmedbasic, a Muslim man, aged 27 in June 1914, had already tried to involve himself in assassination plots. He had thrown the dagger and poison he planned to use on General Potiorek, the governor of Sarajevo, out of a train window on the way home from a meeting with Vladimir Gacinovic in Toulouse, France that January. There were suggestions he had later got hold of a pistol and gone to Sarajevo to shoot Potiorek, only to be sent home to Stolac in Hercegovina by Danilo Ilic and told to wait for his chance to assassinate the Archduke instead.

In court, Ilic claimed he had been invited to Mostar by Mehmedbasic to discuss the Muslim man's plans for assassination, but there seems little doubt he was lying, and the meeting was initiated by Ilic himself, in mid-May, as he began work on organizing a second troika. In any event, they seem to have agreed that Mehmedbasic would wait to be summoned by Ilic, nearer the time.

To complete the second cell, Ilic deliberately turned to the even younger generation of Young Bosnians in Sarajevo, the schoolboys aged 16, 17 and 18 who, while undoubtedly radical, rebellious and determined were also quite jokey in their attitude and didn't always seem to take the plot so seriously.

Ilic's first approach was to Lazar Djukic, one of the main organizers of this younger group, an eighteen-year-old student in the second class of Teachers' School, where Ilic himself had studied some years before. Djukic had earlier studied at the same school as Gavro. Djukic was a member of the group that had organized the selo attended by Gavro to support Serbs and Croats: Srkpska-brvatska nacionalisticka omladina (the Serbo-Croatian Nationalistic Youth). Though he would claim at the trial to be a contented monarchist who had nothing against the 'Almighty Ruling Dynasty' Djukic had actually been involved in one of the earlier plots, in 1912, when a plan was hatched and then abandoned to shoot the emperor himself, Franz Josef, on his state visit to Sarajevo. Djukic would then have been just 16 years old.

He and Ilic met one day in Sarajevo and as they talked Ilic told Djukic about the planned attempt on the Heir Apparent. Djukic said it was hard to get weapons and Ilic told him, no, that bit was easy. Ilic spoke about Serb nationalism and how an assassination might enhance the militant spirit among the young people. He said the youth would be invigorated if there was an assassination. Djukic would later claim he didn't know what that meant, but this was clearly the belief Ilic then shared with Gavro, that the assassination might be the spark for social change, or even revolution.

But when Ilic then asked Djukic if he would be willing to take part in the assassination Djukic immediately said, no. Apparently, he did not want to risk getting directly involved. He agreed instead to help find some other participants for Ilic, but then every time he saw Ilic, the older man would ask if he had found anyone yet. This happened on several occasions before Djukic was able to give him an answer. Djukic claimed in court he did not take the plot seriously, and never believed there would actually be an assassination. He thought that, for some reason, Ilic was simply putting him to the test.

The students liked to promenade on the main streets of Sarajevo, in the early evenings and at weekends, walking around the market streets and along the road that ran beside the river Miljacka, Appel Quay. Djukic saw Vaso Cubrilovic there one evening. He was the younger brother of the teacher gentleman, Veljko, and he had not long since transferred to school in Sarajevo after being expelled for making an anti-Habsburg protest at school in Tuzla.

Though he was not quite the youngest participant, the court, at the trial, still seemed astonished by his age: How is it, the prosecutor asked Vaso, that a youngster of 17 can think of carrying out an assassination? Tell us?

Vaso was an active Young Bosnian and believed in the political and cultural unity of the Serbs and the Croats. He was, he would say, a Serbo-Croatian, fighting for the equality of his people. 'I considered the Heir to be an enemy of the Slavs and in general because he was a representative of the regime which most greatly oppressed Bosnia & Hercegovina by means of the "exceptional measures" and by all other harassments.'

He was asked in court, in October 1914, after the Great War had begun, if he believed in God and answered that he had to have some faith. Then what faith do you have? I believe in everything. The prosecutor seized on this: 'A religious person would never go so far as to kill anyone, because he knows that the commandment is, "thou shalt not kill".'

Vaso said, 'and why then do millions die on European battlefields? I may feel sorry', he added, 'for the Heir Apparent as a human being but as the Austrian Heir I cannot. I can pity millions of our peasants.'

In a 36-page letter to his sisters Staka and Vida, written from prison in 1918, Vaso described the assassination and how it happened. The letter remained in his family, and was never published nor made available to historians until shortly before Vaso's death in 1990 at the advanced age of 93. They were a long-living family, those Cubrilovices. Those of them who were not executed.

The contents of the letter have so far only been known to a small group of academics within Serbia.

Explaining the background to his involvement, Vaso said he first thought of assassinating the Bosnian governor, Oskar Potiorek, in October 1913 after the announcement of emergency measures. He was still in Tuzla then and he was thinking about it all that winter, and even made enquiries when he visited Sarajevo at Christmas to stay with his sister Vida.

Then he was thrown out of school in Tuzla and came to live with

Vida in early 1914 and began studying at the high school in Sarajevo where he soon met like-minded students such as Lazar Djukic, Cvjetko Popovic, Marko Perin, Dragan Kalember and others. They were in the Yugoslavian Students Association and Vaso heard about some of the protests they had made and other activities in which they had been involved. Perhaps because his political activities were getting in the way, Vaso began struggling with some of his studies, and failed a maths exam, after which he started getting extra tuition from Kalember.

Vaso remembered reading in the Serb radical papers such as *Serbian Word* and *Brotherhood* that Ferdinand would come to Sarajevo and how, straightaway, he thought of this new target for assassination. He wondered where and how he might obtain weapons and considered going to collect some in Tuzla but rejected that as too difficult, because he could never hide them in his room at his sister's home, since Vida was always searching his room for tobacco and she would have been bound to find the weapons and that would have been a comedy.

He was certain other students would be planning assassinations too and rightly guessed that Lazar Djukic would know if anything else was going on, knowing that Djukic had been in the 1912 plot against the emperor. They talked about that, one day, when they met while strolling, and Djukic told Vaso how the schoolboys of Sarajevo had been paraded in front of the emperor, as a supposed display of loyalty, when in fact some of them had been hoping to kill him.

Vaso thought he might persuade Djukic to assist him now with an attempt on the Heir Apparent and maybe hide some weapons for him, if he could bring them in from Tuzla.

Vaso said, 'And now Ferdinand is coming …' 'Yes,' said Djukic. 'It would be good to await him,' said Vaso, knowing that Djukic would understand what he meant by 'await' and not think Vaso wanted to stand and cheer, 'long live, the Heir Apparent!' It was only a half-serious, almost teasing conversation. Djukic said, 'if only there were people for that.' Vaso told him, 'people could be found, if only we had something to do it with.' 'Weapons could be found if someone was willing,' said Djukic. At that moment, their light-hearted chat became suddenly earnest and Vaso said he was willing, and in fact had already decided on it but had difficulty finding weapons. Djukic told Vaso he would introduce him to someone who could give him weapons.

Some days later Djukic and Vaso were on the Quay together and met Ilic, and Djukic introduced them. The two men, an ex-teacher of 24 and a 17-year-old schoolboy, went to a kafana in the hills over Sarajevo where they sat and discussed the assassination to come. Vaso said he did not want to know the identities of any others who were involved, only Ilic, and, in return, wanted no one to know about him either. He had complete trust in Ilic and never believed he would betray him.

They spoke from the beginning about where the attempt would be made, and agreed that the best place would be near the railway station, where the Archduke would arrive in Sarajevo because there was a very narrow street there with an elevated path and it would be easy to throw a bomb into his carriage.

Both Vaso and Ilic imagined the Archduke's visit would be full of pomp and that he would be well protected. Ilic even asked Vaso if he would be willing to leave Sarajevo and take a position on the railway line where a cavern might be dug beneath the track. Vaso must have been glad not to hear any more of this particular idea.

Ilic told Vaso the weapons were coming from Serbia, but from unofficial Serbian sources and they must be careful that official Serbia did not find out about the planned assassination, as they would be bound to consider it harmful to Serbian interests. When he was asked during the trial about this aspect of their exchange, Ilic said he had talked so much about the assassination that he couldn't remember whom he had talked to or what he'd said.

In his 1918 letter Vaso initially says he agreed to find two more people for the assassination, which suggests that Ilic was not convinced about using Mehmed Mehmedbasic. But, writes Vaso, though he knew many students, none of them seemed cut out for the task. There was one possible candidate, Cvjetko Popovic, who had just turned 16 in March 1914 and was in his third year at the Teachers' College. His mother was dead and his father, a retired school director, had remarried.

It was only after he had begun to consider him that Vaso discovered Popovic had been arrested and jailed briefly, along with a Young Bosnian activist, Milos Pjanic, a year or two earlier. Popovic considered himself innocent of any offence – he had never been charged – and was aggrieved at being jailed by the Austrians. He wanted revenge.

Vaso studied Popovic carefully for a few days and took a liking to
him. He decided he would take a chance and invite him into the plot.
If he refused then Vaso would try his luck among friends in Tuzla.
Around about 20 May, while Gavro was still in Belgrade waiting to
receive the weapons, Vaso took Popovic for a walk and steered the
conversation to his chosen theme.

Vaso: It would be good to await the Crown Prince.
Popovic: With what? You certainly won't kill him with mud.

As he wrote in his letter, Vaso immediately knew what time it was,
meaning he knew the score, and so did Popovic. Vaso told him he
knew a man who would take care of everything. He later told Popovic
the man was Ilic and that they would carry out the assassination with
guns and revolvers.

Once again, the trial could not believe that such a young boy as
Popovic had so readily signed up to an assassination. He was asked,
'when you met with Cubrilovic and he said that one must lie in wait
for the Heir Apparent, did you immediately agree?'

Yes, said Popovic.

Popovic later gave this account of how he then felt:

After I gave my word to join the plot I spent the whole night
thinking and dreaming about the assassination. In the morning
I was quite a different man. Convinced that I had only until 28
June to live, Vidovdan – St Vitus Day – I looked upon everything
from a new angle. I left my school books, I hardly glanced at the
newspapers which up to that day I read with interest. I almost
failed to react to the jokes of my friends at which the day before
I would have exploded. I tried to make jokes. Only one thought
tormented me: that we might not succeed and thus make fools
of ourselves.

When Vaso told Ilic that Popovic had agreed to join them, Ilic
said he need not look for anyone else because he had already found
someone, though he wasn't absolutely sure about him. That must
have been Mehmedbasic.

Vaso was concerned that he would have nowhere to hide his

weapons when he received them. At that stage, in the third week of May, Ilic expected the weapons any day and was unaware there had been a delay. He had told Vaso the weapons would be distributed immediately they arrived and now suggested Vaso choose a quiet student friend who would not be noticed to hold the weapons for him. Vaso asked his friends Dragan Kalember and Marko Perin but both refused so Ilic said he would keep the weapons himself, until the assassination.

Vaso did not at first tell Popovic about Ilic. Neither Vaso nor Popovic were very secretive about their involvement and almost boastful in their supposedly 'discreet' mentions of it among their peers, who often had a laugh at their expense, and clearly found the idea of their two schoolboy friends becoming assassins quite risible. As Vaso said in his letter,

> The worst thing about the conspirators was that there was not a single mature man among us. Ilic was the oldest and he was only 24 years old which is practically a child. [Actually, Mehmedbasic was older, at 27, but he was the most remotely involved of all the conspirators.] It was especially difficult for Popovic and myself. We were left to ourselves. In truth, we were firmly decided on the assassination. We hated Ferdinand and Austria just as much as Princip, but really we were far too young for such things. Maturity, nerves of steel, caution are a must for such ventures, which we could not have at 17–18 years of age. Aside from that we had no one to talk to or to give us encouragement. Not like the other three who had prepared themselves in Serbia.

Though Vaso and Popovic both now knew of Ilic's role in the conspiracy they were entirely unaware of the identities of the other trio. Vaso had told Ilic he didn't want to know, but of course curiosity got the better of him and he and Popovic could not help speculating. One day they saw Ilic out walking with Gavrilo Princip. Could he be one of them, Vaso wondered out loud. 'If Gavro is first', said Popovic, 'then we don't even have to go, because Ferdinand is a dead man.'

Vaso appears to have had many anxieties in the days leading up to the assassination. He shared Ilic's dismay that the bombs they had received were the wrong kind of bombs. Ilic had hoped for grenades that exploded on impact, but these Serbian military bombs, with their 12 seconds delay, were more primitive and more difficult to use effectively. He told Vaso who was angry because it would be harder to deploy these in an assassination, when every second counted.

Vaso had no idea how the weapons had been smuggled into Sarajevo but often wondered who had brought them. He once laughed out loud, when he was thinking about it. Just imagine, he thought, if it had been Veljko who helped smuggle the weapons, never guessing they were for his little brother.

While he portrayed himself in his subsequent 36-page account of the assassination as solid, dependable and determined it appears that Vaso more than once changed his mind about taking part and at one stage told Ilic he was withdrawing because of his sister. Presumably, because he was staying at her home, he feared that she too would be arrested and jailed. Or perhaps it was just an excuse, and he had lost his nerve. Ilic answered him, 'So what?!'

He wrote in his letter to his sister that he had planned to leave Sarajevo at one stage and live outside the city until 28 June. This had been Ilic's idea, to send him and Popovic to lie low in nearby villages. 'I wanted to avoid bringing any troubles on you,' he told his sister in the letter. But this had not stopped him talking with others about the assassination – only then to worry that he might be betrayed by them.

Having failed to find anyone to look after their weapons before the assassination, Vaso began to worry about what he would do with them afterwards, if, for example, someone else shot the Archduke before they had a chance to. He discussed this worry with Popovic and they agreed to ask a friend to look after the weapons for them.

Here entered 19-year-old Ivo Kranjcevic, a business student and a member of a Young Bosnian nationalist association. He had been walking on Cekalusa Street in central Sarajevo one evening when he saw Popovic and they began to talk and Popovic told him he intended to assassinate the Heir. 'I wouldn't do that, because it's dangerous,' said Kranjcevic, 'and would we gain anything by that?' Popovic shrugged his shoulders and they changed the subject.

Then a few days later Kranjcevic saw Vaso who said, 'Ivo, I too am thinking of doing the same thing.' Kranjcevic told him more or less what he had told Popovic: 'It's stupid to do that when you don't know what the consequences will be.' He remembered walking to a meeting once with Vaso, and how Vaso had been telling him how free it was in Serbia – by contrast with Bosnia – and how King Petar was friendly with the people and had fought alongside them before he became king. It was so much better in Serbia than in Bosnia where everything was held back.

Kranjcevic asked Vaso where the weapons were coming from for the assassination attempt and he said he wasn't sure exactly but that some kind of guerrillas might have them. Vaso asked his friend if he would keep the weapons afterwards and Kranjcevic said he would, but only if they had not been used.

Not long after this Vaso came and told him he was leaving Sarajevo altogether and would not take part after all. Kranjcevic even went with him to get the permit to travel, but still Vaso did not go. The day before the assassination he came and asked Kranjcevic to wait for him the following day on Skenderija Street.

Brought to court afterwards and asked to explain why he did not denounce the assassination to the authorities, Kranjcevic initially said if he had done that none of his friends would have spoken to him. He eventually admitted that he believed a protest, a warning was necessary against the German [Austrian] influence that was destroying the Bosnian people. All the persecutions of the Slavs came from Germany.

When he and Popovic had discussed this they had envisaged a new, unified state which would be ruled over by King Petar of Serbia and be called Great Yugoslavia.

Kranjcevic would then tie himself up in knots, claiming he believed in the assassination of the Heir as a protest but did not agree with it because the Heir was a friend of the Slavs and had often interceded on their behalf. Kranjcevic himself was a Catholic Croat and the Heir was definitely a friend of the Croats.

It was somewhat embarrassing for the Catholic Croat community in Sarajevo that one of their own should be involved, albeit indirectly. Indeed, the shame was all the greater because Kranjcevic's father was a retired sergeant in the Austrian Bosnian police force. The Austrian Catholic newspaper reported the dilemma and presented a handy, if spurious, get-out for the Catholics – Kranjcevic was not so Catholic after all, as his policeman father had married a Vlach, a Romanian

Christian, and so Ivo and all their other children were in fact Greek Orthodox.

Did he agree or disagree with the assassination? he was asked in court. He disagreed. Then why had he said he agreed with the assassination as a form of protest? He did not understand the contradiction and so could not explain it.

He was asked, 'why did you allow this friend of the Croats to be killed as a means of protest against Germanization?' He replied, 'His Highness is not our enemy but the Slavs are persecuted anyway.'

The prosecutor was losing his patience. 'Then, God help us, you would approve also an assassination of His Highness?'

'That's not so. I wanted the assassination of a leader. I approved of the assassination of a minister. But not of the Archduke. If someone wanted to risk his head for the sake of protest, then I agreed.'

Kranjcevic had told Popovic: if you think it will do any good, then go ahead.

In fairness to Kranjcevic, there was a lot at stake after the assassination. The mood of the trial was vengeful and, after what later happened with the weapons, he was in a great deal of trouble, wriggling on the hook of a long sentence.

Vaso met an 18-year-old student, Branko Zagorac, while strolling in Sarajevo and told him there would be an assassination. They met again and Vaso now told him he was to be the assassin. He said their mutual friend Lazar Djukic, who had introduced Vaso to Ilic but declined to take part in the plot himself, was a coward. Zagorac asked Vaso how he planned to carry out the assassination and Vaso said, 'that's easy, there are weapons.' Branko said nothing but noted Vaso had spoken without feeling and therefore assumed he didn't mean it and was just joking.

Vaso had bragged before that he was a kind of hero, according to another Young Bosnian, Marko Perin, and now here he was claiming he would kill the Heir. His friends took it as a joke. Perin was amused. He was one of the students who had refused Vaso's request to hide the weapons before the assassination.

When he saw Vaso, while on the street with his friends, Perin teased, 'here's the one who thinks he is going to assassinate the Heir!' Perin and his friends had been discussing the poor state of their finances and how they all needed some money. One of them, Nikola Forkapic said, 'this man is rather suspicious, perhaps we should denounce him to the police and get a few hundred crowns.'

Vaso said, be free to announce it, but take the responsibility on yourself; if you give it away, you won't see the bullet that kills you. This made Perin, for one, uneasy and he began to wonder if the plot was not a joke, after all.

Dragan Kalember, sixteen years old, laughed out loud when Vaso first told him he was going to assassinate the Heir and refused to believe it would happen. When they met on the Friday, two days before the assassination, Vaso said, 'I can't do it because a detective is following me and I am being expelled from Sarajevo in 24 hours. If I do not leave my sister will be held responsible.'

Vaso said he told some people he was leaving in order to make them think he was no longer going to be involved. If this was true, it did not last long. He met his sceptical Young Bosnian friends on Saturday, 27 June. That evening, Marko Perin and Dragan Kalember were strolling and encountered Vaso by the cathedral. They went to a pastry shop in the old Turkish marketplace and as they sat eating ice cream, Vaso told them he was carrying a gun and a bomb. When they were paying and getting ready to leave, Vaso showed them the handle of the gun which was tucked into his waistband and asked if they would like to hold it. They declined. Vaso told them, 'keep off the Quay tomorrow, if you want to stay alive.'

The talk among the students of denouncing Vaso for a reward was part of a running joke, which had first arisen earlier in the year, following a series of incidents in which German-language signs on shops and public buildings had been defaced, sometimes with paint, sometimes with ink poured on them, and sometimes with acid.

While the authorities tried hard to catch those responsible, rewards had been offered through some of the Austrian-leaning local newspapers. No one had ever been caught, though of course, all the students knew that Young Bosnians were responsible for this anti-Austrian subversion. 'Is that reward for the assassination or for the signs?' said one of Vaso's friends. 'It would be good if the one who reported it got 300 crowns.'

A newly published radical journal, *Zvono*, had written about the defacings in mid-May.

In Sarajevo there were numerous demonstrations against foreign, especially German, store signs. We will not venture to say whether that damage to the signs infringed the laws or not; but we wish to point out the fact that the foreign influence among us, reinforced by the law, has come to such a pass, that it begins to provoke the angriest protests and, conversely, the forceful repression of their dangerous influences.

Those foreigners, and especially the Germans, are so obtuse that they don't even bother to use signs on their businesses in the language of the people among whom they live and whose bread they eat. We know the contempt in which they hold us in our own land and, despite our tremendous patience, by holding themselves aloof and dishonouring our hospitality they provoke justified hatred and protest against themselves. We want to be masters in our own homes.

16

June 1914 – a Morbid Yearning

Zvono – The Bell – had in fact been launched by Danilo Ilic, acting as associate editor, along with a colleague, Jovan Smitran, acting as editor. Ilic seems to have worked hard in his contributions to the journal, as both editor and writer, in the weeks before the assassination and some of his writing may reflect the apparent crisis he was suffering, as he backed away from the idea of the assassination and tried to prevent it happening.

There is no doubt that, even as he continued to arrange the assassination, he was also trying to argue Gavro and Grabez out of it. The motive for his change of heart is unclear – was it his conscience, his personal fear or was it, as others suggest, some advice or instruction he was given by a messenger that Colonel Apis had sent from Belgrade? The truth is now unknowable and it is possible to make each case with some conviction. Perhaps it was a mixture of all three. Here are the origins of the belief that Ilic was first the creator of the plot and then its traitor.

While Ilic was desperately trying to write himself out of the plot at the trial, he received some generous support from his friends Gavro and Grabez who both acknowledged that he had tried to dissuade them.

Gavro said Ilic had told him that now was not the time for the assassination and that it could have bad consequences, that there would be persecution of the people. Gavro disagreed. He claimed he never imagined the consequences would be as great as they were and said at the trial he never foresaw there would be a war.

But that was not what he had said during his talks with Ilic, when he had apparently used the phrase, 'après mois, le déluge'. This was reported at the trial by Grabez who said he had come to town from

Pale three days before the assassination and met Ilic and asked him how things were going with the assassination and Ilic told him there would be no assassination. Then he began to talk as if he was against it, which made Grabez suspicious of him.

Ilic said he hoped there would soon be some improvement in their situation in Bosnia so that the assassination would not be necessary. He had no responsibility, he said, for what was happening.

Grabez perhaps knew of some of the antics of the younger men, the schoolboys such as Vaso and Popovic and said he thought it was a terrible thing the high school students were doing and it was bound to end in a high school student way. Grabez suggested drawing lots, to decide who would be 'the one'. Ilic said he was wasting his time as Ilic had already spoken at length to Princip who wouldn't listen.

Curiously, Grabez said that by the same afternoon Ilic was now telling him a decision had been made that five would carry out the assassination and under no circumstances should Grabez take part. Grabez said he agreed.

This was more or less what Ilic had tried on Gavro after failing in his lengthy attempts to persuade him against the assassination. All right then, Ilic had said to Gavro, 'let the other five do it, just you don't'. Gavro fell silent and, for once, did not directly object, so Ilic allowed himself to believe Gavro had agreed with him and thought now he wouldn't take part. Or so he said, in court.

Gavro had earlier said that Ilic spent ten days saying they should not attempt the assassination because the present time was not favourably chosen and they would have no profit from this assassination.

'But', said Gavro, 'I was not in agreement with the postponement of the assassination because a certain morbid yearning for it had been awakened in me.'

Ilic was eventually asked the obvious question at the trial: if he had been so against the assassination, why did he not hide or dispose of the bombs and guns, instead of handing them out to the assassins. He said that was because he knew the bombs had come via Milan Ciganovic from Major Tankosic the guerrilla leader. 'I was afraid by my conduct I would become the object of open hostility.'

Dedijer, in his book *The Road to Sarajevo*, characterized Ilic's dilemma in more philosophical terms, as an inner torment, political, spiritual and moral, which he tried to work out with Gavro and through some writing of letters and his contributions to his new socialist journal, *Zvono*. As his earliest contributions showed, Ilic had lost none of his anger towards the Austrians and was relishing the chance to express it through biting satire. This article by him was headlined, 'Oh These Poor Birds' and was a response to Austrian reports of an increase in songbirds in Sarajevo:

> To the great joy of the whole people in Bosnia & Hercegovina, the provincial government has issued an important announcement that the number of singing birds in Sarajevo has increased. For this extraordinary step forward in the cultural life of our fatherland, we must be grateful to the industrious sacrifices of the municipal authorities who have painstakingly constructed, in gardens and parks, shelters were the poor magpies and sparrows are fed in winter.
>
> And you poor, suffering people who bear on your bowed backs the whole weight of the social edifice, in vain you have waited for years for somebody to take care of you and to build proper houses with sweated tax money so that you do not have to die a miserable death in filthy hovels.
>
> Why are we not birds too?

There are, as Dedijer points out, some further clues to Ilic's troubled state of mind in the essay he wrote about the Russian revolutionary writer, Leonid Andreyev, who was widely admired among the Young Bosnians, especially for his story 'The Seven Who Were Hanged' which was partly a protest against capital punishment but also considered the young heroes as they awaited execution for an assassination attempt, and did not dwell on what they had done so much as contemplate the death that awaited them.

Ilic would soon be so desperate to avoid execution himself that he would, apparently, make wholesale betrayals of his colleagues, selling his soul, as it were, for his own salvation. Was he thinking of his own future plight or troubled being when he wrote how Andreyev's 'descriptions of man's darkest feelings' placed him at the top of Russian literature?

This deep spiritual analysis, the specific notion of life and a kind of mysticism, of fatalism which runs like a red thread through all his writings ... his love for humanity, his enlightened and libertarian views, his protest against the tyranny which reigns in his own country – these are the main reasons for his great literary success in Russia ...

He likes especially to portray the heroes of the 'period of liberation', revolutionaries with whom he himself actively participated in the revolution. The deep spiritual crises, the tremors and breaks which are going on in the souls of these great idealists and apostles of liberty, Andreyev described with especial love, with greater realism and artistic force.

Turning at the end to 'The Seven Who Were Hanged', Ilic cited a letter from Andreyev himself, about the story and some of its characters:

It is my intention with this story to point out the horror and impermissibility of capital punishment. The death penalty confuses the conscience even of resolute men; it results in much greater havoc among the weak. Werner can pit his intelligence and will power, Musya her purity and innocence, against this last instinctive horror of inevitable death; what is left for the weak and sinful? How can they face it? Unless at the cost of their rational consciousness, ravaged to the depths of their souls.

The Archduke was facing his own death sentence, of course, and so too, soon, would Ilic, the Tuzla cinema owner Misko Jovanovic and his teacher gentleman friend Veljko Cubrilovic. It is certainly tempting to see Ilic exercising his own crisis in his writing.

He and Gavro wrote a joint letter to their guiding light in Switzerland, Vladimir Gacinovic. It was a letter written by Gavro but with a few sentences added by Ilic. Gacinovic wrote about it for Leon Trotsky, a year later, saying how he had received the letter just a few days before the assassination and how it had informed him of internal differences that had arisen as if some comrades were against the assassination and trying to put moral pressure on the group 'which had been determined to act at all costs'. Gacinovic had felt uneasy reading this disturbing letter and planned to write and tell them to cool off, 'but Princip's deed echoed through the whole world'.

Writing soon after the assassination, Gacinovic told a girlfriend in Hercegovina that he had received two comradely letters from Ilic and Princip and saw that they were nervous and impatient and that 'there was a kind of quarrelling between them'. Gacinovic had been distracted by his own studies and did not notice that 'we were on the eve of a great catastrophe'.

There was a shifting mood among the young radicals against political assassination. Some of Gacinovic's colleagues were in Vienna on the very day of the assassination, at a student conference where there were secret and open meetings and, in the secret sessions, a resolution was proposed against individual terror. A committee was still drafting a further resolution against political assassination when news came through from Sarajevo that the Heir Apparent was dead.

Back in the previous year, Ilic and Gavro had planned and then abandoned an attempt on the life of the governor, Potiorek. Ilic had wanted to create a new pan-Slavist organization as a prelude to any act of terror, perhaps imagining it could step into a void, or force itself into a position to lead a revolution.

He may have still been waiting for such an organization to be formed, and perhaps *Zvono* – The Bell – at its launch in mid-May 1914 was preparing the way for a new socialist group and would have become its voice, just as *Pijemont* was speaking for The Black Hand, and other radical journals proliferated as voices of the disenfranchised.

Gavro told Pappenheim that Ilic had no energy, that reading had – Ilic confessed – made him quite slack. Gavro had lived with words long enough, now he wanted action, had a 'morbid yearning' for it.

At the trial Ilic was asked why he had run away to Bosanski Brod after the assassination, but he hadn't, as he pointed out to the prosecutor. He had actually gone to Brod before the assassination, and returned, he said, to stop the assassination. He never said precisely what he was doing there but it appears that he may have gone there to meet the messenger sent by Apis to call off the assassination.

Apis later claimed, as described in chapter ten, he had been told about the plan by Tankosic and given his approval without really taking it seriously. Then later, on reflection, he changed his mind and sent Djuro Sarac to Bosnia to try to call it off, but it was too late. Apis could not have known how determined Gavro was and this may be seen as good evidence that Gavro was not a member of The Black Hand. If he had been, surely, he would not have gone against Apis.

In some accounts, Apis never informed the central committee of The Black Hand about the assassination, and the decision to send Djuro Sarac to try to stop it was entirely his own. A counter-theory has him belatedly informing the central committee and the committee overruling Apis and ordering him to prevent the assassination and this was why Sarac was dispatched.

Sarac was too well known in Sarajevo, it was said, so Ilic left the city to meet him instead in the nearby town of Bosanski Brod. There is no account of this meeting or what was said. It may never even have happened. That's the hidden history of the assassination, the lost truth that can never now be recovered. You could very easily tie yourself in knots trying to make sense of it all.

Indeed, the normally thorough Dedijer contradicts himself, comprehensively, in his own book. On page 309 he can be found writing about the 16 June meeting between Sarac and Ilic at Bosanski Brod. Here Dedijer disputes that Ilic acted after 'receiving orders from Belgrade'. On this page he thinks Ilic's main motive for turning against the assassination was 'his own philosophical and political considerations'.

Eighty pages later he has Ilic again leaving Sarajevo to meet Djuro Sarac but now it is 'a few days after 15 June' and he does not go to Bosanski Brod, but goes to the riverside town of Sabac where Sarac gave him the message that the assassination had to be stopped.

Here Dedijer says, 'Ilic does not seem to have been a man of weak nerves who was suddenly frightened and decided to quit the plot. Obviously he changed his attitude under the influence of other people.'

Djuro Sarac certainly seems to have known about the assassination. As described earlier, he accompanied Gavro, Nedjo and Grabez to see them off when they left Belgrade on the boat to Sabac at the start of their 'underground' journey to Sarajevo. Sarac may even have played a more direct role in organizing the plot through his own secret society, Smrt Ili Zivot – Death or Life.

In later years Djuro Sarac was suspected of being a spy or agent of the Serbian government, perhaps directly reporting to the prime minister, Pasic. This view gained credence when he became a witness for the prosecution of Apis at the Salonika trial in 1917, which was widely believed to be a 'show trial' of concocted charges intended to destroy Apis and The Black Hand.

The trial was full of unsubstantiated and hearsay evidence that would never normally find its way into court. At one moment Sarac was being questioned on something Ciganovic had once said in his hearing about Major Tankosic, the close colleague of Apis, and his alleged role in some murders or tortures near Belgrade. Apis interjected: That is a lie!

No, retorted Sarac, that is no lie. 'It hurts my soul when I consider what you made of us, and what you still intended to make of us. One can't mention everything here in court. You know that very well. But the time for that will come. I knew no evil before I fell into your hands. Horror seizes me when I think what you made of us.'

There spoke Sarac the former student of theology, who must have been well versed in the unending struggle between good and evil.

Another defendant at the Salonika trial, alongside Apis, was Rade Malobabic, who had been Apis's chief agent throughout the Austro-Hungarian empire and had often been assigned to 'difficult and dangerous missions'. It was Malobabic who had first informed Apis of the Austrian army manoeuvres that were due to take place in Bosnia, which Apis, and others, suspected might be the prelude to an attack on Serbia. These were the manoeuvres that brought the Heir Apparent to Bosnia, in his newly exalted capacity as Inspector General of the Army.

There was evidence that in early June 1914, Malobabic had also smuggled four revolvers and some ammunition into Bosnia, on behalf of Apis who said he was allowing Malobabic to arm his other agents who were working in dangerous conditions in Austrian territory. There was talk of a further suitcase of grenades and guns being delivered to Malobabic but Apis claimed not to know about this.

One source has Malobabic arriving in Sarajevo on the eve of the assassination and meeting with Ilic. Part of the evidence for this meeting relies on Ilic's mother's account of an unnamed visitor with 'big feet' who had been at her home with her son Danilo. Malobabic, apparently, had big feet. In this version of events, Malobabic is countermanding the previous instruction and ordering that the assassination go ahead after all.

Malobabic was by the town hall, watching the Archduke's parade on the morning of the assassination. He was arrested a month later in Belgrade and apparently recaptured after he had jumped from a moving train with no shoes on, while being transported from Belgrade to the town of Nis. He was held in chains on remand for 14 months until released 'more dead than alive' and cared for in his recovery by Apis.

It was only after the Salonika trial had begun in 1917 that Malobabic appeared as a witness, having by all accounts broken down and accused Apis of the fake charges he faced, plotting to kill the Prince Regent, Alexander.

In return, Apis produced his own false admission of his role in the Sarajevo assassination, now naming Malobabic as the man he had appointed to arrange the entire plot: 'Malobabic executed my order, organized and performed the assassination. His chief accomplices were in my service and received small payments from me.'

Malobabic was sentenced to be executed, alongside Apis, and gave a confession to a priest in his cell where he admitted being sent to Sarajevo when the assassination was to take place and then, 'when everything was over' he was ordered back for other missions. As confessions go, it was not much, and did not solve the mystery of why he had been sent to Sarajevo or what he did while he was there.

After the two-hour reading of the sentence, the two men, Apis and Malobabic, embraced and also hugged the third condemned man, Major Ljubomir Vulovic. A witness to the execution described Malobabic blaming Apis for bringing him to this spot, beside the ditch. 'It's fate, Rade,' Apis had replied. 'If you had not been with me, it would not have happened to me either.' After the last embrace Apis turned to face the firing squad and placed his hand on Malobabic's shoulder saying, 'I affirm again that this man was a good patriot and that he has always acted for the welfare of Serbia.'

The guards saw Malobabic turn and look around and suspected he was seeking a means of escape. But he gave up and stepped down into the ditch with the other two. He asked to be spared the blindfold but Apis told him not to argue: 'Let them do it, Rade, the law requires it.' Malobabic did not cry out, 'Long live Serbia', as Apis did. He did not cry out at all, nor even answer Apis as he said, Adieu Rade. He fell after five shots.

One man who was lucky not to be in that ditch with Apis and

Malobabic was Mehmed Mehmedbasic, the sixth would-be assassin of Sarajevo and the only one who was never caught and tried for that crime. Instead he found himself hauled into the Salonika trial in 1917, accused of participating in the non-existent plot against the Prince Regent.

Mehmedbasic had signed up to the Serbian army at the outbreak of the Great War and become a close associate of Tankosic. He had been involved in an Apis-inspired plot in 1916 to assassinate two figurehead allies of Kaiser Wilhelm, the emperor of Germany, who was Austria's wartime ally. Mehmedbasic had gone to Athens to kill the Greek King Constantine and had waited for him in a theatre, apparently to carry out an Abraham Lincoln-style assassination, unaware the king was ill and not coming.

Arrested by police in Serbia in 1916 and questioned about the one assassination – the attempt on the Prince Regent – he had not been involved in, he had not been so easy to break as Malobabic, and resisted both threats and torture as he kept insisting, 'there was no idea behind this so-called attempt, and therefore I could not take part in it.'

He was only one of two among the eleven defendants who were not sentenced to death, though six were later spared with life sentences. Mehmedbasic was sentenced to 15 years.

In June 1914 he was waiting at home in Stolac for the summons from Ilic, which finally came in a telegram on 26 June. Needing a pass to travel, Mehmedbasic told the police he would visit a dentist in Mostar. From there he went by train to Sarajevo and booked himself into the Hotel Sarajevo. He and Ilic and some others, unnamed, sat up until 3am while Ilic told stories of Russian revolutionaries.

Gavro may have been there as he said at the trial he knew one of the conspirators was a Muslim, after meeting him a short while before the assassination. Mehmedbasic subsequently said he had been introduced to Gavro by Ilic in a Sarajevo café: 'Mehmedbasic who tomorrow is to be with us'. The three of them signed a joint postcard to Vladimir Gacinovic in Lausanne, Switzerland.

Mehmedbasic said there was no sign of Ilic's change of heart: 'It is not true that at the last moment Ilic tried to persuade us not to carry out the deed; he simply expressed the fear that the police had somehow got wind of something and might manage to hinder us. On the actual day of the outrage he was on the street where the assassins had gathered and went from one to the other. He came to me too, and said, "be strong, be brave".'

Danilo Ilic infuriated the prosecutor at the trial, eliding and evading in his desperate attempts to save himself. He had given some of the conspirators weapons the day before the assassination, he was asked, 'and now you want to say you withdrew from the assassination?'

Ilic: 'I did not directly withdraw but that is already a withdrawal when I did not give them the arms before ... at first I was for the assassination and then I worked against it.'

Prosecutor: 'When you give bombs to someone you don't work against assassination?'

Ilic: 'But I was convinced that they would not carry out the assassination ...'

Pr: 'Better admit the truth. It is obvious that you don't admit the truth. You didn't say a single word that you wanted to divert Cabrinovic, Cubrilovic and Popovic?'

Ilic: I did not dissuade them but I was firmly convinced that they would not carry out the assassination. I got the impression from conversation that they were not fit for the assassination ...'

Pr: 'Because you have fooled around enough today, say whether it is true, whether you, when you gave the revolvers to [Vaso] Cubrilovic and Popovic, showed them how to shoot those revolvers in a tunnel?'

Ilic: 'I don't remember now. I think I didn't.'

It was certainly true that Ilic had waited until the last minute to distribute the weapons for the assassination. They were sitting there, all that time, in the Gladstone bag beneath Gavro's bed in the room he shared with Ilic at his mother's house on Oprkanj Street, where Ilic was keeping the door closed to keep his mother from discovering the six bombs and four pistols while cleaning her boy's room.

On 27 June, Vaso met up with Popovic and the two of them went to Bembasa, a quiet area by the Miljacka river on the outskirts of Sarajevo, where they met Ilic. They went to the park where he gave each of them in turn a gun and a bomb, showing each of them, again in turn, how to use it. He took the gun from Popovic and fired it into the tunnel at the Kozija Bridge. 'Where this one hits', said Ilic, 'no medicine can help.'

Vaso wrote in his letter to his sisters that he kept the gun in his pocket all the time, after he had received it, though he went home and put the bomb in a drawer in his desk, while worrying that his sister might find it. Later though, as we heard earlier, he was in the pastry shop eating ice cream with friends, boasting that he had a gun and a bomb in his pocket.

He said that Ilic had assigned them positions along a 300-metre stretch of Appel Quay beside the Miljacka where all the armed conspirators would stand, one after the other but some distance apart. A Bosnian newspaper had conveniently published the route the imperial procession would follow. This instruction upset Vaso and Popovic who may have been expecting to choose their own locations for the mass attack that was planned on the Heir Apparent. Ilic told them this was just for form, and that afterwards they would all be free to take up a position of their choice.

Ilic asked Vaso to stand by the front of the home of Danilo Dimovic, which may have been a satirical touch as Dimovic was the head of the Serb collaborators in the Sabor puppet parliament, the 'government Mamelukes' as Nedjo had called them, wishing he could throw a bomb into their midst. Popovic was given a place further down, outside the school's residential home. 'Of course', Ilic told the trial, 'I knew that he wouldn't shoot, that he is not capable.' He still gave the two boys the weapons, though, along with instructions on how to use them.

Later on, in the early evening, Ilic met Mehmedbasic at the Mostar Café and went with him back to his room at the Hotel Sarajevo, handing him a bomb as they walked together, along with some instruction on how to use it.

Gavro spent much of his last month in Sarajevo with a different group of people from his normal associates. He did this, he said, only in order not to arouse suspicion. Notably, for him, they were 'fellows who liked to drink', which ordinarily Gavro would avoid. These too were Young Bosnians but not of the same ascetic mould as Gavro. 'These fellows were for the most part incapable of a great idea,' said Gavro, perhaps a little pompously. Among them was Borivoje Jevtic who would later make a reputation for himself as a writer of fiction but was then leading a bohemian kind of life. He had roomed with Gavro back in Belgrade and had been a correspondent of Nedjo's during his travels.

Dedijer, in *The Road to Sarajevo*, disapproves of Jevtic as showing a novelist's disregard for the facts and shaping events afterwards according to his own prejudices. But Jevtic was there, not Dedijer. Jevtic was perhaps lucky not to stand trial himself. Afterwards he complained that he had never known anything about Gavro's revolutionary ideas and would have dissuaded him, had he known, from the assassination, as killing individuals could not eliminate a system. It was a reasonable point, but seemed in contrast to his role as an active Young Bosnian, corresponding with Nedjo and also, apparently, with Gacinovic.

No doubt, like many others, Jevtic was desperate to save himself from prison or worse. Gavro had moved among them, he said, 'because we are poets and futurists, eager to live, but Princip tried to hide behind us and now we are all suffering because of him.'

Jevtic described a kind of farewell party attended by Gavro on the last night of Saturday, 27 June when they gathered at Semiz wine shop, which was popular for its range of Mostar wines, where they sang Serbian songs and drank red wine.

A contemporary photograph of the exterior of Semiz reveals the likely truth of its description as dark and poorly lit inside with only one window to bring in daylight. It looks Moorish with its shabby whitewashed walls but it was close to Appel Quay and, especially, the Lateiner Bridge, which could be seen from its single window, so that you could probably have looked out from that window and watched the assassination, the following morning.

We have Jevtic to thank for the observation that Gavro was preoccupied that night with his own thoughts and not very sociable. He gulped down a glass of wine apparently and finally responded when friends told some jokes against the Austrians. Gavro walked two other men home afterwards and left them at their door with an embrace, urging them to go inside quickly and not be seen with him. Perhaps it was now, certainly it was at some point that afternoon or evening, that Gavro went to the cemetery of St Mark's and found some flowers to decorate the grave of the martyr Zerajic.

Unlike Nedjo, Gavro had already seen his prey. That Thursday, 25 June, following his arrival at the Hotel Bosna in Ilidze, the Archduke must have been feeling very cheerful and well disposed towards the trip ahead as he decided on impulse to break into his carefully planned schedule and take a trip into Sarajevo for some shopping.

They arrived by car in the late afternoon and spent over an hour looking at the shops and, true to his natural acquisitiveness, the Archduke and Sophie made many purchases. A large crowd gathered and made it difficult for the royal couple to make their way through the narrow lanes of the Turkish market, the Carsija with its stalls and shop fronts full of brightly coloured displays. There were cheers, apparently, none of the boos the Archduke might have feared. That evening Gavrilo Princip would tell his new-found wine shop friends that he too had been there by chance and seen the Heir and his wife just as they entered the Kabiljo carpet shop, getting so close he could have shot the Archduke there and then. He was reported to have said he couldn't do anything because a policeman was right behind him. Then according to another account he later claimed he did not want to fire in the small shop in case he hit the Heir's wife, Sophie.

But, in truth, he was not yet armed, the guns and bombs still in the bag under his bed, so this was simply an illusory assassination, an imagining of the real thing to come.

17

The Smell of Gunpowder

Had they known the reality behind the Austrian troop manoeuvres which the Heir Apparent was planning to attend in
Bosnia that June, the Serbs who feared them as a pretext for war
would surely have put their anxieties aside.

One writer likened these unlucky Austrian troops stationed in
Bosnia, the 15th and 16th army corps, to the British forces in India,
both armies being deployed in remote parts of their respective empires in difficult conditions, among sometimes hostile people whose
languages they did not speak. They were the 'forgotten' soldiers and
in the case of the Bosnian forces they needed the morale boost of an
imperial visit. Though perhaps, too, the Austrians were mindful that
even a small show of strength would make itself felt in neighbouring
Serbia. There was a buoyant mood among the Serbian military after
the recent victories against Turkey and Bulgaria, in successive Balkan
wars, and there were those among them who would have invaded
Bosnia tomorrow, if they could.

The Austrian-imposed governor of Bosnia, Oskar Potiorek, had
applied to the Archduke's chief of staff, General Conrad, for a budget
of one million crowns to put on four days of manoeuvres. He wanted
a display that would demonstrate the 'power of the dynasty and the
Monarchy'. Conrad had cut the budget in half, saying it was too
expensive, and said a two-day spectacle would be enough. The Heir
himself later ordered the troops not to wear their best uniforms, as a
further economy.

Perhaps then, Potiorek proposed, the Archduke could make an
extended visit to embrace outlying areas of Bosnia where he could
be seen and appreciated by the people, especially the Muslims and
the normally loyal Catholic Croats who had been wavering in their

support. Potiorek included in his plans a series of excursions and shooting expeditions to tempt the Archduke. His plans, he was told by reply, had been received with interest, but the Archduke's stay must be limited to the two days of army exercises and a brief trip to Sarajevo. He might return later in the year for a more informal visit to the regions.

The dates took a while to be fixed and Potiorek became concerned that the imperial party was considering a late departure from the Hotel Bosna, the central hotel in Ilidza. The spa season was due to start on 1 July and, as Potiorek wrote to the Archduke's staff, there would be 'much unpleasantness' if they had not left by 29 June. While he was confident in taking 'full responsibility' for the official visit, having plenty of advance notice to plan security measures, he could not provide the same guarantee for any later unofficial trip that might happen at short notice.

The broad schedule was finally agreed in March 1914 – the Heir would arrive on 25 June, attend two days of manoeuvres, 26 and 27 June and then visit Sarajevo on Sunday, 28 June. He would be gone before the start of the spa season.

For some weeks after that, in the spring of 1914, the health of the emperor Franz Josef had been in serious decline and it looked as though the trip would have to be cancelled, that the Heir might be assuming the crown sooner now rather than later. Despite his advanced age of 83, the emperor remained a robust character and at the end of May his doctors issued a bulletin saying he was fully recovered. The official announcement of the Bosnia trip was made on 4 June.

In reality, the fine detail of the planning was already being considered, under the pedantic eye of Potiorek – suggestions, questions and instructions flew back and forth between Sarajevo and Vienna, in letters and telegrams. What route would the Heir follow to Bosnia, and then while in Bosnia? What about photographers? Two pennants for the Archduke's car? An official from Vienna to supervise catering at the Hotel Bosna in Ilidza? And would the Archduke's riding saddle be sent from Austria? If not, one could be provided. Telegram. 21 May. 'Request to be informed the weight of His Imperial Highness, also length of stirrup he uses …' The reply was that the Heir weighed 83.5 kilos. The stirrup should be 72 centimetres long.

Less than three weeks before the trip was due to start, there was a note asking if the Archduke would like to hear music during lunch at the Konak, the official residence of Governor Potiorek. The reply was that a 'small string quartet' should be chosen, to play only light Viennese music.

The menus, the wines … chilled or room temperature, sweet or dry? The Archduke liked his wines dry. Plus of course the matters of protocol: who should be invited and where should they sit? At least, on this occasion, that would not inflict any great ignominy on the Archduke's wife. On this visit, Sopherl, as he called her, would enjoy all the reflected status of her husband's title. Though the guard of honour at the hotel where they would stay were told not to present arms to her when she passed. That privilege was reserved for the Heir Apparent.

Perhaps Potiorek's concern to get things right was partly inspired by the widespread fear of the Heir's temper tantrums, which had not abated as he advanced in age. Just recently he had bellowed at senior officials on at least three occasions, sometimes in full view of others. Actually, it had been the same official in all three instances: General Conrad, his chief of staff. This gave the lie to those close to him who believed the Archduke, 'in spite of his complex personality had come to terms with himself'.

A year earlier the Austrian army had uncovered one of its most brilliant officers, Colonel Redl, as a traitor, selling secrets to foreign powers. On the orders of Conrad, Redl had been interrogated lightly before being given a revolver and left alone to do the decent thing and shoot himself. Only then had the full extent of his treachery – and his homosexuality – been discovered. Conrad later described his carpeting by Ferdinand for this matter as the worst experience of his career. He had thought, he said, the Archduke was going to choke on his own rage.

Then, in September 1913 Conrad had been reproached 'with unparalleled anger, even brutality' for failing to attend Mass. Finally, the Archduke had verbally abused him at a banquet, in full view and hearing of the Kaiser, among others.

There were rumours that Ferdinand was going mad. Even Conrad, who did not believe he was mad, thought at least the Archduke must be ill.

In early June 1914 he reportedly tried to get out of the trip to

Bosnia, seeking an audience with the recently recovered emperor and suggesting someone else go instead as he was not sure his health could stand the heat of the Bosnian summer. The emperor broadly told the Archduke he could do as he wished, but seems to have subliminally made his feelings known, that he thought the Archduke ought to go. Ferdinand then asked if Sophie could accompany him, to which there was no objection.

Some suggest that it was Sophie's anxieties which prompted Ferdinand to approach the emperor. It was she who was troubled by the effect of the heat on his health and perhaps too she was afraid for his safety, insisting that if he was going, she would go as well.

In a later version, given by Max, the Archduke's son, it was actually the emperor who tried to stop him going and the Archduke who insisted the trip must continue. 'I am Inspector General of the Austro-Hungarian armed forces,' he was supposed to have said, 'I must go to Sarajevo. The soldiers would never be able to explain my absence.' Perhaps he was being a brave trooper for his children when he told them this.

Max's parents spent the last days before the trip at their estates in Bohemia, the homeland of Sophie's family, the Choteks, who were there in unusually high profile for the visit on Friday, 12 June and Saturday, 13 June of Franz Ferdinand's friend and ally, Kaiser Wilhelm II, the emperor of Germany.

Again the presence of the Choteks at the Friday night dinner signified the Archduke's attempt to bring his wife to the forefront of court life – and also signified how much easier it was to do this outside Vienna.

He and Wilhelm had forged a good relationship during their past encounters and Wilhelm obviously wanted to nurture his alliance with the future Habsburg emperor. The Archduke's attempts to create his own individual ties with foreign powers were sometimes called his 'shooting box diplomacy'. He had already lined up the British King George and his wife Queen Mary for a visit in the autumn. Some thought he was hoping the Kaiser would return then too.

There would later be claims that the Heir and the Kaiser spent their time plotting a quick European war, which would be provoked by Austria invading Serbia with a swift rout of Russia and France to follow, while Britain stayed neutral. That would leave the Germans and the Habsburgs to reign supreme with enlarged territories in Europe, enabling Franz Ferdinand to take on new sovereignties which could then be passed to his eldest son Max, after his death. The evidence did not support the theory, but amid the rampant speculation and propaganda that would soon engulf Europe, this had some credence for a while.

In truth, a European war had been envisaged for at least two years and had been foreshadowed by the British politician Winston Churchill as far back as 1901, during his maiden speech as an MP in the House of Commons when he warned against the glib talk of a European war and cited his own observations as a reporter at the recent Boer War in South Africa as a reminder of how cruel and heartrending a new conflict might be. Such a war would demand 'perhaps for several years the whole manhood of the nation, the entire suspension of peaceful industries, and the concentrating to one end of every vital energy in the community'.

By 1912 Churchill had become First Lord of the Admiralty – head of the navy – and was engaged in a rivalry for naval supremacy with Germany. In a world carved up by the so-called Great Powers, Britain, with its vast empire across India and much of Africa and elsewhere was the Superpower of the age, heavily reliant for its continuing author-ity on the largest fleet of battleships at sea. Germany's more modest empire, argued Churchill to the annoyance of the Germans, made a good-sized fleet a mere luxury.

Britain had good reason to fear German plans for expansion, not just of its navy but of its land troops too. Even as Churchill and others were seeking diplomatic agreements, a pause in both their expansion plans – a naval holiday – some senior Germans were advocating war.

In his first volume of *The History of the Twentieth Century*, Martin Gilbert cited a retired German General Bernhardi who was already writing a book called *Germany and the Next War* in which he said his nation must claim 'not only a place in the sun but a full share in the mastery of the world', destroying the old order, recognizing Britain as the enemy, and beating it at sea.

Other influential Germans sounded more conciliatory, the Chancellor Bethmann-Hollweg saying that none of the powers wanted war, although often wars were not planned and caused by governments but by 'noisy and fanatical minorities'.

Germany feared the long-standing alliances that Britain maintained with France and Russia. It knew that France still resented German control of the border regions of Alsace-Lorraine. Germany's own allies, Austria-Hungary chief among them, had grave problems on their hands, largely, of course, arising out of the Balkans. The German people had a thousand-year enmity with the Slavic races. Those hostilities were still very much alive.

The Balkans were the key to everything. Without a share of them, Austria-Hungary would be land-locked and powerless. Turkey was still keeping a foothold while the Slav states themselves, Serbia, Montenegro, Bulgaria, Greece would happily drive Turkey from the region altogether.

Italy had its own aspirations in the region, which threatened its Triple Alliance with Germany and Austria. Both Germany and Austria tried to stop Italy moving against Turkish territories to which Italy laid claim. Italy responded with a show of strength and there were anti-Austrian demonstrations in Italy itself. Finally, fearing the loss of the Triple Alliance, Italy drew back and was rewarded with a renewed Alliance.

Still, there had been war in the Balkans that October which Austria and Serbia's natural ally Russia had been powerless to prevent. First the Serbs and the Bulgarians had fought and then they had joined together and formed The Balkans League with Montenegro and Greece to take on Turkey.

When Serb forces succeeded in pushing back the Turks first from Macedonia and then from Albania, Austria could not stand idly by and so turned once again to seek the support of the Kaiser who showed himself highly alert to the prospects of a wider war. The Kaiser told his senior aides that 'Austria had to act vigorously against the foreign Slavs because she would otherwise lose her power over the Serbs in the Austro-Hungarian monarchy'. And if Russia supported the Serbs, the Kaiser observed, then 'war would be inevitable for us' and, equally inevitable, Germany would also find itself at war with Britain on the seas. The Kaiser and his aides agreed to begin a domestic propaganda campaign, to prepare the German people for the idea of a war in the national interests.

Vienna could not countenance the unification of the south Slavs, especially with Serbia at its head. General Conrad, his chief of staff, had warned the Archduke that such Serbian ascendancy would 'relegate the Habsburg monarchy to the status of a small Power'.

Serbia wanted to absorb Albania – Austria was determined that Albania should remain under Turkish control or become independent. Such a stand-off could easily have led to a war but, fortunately, the Russians urged caution on Serbia who could not maintain their determined position without Russian support and so withdrew from Albania for the time being, leaving the Turks with a small stake left in Europe.

Russia had domestic problems of its own, with growing discontent at the harsh policies of the Tsar. Workers were forced to labour in poor conditions and brutally repressed if they complained. Strikes were outlawed. The Russian government sensed the mood of rebellion and revolution and attempted to introduce some welfare reforms, but they did nothing to quell the rising desire of the masses to smash capitalism.

Back in January 1912, a small breakaway group from the Russian Social Democratic Labour Party had met for the first time in Prague. They were the Bolsheviks, all of them in exile, the meeting organized by Lenin who co-opted two additional members to the newly formed Central Committee, one of them a Georgian, Josef Stalin.

Just as the Tsar's position was coming under increasing threat, so too was Turkey's lingering role in the Balkans and a renewed war in March 1913 again saw the Balkans League alliance acting together against the common enemy. Bulgaria made the first attacks but it was Montenegrin and Serbian forces who made the most inroads, once more in Albania. Greece too was involved and, finally, Greece and Bulgaria began fighting between themselves.

An independent Albania was declared but not initially accepted until the Great Powers applied pressure (acting in concert in their own interests for once) and Serbia and the rest of the Balkans League allies relented on the implied threat of an attack by Austria with no intervention by Russia.

Peace treaties were signed and soon broken when the Bulgarians attacked Greek and Serbian troops in Macedonia in June 1913. There were losses and gains on all sides and a rising trend of cruelty and terror which created widespread shock and revulsion and seemed, for a while, to have killed the European appetite for war.

A French official leading a commission of inquiry into the atrocities noted the change of heart and said that the Balkan wars had finally brought war itself into disrepute (an odd sentiment, you might think, as if war was ever anything but unpleasant).

The Great Powers, he said, were now manifestly unwilling to make war. Germany, France, Britain and the United States had 'discovered the obvious truth that the richest country has the most to lose by war and each country wishes for peace above all things … the dread of socialism and of the unknown, have been more efficacious in forcing the governments to think than any exhortations.'

The official also pointed out the vast costs of war, of maintaining and expanding national military might and asked people to imagine what a 'United Europe' might have done with those millions in promoting freedom, education and security.

Despite these fine words skirmishes continued in and around Albania. There were concerns that Austria might act on its own and intervene. That could be disastrous. German ministers issued clear warnings to their Austrian counterparts not to go to war with Serbia. The Germans, it now seemed, knew that war would come but wanted to be ready for it. The German people would have to be prepared to make sacrifices and show popular enthusiasm for conflict, which they were not yet doing.

Germany proclaimed fresh military expansion, saying it had been made necessary by continuing instability in the Balkans. Germany also spread its military influence to Turkey, provoking complaints from Russia.

The German chancellor Bethmann-Hollweg made a significant speech in April 1913, introducing his new army bill to the Reichstag, noting that there had been a 'state of tension' for many months within Austria and Russia over the Balkans and only the 'moderation and sense of responsibility of the powers' had prevented war. Nobody, he said, could conceive the dimensions of a world conflagration and the misery and trouble it would bring upon the nations. All previous wars would probably be as child's play by comparison.

The tone of the speech was calming, mostly, but he singled out the chauvinism of a French minority who boasted of their own superior military power and saw visions of Germany overrun by masses of Russian infantry and cavalry. Both Russia and France wanted to be as strong as possible, the German chancellor acknowledged, and Germany had to do the same. Germany wanted peace – but if war came it wanted to win.

Ironically, Churchill's offer of a 'naval holiday' was still on the agenda, though his German counterpart Admiral Tirpitz believed Churchill was only advocating such a plan because he feared losing naval superiority to Germany. The Kaiser succumbed to such hawkish talk and was increasingly sure of Germany's military domination.

Serbian troops were still in Albania in October 1913 when Austria issued an ultimatum, ordering a withdrawal within eight days. This was Austria going it alone, without the support of its allies or indeed any of the Great Powers. A dangerous game of brinkmanship and noted as such by both British and German officials, as well as the Russians who stayed quiet once more.

When Serbia complied and withdrew, fearing attack, the Kaiser sent telegrams of congratulations to both the Austrian emperor and his Heir Apparent, the Archduke. Austria knew it could rely on Germany – the Kaiser would not shirk from war.

The Kaiser told the Austrian chief of staff General Conrad that, if it came to it, 'within a few days you must be in Belgrade. I was always a partisan of peace; but this has its limits. I have read much more about war and know what it means. But finally a situation arises in which a great power can no longer just look on, but must draw the sword.'

Privately, the German chancellor wished everyone would calm down and war could be avoided. An explosion would be to the detriment of them all.

In March 1914, the British Admiralty published its own list of the naval strengths of the Great Powers. Britain had 58 battleships less than 20 years old, Germany 35, the United States 30, France 21, Japan 17, Austria-Hungary 14, Italy 9, Russia 8. The British announced plans for its greatest ever naval expansion, designed to maintain 60 per cent superiority over its nearest rival. So much for a naval holiday ...

The Germans feared Russian expansion. Apparently oblivious to the social upheavals there, the protests of a million workers on strike, the clamour for revolution, the German chief of staff told the Austrian, Conrad, that they could not afford to wait to wage war with

Russia, that any delay would lessen German chances as they could not compete with the Russian masses.

It took an outsider to summarize the state of affairs in Europe, an American diplomat, Colonel House, writing to his own President Wilson in May 1914 from Berlin: 'The situation is extraordinary. It is militarism run stark mad. Unless someone acting for you can bring about a different understanding there is some day to be an awful cataclysm.' There was no one in Europe who seemed capable of stopping the inevitable: 'There is too much hatred, too many jealousies. Whenever England consents, France and Russia will close in on Germany and Austria. England does not want Germany wholly crushed, for she would then have to reckon alone with her ancient enemy, Russia; but if Germany insists upon an ever-increasing navy, then England will have no choice.'

While some socialists and anarchists, in Italy and further afield, protested in vain against militarism, others noted the paradox of the developed nations, the Great Powers, on the one hand sharing interdependence and common aims in trade and industry and on the other, being apparently ready to destroy each other.

Kaiser Wilhelm's visit to his Austrian imperial friend took place at the Archduke's primary Bohemian residence, the castle at Konopischt where he employed a small army of gardeners to tend the grounds, especially the expansive rose beds. This was the ostensible motive for the visit, the Archduke's opportunity to show off the newly bloomed roses as the glorious centrepiece of his 500 acres.

The Kaiser had brought with him another keen gardener, the German Grand Admiral, Alfred von Tirpitz. The presence of this powerful military figure certainly aroused suspicions that something more than roses was being discussed. 'The ravishing aroma which rises out of the flowerbeds has suddenly taken on the smell of gunpowder' as one Viennese newspaper put it.

While their brief political talks centred on the strength and solidarity of their allies, Hungary, Italy, Romania, the Archduke apparently raised the idea that a title in the Kaiser's gift might be given to Ferdinand's dispossessed son, Max. He could become Duke of Lorraine, a territory taken from the French by Germany in the last century. The idea foundered with the death of Max's parents.

The Kaiser showed every respect to Sophie, taking her into dinner where she sat beside him. Her sister and several other relatives were among the 26 diners. There was a further dinner the following evening, with marching band music and hunting songs, before the emperor's party left at 9.30pm.

A few days later on 20 June the Archduke and his family moved to their other Bohemian estate, Chlumetz, where he had 'shot out the deer and stags completely' to preserve the woods and grounds as part of his inheritance for his children.

On Sunday, 21 June the Archduke was sitting in a car overlooking the meadow when a cat began to walk across the grass. He took out his pistol and steadied his arm on the back seat as he shot the cat and killed it outright with a single bullet.

The shot that killed the cat was the last shot the big game hunter ever fired.

If it is not just the historical wisdom of hindsight, there is some evidence that the Archduke expressed foreboding about the trip to Bosnia and, in one account from a relative, after supper one evening in May 1914 he actually gave a hurried premonition while his wife was out of the room: 'I know I shall soon be murdered.' After all, he was said to have added, 'the crypt at Artstetten is now finished'. The crypt is where the Archduke and the Duchess now reside, in perpetuity.

Dedijer suggests the Archduke's superstitions were the result of his mediaeval upbringing. He cites the memoir of one of the Archduke's advisers who was told by the Archduke 'how a fortune teller once predicted that "he would one day let loose a world war"'. The adviser said that although to a certain extent the prophecy flattered him, containing as it did the unspoken recognition that the world would have to reckon with him as a powerful factor the Archduke still 'emphatically pointed out how mad such a prophecy was'.

In all other respects the Archduke seemed cavalier about his personal safety, often shrugging off concerns for his protection. That spring he had been driving on from the Austrian imperial port of Trieste through an area where Italian nationalists had resorted to violence. As they headed towards the town of Cividale someone asked if the journey was wise, and suggested they notify the police. The Archduke said, 'But of course we are going to Cividale! Precautions? Alerting the police director in Trieste? To me that's all rubbish. We are at all times in God's hands. Look, some rogue could have a go at me now, coming out of that brushwood. Worry and caution paralyse life. To be afraid is always a dangerous business in itself.'

Yet his physician, Dr Eisenmenger, who at least thought anyone who believed the Archduke was mad should have their own head examined, reported the Archduke complaining about having to go to Bosnia and wishing his uncle the emperor had entrusted it to someone else. Another source has him 'extremely depressed and full of forebodings' in late June.

Leaving Chlumetz, saying goodbye to their children, promising to see them again in a week's time, setting off to the railway station to begin the long circuitous journey to Bosnia, via Vienna, Ferdinand and Sophie immediately discovered that they would have to abandon their private train carriage as one of the axles had run hot and caused the grand saloon-car to overheat. 'Well, well,' the Heir said with heavy sarcasm, 'this journey is getting off to a really promising start.' He turned to his aide Baron Morsey, 'you see, that's the way it starts. At first the carriage running hot, then a murder attempt in Sarajevo and finally, if all that doesn't get anywhere, an explosion on board the *Viribus*.'

The *Viribus Unitis*, a battleship, was the pride of the Habsburg fleet, maintained at Trieste. Ferdinand would go first to Vienna with Sophie, but there they would part, she to go by train to Budapest and Brod and on to Ilidza and he to Trieste to take the battleship down the Adriatic coast to the Croatian town of Metkovic where he would travel by train to Mostar and into Bosnia to rejoin his Sopherl.

By the time he reached Vienna that first evening, a new imperial carriage had been found to replace the one that was overheating, but as he boarded the new one he learned that the electricity had failed and it could only be illuminated by candles. 'How do you find this lighting?' he said to his private secretary who had come to see him off, 'like in a grave isn't it.'

During the sea journey through the Adriatic, Ferdinand was informed in a telegram that King Petar the Serbian monarch had abdicated in favour of his son Alexander who would now reign as Prince Regent. The Serbian government had been dissolved, leaving the country in brief turmoil which would distract it from any intentions it might have been harbouring towards Bosnia. The source of the difficulty involved Apis and The Black Hand and was effectively a power struggle between the civilian government and the army. When the government won, the prime minister, Pasic, dissolved the government to obtain a new mandate. King Petar, who had briefly aligned himself with the military, was left stranded and bound to do the honourable thing.

A guard of honour and a band playing the imperial anthem greeted the Heir as he arrived at Ilidza station in the afternoon of Thursday, 25 June. The royal party had taken over the Hotel Bosna, which had been subjected to extensive refurbishments, including the conversion of a guest room into a chapel, at the cost of 40,000 crowns. The royal suite was decorated in an Ottoman fashion and furnished accordingly with Turkish carpets and other ornaments from a store in the Sarajevo bazaar, the Carsija, including carved tables inlaid with mother of pearl. Supposedly, it was their admiration for these adornments that prompted the couple's unscheduled shopping trip to Sarajevo, where they were seen by Gavrilo.

The Archduke sent a telegram to his 13-year-old daughter, named Sophie for her mother, back at Chlumetz. 'Safely arrived in Ilidza. Found Mama very well. Very beautiful and pleasant here. We have splendid quarters. Weather very nice. Good night, fond embraces to you and your brothers.'

It began to look as if the trip would be a great success, perhaps even a triumph. The crowds cheered and the commentary, in most papers anyway, was supportive. The Catholic *Hrvatski Dnevnik* headlined the report of the Heir's arrival, 'Hail, Our Hope' and lauded his visit: 'he is coming to Bosnia as the Commander in Chief of all the armed forces of our Monarchy ...' This was not strictly true, of course, he was actually only the Inspector General. '... This is his first official visit to this country. We feel that he is sending to us and all our enemies the following clear message: Never will Bosnia leave the Habsburg Monarchy. The whole armed forces of the Monarchy will defend the Bosnian possessions to the last ounce of strength. He came here in order to stand up at the head of two Army corps of 50,000 men, showing us what he intends to do in the event of a reality of bloodshed.'

The royal couple parted ways for most of the next two days. The manoeuvres had been planned by Potiorek himself and actually involved around 20,000 troops under his command. The 16th corps had been marched across from Dalmatia to join the 15th corps assembled in Bosnia. Keeping them far from the Serbian frontier, where they would certainly have been considered provocative, Potiorek had planned the manoeuvres in hilly terrain west of Ilidza and had devised them not so much as an offensive, but as a defensive, to show how the troops might fare in repelling an attack on Sarajevo by forces advancing from the Adriatic.

The Archduke was on the road before 6am, and was spared the debilitating heat he had feared might affect his health – it was bitterly cold and wet and there were even some showers of snow. He watched through binoculars, some of the time on horseback, from high in the mountains as the mock battle was played out like a board game, 'blue armies' against 'red armies'.

There was a brief moment of anxiety when a civilian appeared from behind a thicket, as if in hiding, and came towards the officers grouped with the Heir Apparent. The man was carrying something that might have been a weapon. An officer grabbed him, fearing he was an assassin. The Archduke laughed. 'But that's the court photographer. Let him go. He's only doing his job and we all have to live.'

Ferdinand must have been in a cheerful mood and was full of admiration for the manoeuvres he had seen. On the second day, 27 June he returned early to Ilidza having called a halt to the mock battle around noon. The troops had been on the march since 4.30am and he felt they had done enough. He issued an Order of the Day which stated that the soldiers had justified his high expectations and commanded that the Order be translated into the many different languages spoken by these soldiers of the empire.

Back at the hotel, at about 4pm he dictated a telegram to the emperor in which he said the performance of the troops had been outstanding beyond all praise; they were highly trained, very fit and their morale was first class. He was visiting Sarajevo tomorrow, he told the emperor, and would be gone by the evening. Then he changed for dinner.

Sophie had been fulfilling the engagements her husband couldn't attend personally, which were of course, by comparison with playing soldiers, the more unmanly of the royal duties. As the Duchess of Hohenberg she had the benefit of the services of Baron Andreas von Morsey from the Archduke's personal staff. He had been assigned to accompany her on her duties in Sarajevo 'and in particular to make sure that no official, no nationality and no religious denomination was overlooked'. Not giving offence was no easy matter in a city of such complex identity.

There were visits to the Catholic children's home where she had been a patron for two years, to schools where she distributed sweets and photographs of her family, to a carpet factory, to both the Catholic and the Serb Orthodox cathedrals and various mosques.

Writing after the assassination, Morsey complained of the 'extreme incompetence' of the Sarajevo police who had watched and done nothing as the imperial detectives had struggled to push back a crowd of spectators who were crowding in on the Duchess. She was not troubled and 'took the keenest interest in everything she saw'.

Dinner at the Hotel Bosna on 27 June took place in the early evening, with 40 guests from the upper echelons of Sarajevo society. There was soup and local fish and three meats for the main course with asparagus, salad and sherbet followed by desserts, cheeses and candies. The extended wine list embraced champagne, clarets and both German and Hungarian wines. Apart from the trout there was scarcely any taste of Bosnian culture, until the Zilavka wine right before the brandy.

When the meal was finished the guests wandered into the hotel foyer where the Archduke and the Duchess mingled and talked easily with the guests. Sophie recognized the name of Dr Josip Sunaric when he was presented to her. He was the Croat vice-president in the Sabor and had been a voice of doom, urging Potiorek to cancel the imperial visit because he feared the mood of revolt among the Bosnian Serbs.

'My dear Dr Sunaric, you are wrong after all,' she said. 'Things do not always turn out the way you say they will. Wherever we have been everyone, down to the last Serb, has greeted us with such great friendliness, politeness and true warmth, that we are very happy with our visit.'

'Your highness,' Dr Sunaric replied, 'I pray to God that when I have the honour of meeting you again tomorrow night you can repeat these words to me. A great burden will be lifted from me.'

No one could say the Austrians hadn't been warned. There was evidence that a Serbian minister had alerted his counterpart in Vienna to the specific threat of assassination during the visit. Austria would expend enormous energy, afterwards, in attempting to prove official Serbian involvement in the assassination, but it could not ignore the evidence of its own complicity. Various officials, but especially General Potiorek, the Bosnian governor, had been determined that the visit should go ahead at almost any cost, and had conveniently dismissed or overlooked any suggestion that there would be trouble.

Dr Sunaric had warned against plans for a visit by the Archduke three years earlier. 'I know the Serbs,' he had said, 'I know that they will wait for him in ambush as murderers.' In the run-up to the June 1914 visit he had again made persistent warnings and had even telegrammed one of the senior ministers in Vienna, Bilinski, to warn him of the dangers the Archduke and Duchess might face. It was this telegram that had prompted Sophie's comment to him, her remarks in reality a reprimand. He should have known his place and kept quiet.

Governor Potiorek had seen a special report by a Bosnian civil servant, Count Carlo Gallas, which detailed the increasing activities of the Young Bosnians. Potiorek had criticized Gallas for 'having a fear of children'.

He had similarly ignored the warnings of the Sarajevo chief of police, Dr Edmund Gerde, who believed the atmosphere in the city was tense and there could well be an assassination attempt. He alone seemed to notice that choosing St Vitus Day, 28 June, was especially provocative. Having no joy with his own superior, Gerde appealed to the town's military committee and was ridiculed for his trouble: 'Don't worry, these lesser breeds would not dare to do anything.' Gerde insisted his concerns be minuted but even as they were written down he was still being mocked. 'You see phantoms everywhere,' the committee chairman said.

The committee also rejected a request that a cordon of soldiers be drafted in to line the streets, as it had done during the official visit of the emperor four years earlier. Then, in fact, there had been a double cordon, while hundreds of 'suspicious' residents had been kept under house arrest for the duration of the emperor's tour. There were no such measures this time. Dr Gerde had asked not to publish the route of the parade through Sarajevo until the day before, but this too was ignored. He pleaded with his superior to appeal directly to Potiorek, not once, but twice, and both times was told 'the Archduke is coming here as a general and it is none of your business to take care of this visit'.

Dr Gerde had 120 men in his police force and a request for reinforcements to be brought in from Budapest was abandoned on the grounds that the cost of 7,000 crowns would be too much. Gendarmes from the countryside around Sarajevo were drafted in, instead.

The police had at least managed to implement an instruction for the schools to close in mid-June and all non-resident students to leave the city. As a last measure they ordered the 120 police officers, and their few additional colleagues, to make sure they turned and faced the crowd as the imperial procession passed. Otherwise, as one of Gerde's colleagues remarked, 'security measures on 28 June were in the hands of Providence'.

When the dinner was over and the guests had departed, many of the Archduke's staff left too, for various other duties, and some of those who remained began to suggest the tour could end there, now that the main object of the visit, the manoeuvres, had finished. The Archduke listened, apparently open-minded as the discussion gained momentum. His head of household had been worried about hostile demonstrations and saw no reason to tempt fate with another day in Sarajevo. After all, Sophie had spent much of the last 48 hours there and Sarajevo could not complain of being ignored.

The Archduke seemed swayed by argument and on the point of agreeing to pull out that night, until General Potiorek's adjutant Colonel Merizzi pointed out that an early departure would especially offend the loyalists, the Croats whose support was so dearly needed. It could be seen as an insult to the governor himself and even as an admission of defeat.

So the day in Sarajevo would go ahead after all. No one was too sorry, and a group of them, including the Archduke, sat up until after midnight talking and drinking cognac.

The itinerary for the following day was typed up on a sheet of A4 and can still be seen in a display cabinet in the small family museum at the Hohenbergs' Austrian castle, Artstetten.

Mass at the new chapel in the Hotel Bosna was scheduled for 9am after which the royal party would leave on the special train to Sarajevo at 9.25am and by 9.50 they would be at Sarajevo station allowing ten minutes to get into the fleet of cars that would take them to the military barracks close to the station for a brief inspection of the troops followed by the ten-minute drive down Appel Quay to the town hall, past various sites highlighted in advance on the itinerary – the garri-son, the post office, the gendamerie – then a twenty-minute reception with speeches at the town hall before a 10.30am departure for the drive back down Appel Quay, and a right turn into Franz Josef Street to reach the ceremony for the opening of the new museum with a speech by Dr Gerde and a tour of the exhibits, then at 11.30am the drive back to the governor's palace, the Konak, for lunch at 12.30pm, leaving at 2pm to visit a carpet factory on the way back to the station to return to Ilidza for supper at 7pm, before departure at 9pm, out of Bosnia, the visit over.

And so, on the day of their deaths, the royal couple exchanged their last words with their God in the expensive hotel chapel. The Archduke then dictated two telegrams to Baron Morsey, one for a servant at Konopischt and the other to his teenaged daughter Sophie. His last words to her were, 'Mama and I are very well. Weather warm and fine. We gave a large dinner party yesterday and this morning there is the big reception in Sarajevo. Another large dinner party after that and then we are leaving on the *Viribus Unitis*. Dearest love to you all. Papa.'

After several days of rain, the weather had indeed changed and it was clear and sunny over Sarajevo, where, by now, the Archduke had every reason to expect an enthusiastic welcome. The main road had been renamed Franz Ferdinand Strasse. The town had been given a facelift and the Lord Mayor had issued a request or proclamation for everyone to demonstrate their 'gratitude, devotion and loyalty' by fly-ing flags, decorating their houses. In addition the loyal citizens of the empire had been urged to come out of their homes, or travel in from outlying areas, to watch the procession. A gala day was anticipated.

The Archduke and the Duchess set off for the station in their colourful finery, which the surviving black and white photographs cannot quite convey. The Archduke's shiny peaked hat sprouted an exotic, bushy plumage of light-green peacock feathers. He was dressed like a general in the hussars, with white gloves, silver spurs on his polished black boots, a red stripe down the outer seams of his black trousers, three stars on the raised collar of his blue serge tunic, a row of medals above his left breast and a waistband from which dangled at his left side a gold braided ribbon with tassels. He looked well fed, with his tunic stretched taut over his portly, 50-year-old's physique, the buttons appearing to strain a little in their buttonholes. His thick, upturned moustache was clipped and tidy, in the military fashion of the times.

The Duchess looked milky and unblemished, all in white, from her wide-brimmed hat with its cluster of dark ostrich feathers over a white veil to her full-length white dress fitted at the waist with a red sash. A posy of flowers was tucked into the sash, and the Duchess had various accessories, a white parasol, white gloves, a dark fan, a fur of ermine tails.

Potiorek was waiting for them at the station with the fleet of seven cars that would provide the convoy for the procession along Appel Quay to the town hall, known as the Beledija. After a guard of honour had presented arms the party travelled the short distance to the army barracks for the brief inspection of the troops.

As they prepared to leave there was some jockeying for position which saw Sarajevo police officers outwitting a group of the Archduke's private detectives to grab seats in the front vehicle. The detectives were left behind as the procession set off, the vehicles spaced some 50 yards apart.

The second car carried the Lord Mayor, Fehim Effendi Curcic, a Muslim who was wearing a fez and the chief of police, Dr Edmund Gerde, the man who had long since entrusted the protection of the Archduke to fate.

The royal couple were in the third vehicle, a convertible, open-topped sports car made by Graf and Stift the Viennese automobile manufacturers. The car was known as a double phaeton, as it had two bench seats, one up front for the driver and a passenger and one at the back, facing forward, for two further passengers. In addition it could become a six-seater with the use of the two rear-facing pull-down seats, behind the driver.

The trio of Graf brothers had not long since been bicycle manu-facturers before joining forces with businessman Willy Stift in 1904 to start producing their range of luxury limousines. This particular vehicle had been bought four years ago in 1910 by Count Franz von Harrach, an officer of the Austrian army transport unit. Harrach was sitting up front beside the chauffeur, Leopold Lojka. Behind them, in a pull-down seat, was the governor, Oskar Potiorek, facing the Archduke who was sitting to the left of the Duchess. The car was flying a Habsburg pennant from its hood in front of the high wooden steering wheel. The convertible top was rolled back behind the royal couple.

Behind them were four more cars containing officials from the governor's staff, various aides of the Archduke and some other notaries, including the head of the Fiat works in Vienna.

The Archduke had asked to proceed slowly along Appel Quay so that he could take in the surroundings. He would have seen the displays of flags – the Habsburg's black and yellow banner with its red border and Austrian eagle at the centre; the red and yellow of Bosnia. Some buildings were displaying the Archduke's portrait in their windows.

The 24-cannon salute from the fortresses above the city must have echoed around the valley below. Though the crowd on Appel Quay was far from huge, there were some cries of Zivio! Long may he live! By mid-morning it was really quite hot and the crowd was mainly gathered in the shade of the houses and trees along the city side of Appel Quay. On the other side only a narrow pavement and a low wall separated the road from the river Miljacka. The river was much lower than the road, and depending on its flow was usually a drop of fifteen or twenty feet from the wall. Only a few observers were standing beside the river, in the full glare of the sun.

Potiorek pointed out to the Archduke the site of the new barracks for the 15th corps, whose troops they had watched on manoeuvres.

At more or less that moment, their chauffeur Loyka saw an object flying through the air towards him. No one else in the car had seen it, apparently, but Lojka reacted automatically. He pressed the pedal with his foot to try and accelerate forward and out from under the object's flight path.

18

June 1914 – on the Avenue of Assassins

Thinking of grainy images, both still moving, of young men in groups, 80 or more years later, arriving at American airports, boarding American planes, or entering a British railway station carrying their backpacks full of explosives, all on their way to commit murder and to make martyrs of themselves, it is tempting to wonder what CCTV cameras peering backwards into history from future technology might have recorded of the appearance and the movement of Gavro and Nedjo and their fellow conspirators on the morning of 28 June 1914.

They would not have been sporting baseball caps and logo tops and leisure wear, that's for sure. The conspirators that day, or many of them, wore their stiff-collared shirts and ties; their suits and their fedora hats. I think it likely their clothes were worn and frayed. Perhaps their suits were dusty and unpressed; perhaps they had holes in the toes of their socks and the soles of their shoes. Or perhaps they put on their church best for this special occasion, setting out to make their mark on history. With one exception there was no record of the young men's appearance that day, so, at best, we are in the realms of informed speculation; though that one record certainly helps.

Like the passengers on the tube trains and the planes, as with the people in the North and South Towers of the World Trade Center, the Archduke and the Duchess had no idea what lay in wait for them.

They might have feared but could never have guessed, as they journeyed slowly down Appel Quay to the town hall in their luxury car that they were passing through 'a regular avenue of assassins', as the Archbishop of Sarajevo would later describe it, when the full story, or as much of it as we can ever now know, became known.

The Archbishop was Josip Stadler, a Croat priest who had revived the Catholic Church in Sarajevo after years of Ottoman rule. He had overseen the building of the cathedral and had been personally appointed by the pope to become the first ever archbishop.

Those assassins had no plans to survive the day themselves. They were all – almost all – ready to die and had the means to do it.

After returning home to leave his dog behind, Nedjo had walked into town and went to the book store of Basagic, which may have been a place where students gathered in the early morning to read the newspapers of the day. This must have been the premises of Safvet-beg Basagic, a renowned Muslim Croatian who was an intellectual and collector of Islamic manuscripts and other books and texts, while also writing a substantial volume of work himself. He later became curator of a prominent Sarajevo museum.

At some point that morning, very likely at Basagic's, Nedjo acquired a copy of *Narod*, the Serb daily, which had celebrated the visit of the Archduke by ignoring it altogether and choosing instead to evoke memories of St Vitus Days gone by. Its leading article was a lengthy editorial commemorating the Kosovo battle of 1389, together with poems – an inspirational read for any would-be martyrs.

While he was there, Nedjo met Grabez who had just arrived from his home town of Pale. Nedjo told him the group was scheduled to meet at Vlajnic's pastry shop, around the corner from Appel Quay at eight o'clock.

The owner of the café, Djuro Vlajnic, later testified that he had seen Ilic arrive there, later followed by two other young men. The waitress and cleaning woman, Erna Atias, believed she recognized Princip.

When Nedjo arrived he found Grabez and Ilic, who was joking with Erna as she served them. Grabez asked Nedjo if Princip had told him where to stand, and Nedjo said he knew. Nedjo sat down with them in the rear room, perhaps the seating area at the back of the shop, where he ate three cakes while he waited for Gavro. When Gavro arrived he quickly handed Nedjo a bomb and some cyanide …

The agreement to commit suicide had been established between the conspirators from the beginning, back in Belgrade, and accepted by those who joined afterwards. Dead conspirators could neither talk nor betray their colleagues. It had been Ciganovic's idea and perhaps he had intended preserving for eternity the secret of his involvement and that of Tankosic and Apis, his Black Hand associates. Even if they did not succeed, Ciganovic had told Nedjo, Gavro and Grabez, they should kill themselves anyway.

He had recommended cyanide, as it was a strong poison and certain to kill them.

Most historians and writers assume the cyanide was actually supplied by Ciganovic, along with the weapons, but there is no evidence for this. Remarkably, none of the defendants at the trial was ever asked who gave them the cyanide. Claiming Ciganovic as the source remains an assumption.

Then too, some writers have described the cyanide as a phial or capsule, but there is no evidence for this either. That too is an assumption. When I was in Sarajevo, in the autumn of 2006 and talked with Ranka Cabrinovic, the daughter of Dusan who was the youngest brother of Nedjo Cabrinovic, she said her father had been good friends in later years with Dragan Kalember, one of the Young Bosnians in Sarajevo who had teased Vaso Cubrilovic when he started boasting to friends that he was going to be an assassin. Kalember had only been 16 in 1914, and was still at school, but he had apparently told Ranka's father that he had then been working at a pharmacy and it was he who had supplied the cyanide that was used, in the form of a powder.

There was no way, now, of verifying the truth of this, but since none of the trio who had smuggled the weapons from Belgrade to Sarajevo ever mentioned carrying with them a poison it made more sense that the poison had been found in Sarajevo, perhaps arranged by Ilic. Kalember had been a defendant in the subsequent trial, for the relatively minor offence of not disclosing to the authorities that he knew about the assassination in advance. If it had been known that he supplied them with poison he would have been in a lot more trouble.

Asked at the trial why he had not been given a Browning pistol, Nedjo simply answered, that was the arrangement. He was pressed further, was it because he was not well-trained? 'With a Browning I would have to commit suicide and I knew that.' It is unclear of the meaning here, as he had accepted the cyanide so was already prepared to die. Perhaps it was the thought of shooting himself in the head that did not appeal.

After he had been given the bomb and the poison Nedjo left the pastry shop and went down to Appel Quay. Nedjo had not even spoken to Ilic and it seems that some enmity had arisen between them. Nedjo would later say it was not until that morning that he discovered Ilic was not actually going to take part himself in the assassination. He told the trial that, back in Belgrade, Gavro had complained about Ilic as unreliable and untrustworthy. Gavro had said, 'it seems to me that Ilic is a snob.' Nedjo probably thought the same thing: Ilic considered himself to be on a superior academic plane – too intellectual to get his hands dirty pulling a trigger or throwing a bomb.

The prosecutor at the trial wanted to know what Nedjo thought Gavro had meant, calling Ilic a snob. Nedjo replied, 'that is said of someone a little higher, who holds himself a little higher.'

Reaching Appel Quay, Nedjo had a chance meeting with his friend Tomo Vucinovic, who was one of those he had been singing with while promenading on the Quay in recent days.

Nedjo was the most uninhibited of the assassins and clearly had a sense of his own impending place in history. He decided he would like to have his photograph taken that morning – 'so that something would remain of me' he said in one statement and, in another, 'I thought that posterity should have my picture taken on that day' – so he invited Vucinovic to join him and they set off to find an open photographic studio. The first one they tried was closed so they walked on to the Cirkus Trg – Circus Square – where they found that Josef Schrei's studio was open and straightaway went in and posed for a photograph. It must have been around nine o'clock. The royal couple would be dead by eleven.

In the cropped version of the photograph that I have seen Nedjo is sitting down and Vucinovic is standing beside him, his right arm resting lightly on Nedjo's shoulder. Both young men are staring directly into the camera but while a slight smile plays on the mouth of Vucinovic, who is not about to try and kill somebody, Nedjo's lips are pursed; he looks tense and uncharacteristically stern. His wavy, swept hair is cut short and neat and he has a clipped moustache with none of the extravagant, bushy extensions favoured by the Archduke and his eminent colleagues.

Both men are wearing suits over what appear, in the black and white image, to be white shirts with stiff collars and dark neckties. There is testimony that Nedjo was wearing a hat – an 'anarchist's cap' – that morning but he is not wearing one in the photograph. Because the image is cropped I cannot see the copy of that day's *Narod* newspaper which was supposedly tucked into the outer pocket of his jacket. Nor can you see, in the cropped version, the bulge of the bomb which was apparently visible from his pocket.

Schrei was able to develop and print copies within the hour. Nedjo asked for six and, telling Vucinovic he was leaving for Zagreb, asked him to give one to his grandmother, one to his sister and send others to friends in Belgrade, Trieste and Zagreb. They strolled around while they waited, meeting a couple of girlfriends of Vucinovic. Nedjo joked with them a little before returning to the studio to collect the photographs which Vucinovic later sent on, as he had been asked.

After that, Nedjo spent his time strolling on the Quay, thinking about where exactly he would stand and wait to throw his bomb at the Archduke, but also taking long strolls so as not to be seen loitering and to avoid arousing the suspicion of the many detectives and spies that he, wrongly, imagined were watching out for would-be assassins.

So he walked between the Austro-Hungarian bank and the bridge, on the sunny side of the street beside the Miljacka. He wanted to pick a spot where there would not be such a crowd as he hoped to kill only the Archduke and not hurt others. At the same time, he needed to stand next to a lamp-post so he would have somewhere to strike the bomb to prime it, before counting the seconds and throwing, as he had been instructed.

He was challenged at the trial on this expressed intent not to hurt anyone but the Archduke. 'You knew that when the bomb exploded she would die too?'

'We were determined to kill only him, but if that were not possible, then we would sacrifice her and all the others. I did not know that there would be some from his escort. I thought that there would only be Potiorek, and his wife with him, and that he would be killed. I didn't know that there were still others. When they approached I was pretty far from the others.'

Ilic did not bring Grabez's weapons with him to the pastry shop, probably because he did not want to take the risk of walking with them. Instead, he took Grabez back to his mother's house, in Oprkanj Street, and there he gave him a pistol and a bomb. He did not give Grabez any cyanide, believing he had persuaded him not to participate.

Grabez changed his mind more than once, in his evidence about what his intentions really were. He described his conversation with Ilic while the weapons were being handed over, saying he had promised Ilic that he would not carry out the assassination or kill himself but would remain for further activity and would continue to work in the same spirit for revolutionary ideas.

But that, he said to begin with, was all a pretence. He left Ilic's home to go to the Quay and carry out the assassination. He said he went looking for Gavro, expecting to find him standing by Siler's. He thought he could throw his bomb to create a diversion and confuse the chauffeur and the public while Gavro carried out the actual shooting.

But when he reached the Quay he was unable to find Gavro. He walked up and down along both sides several times and still could not see him. He convinced himself that Gavro must have been arrested.

Imagining what might happen now, he thought of going to wait by the Careva Cuprija – the Emperor's Bridge – which was the direct route across the Miljacka to the governor's building, the Konak, where a royal lunch was scheduled. The Konak was a walled, secluded palace, dating from the Ottoman period. If Nedjo tried and failed to carry out the assassination then surely the chauffeur would take this route and Grabez would be waiting for him as the car slowed at the corner. Grabez referred to the spot as 'the place of Zerajic' because it was the precise location where the heroic martyr Bogdan Zerajic had killed himself four years earlier, after trying and failing to shoot the former governor, General Varesanin.

He was sure two detectives had noticed him and thought about trying to walk across the Miljacka and back round over the other bridge but there was a huge crowd at the Emperor's Bridge and the way was blocked by police officers. He decided to stand there and wait and was still there a few minutes later when he heard the explosion of the bomb. He did not know who had thrown it but thought it must be Nedjo Cabrinovic as the other assassins were Bosnian Youth of 'weaker quality'.

This was the account that Grabez was to give during his evidence in chief at the trial. Had you decided to commit suicide if the assassination succeeded? He was asked. 'Yes,' he said. 'With what?' 'With the revolver of course.'

At the earlier pre-trial hearing he had told a completely different story and denied he was ready to take part. Then six days later in the trial he changed his mind yet again and said that even though he had stopped trusting Ilic when he tried to dissuade him, Grabez had eventually agreed with Ilic's decision that he should not take part, had never gone to stand at the Emperor's Bridge and had instead only taken the weapons to remove the evidence from Ilic's house. He had wrapped the gun and the bomb into an awkward-shaped package, he said, and had no intention of assassinating anybody.

He claimed he had lied before, about being at the Emperor's Bridge, to hide the identity of someone who had been with him during the morning. The trial team seemed sceptical. 'That's the third time you've changed your story. What are we to believe?'

It's hard to be sure, but I feel certain he meant to take part and lost his nerve that day and again at the trial, when he made a last, futile attempt to save himself from a long sentence.

Only Nedjo and Gavro, it seems, were unwavering in their commitment and their unwillingness to compromise their beliefs to save themselves. On the contrary, perhaps, they alone were determined to martyr themselves for the Serbian cause.

Gavro had collected his own weapons, a pistol and a bomb, from the bag beneath his bed as he left Ilic's house for the last time that morning at about eight o'clock. There is no record that he 'tidied his affairs' or said any special goodbyes or made any other particular arrangements. So far as history knows, he got up, got dressed, got the weapons, went out.

From Vlajnic's he went walking, looking for company that would not be conspicuous. He walked for a while with a schoolboy, named only as Spiric, and then they met another young man, Maxim Svara, and invited him to join them. Svara was the perfect cover for Gavro – he was the son of the Sarajevo Public Prosecutor Franjo Svara, who would soon be leading the case against Gavro and the 24 other defendants at the trial.

They walked to the park and strolled there talking about 'ordinary things', as Gavro described it. They wanted to go back to the town and the korso, the promenade through the city centre. It was time for Gavro to go to his place, so he walked back to Appel Quay and took up his assigned location.

Though there have been numerous attempts to record the exact positions where the assassins were standing when the Archduke's parade passed along Appel Quay, they are all of them inaccurate in some way or other, placing people on one side of the road, when they were on the other, and at the wrong position along the road. It is impossible now to recreate the precise map of their locations, especially since they moved around.

Most maps place Gavrilo Princip on the sunny side of the street, beside the Miljacka just before the Lateiner Cuprija – the Latin Bridge. Grabez, if he is to be believed, is further along, in front of the Emperor's Bridge, the last in the long line of assassins the Archduke would have passed before reaching the town hall.

Ilic told the trial he had discussed the positions with Gavro and Grabez and then assigned the placings himself, putting both Gavro and Grabez beyond the Emperor's Bridge, both of them nearer to the town hall. But Grabez said he expected to find Gavro near Siler's and this is the shop on the corner of Appel Quay and Franz Josef Street, across the road from the Latin Bridge, more or less where the maps usually place Gavro. He was never asked and never gave his own location at this point in the morning's events, before he moved to take up the second position from where he would carry out the assassination.

One writer, Joachim Remak, wrote an account of the assassination in 1959 which was published with a map. He then met Cvjetko Popovic afterwards (perhaps he should have thought of meeting him before he published) and wrote an article describing how Popovic had taken issue with some aspects of his book – 'none of us were Black Hand members, not even Ilic' – including Remak's map, which had placed Popovic too close to Nedjo and put Vaso on the opposite side of the road to Popovic when in fact they had been close together on the same side, the shady side.

Popovic, said Remak, had only once become really violent at their meeting – meaning angry I think, not physically abusive – when complaining that the only trial record available then had quoted him as saying he 'lacked courage' to shoot or throw his bomb. 'What I meant', Popovic said, 'was that there were some people in the way.'

In the full transcript, which is now available, it is quite clear that Popovic admits his nerve failed him. Why didn't you do it? he is asked. 'I didn't have the courage. I don't know what happened to me.' Of course, he was only 16.

Popovic placed himself on the corner of Cumurija Street, the turning off the Quay where Vlajnic's pastry shop was located. Ilic also said that, after walking up and down the Quay he too was at this corner as the Archduke went past.

Vaso Cubrilovic describes in his unpublished letter to his sisters how he was more or less opposite Nedjo. I think it has been possible, comparing the buildings that still stand on Appel Quay – now called Obala Kulina Bana – with photographs taken on 28 June 1914 to position them fairly exactly, just before Cumurija Street, with Popovic I think on the next corner, further up towards the town hall.

Intriguingly, Vaso disclosed in this letter that he and Popovic had been given the cyanide two or three weeks earlier, long before they had received the weapons. He does not say who gave it to them and since the letter was written in 1918 while he was still in prison it seems likely he was avoiding disclosing the source. Perhaps it was Kalember. Vaso subscribes to the view that the cyanide had been ruined because they had been walking around with it in their pockets all that time. Only Nedjo and Gavro ever tried to take the poison so Vaso is perhaps being a little boastful when he writes to his sisters that 'unfortunately none of us knew how to keep it and we carried it in our pockets which ruined it', as if he too had tried and failed to achieve martyrdom.

He describes how he went out with the pistol in his right pocket but found he could not carry the bomb in his trouser pocket because it was too heavy and would have dragged his pocket down. Instead he used his red scarf to make a small pouch which he tied to his belt at both ends. He put the bomb inside so that it would be easy to carry and easily accessible and was barely noticeable at his waist.

Somehow, while he was waiting he fell in with an annoying companion whom he could not shake off. Then the companion pointed to the linden tree near them and said as a joke, look there's a bomb hidden there for Ferdinand. Good, said Vaso, wait there for it to explode. Vaso did not feel the position was suitable as he could not see very far and envied Nedjo his position across the road, at the top of the bend, from where he could see all the way back down the Quay. Vaso could not even see his friend Popovic who was just around the corner, outside the Teachers' School residences.

By ten o'clock, said Vaso, everyone was ready and waiting for the Archduke. Ilic had told him the Archduke would be in the third car – Ilic must have read this detail in the Sarajevo papers that published the plans for the procession – but when the first car appeared it was full of police officers so Vaso discounted it and began to count back at the line of cars he could see, but then suddenly there he was, the Archduke, two cars behind the police.

Writing in 1918, Vaso said he could picture the Archduke and his wife as if they were still in front of him now. He was resting his arm on the folded roof of the car, waving, and his wife was all in white, holding her parasol. Is that them? Vaso asked his annoying companion. The man nodded and Vaso stepped back towards the wall ready to throw his bomb, he claimed, when suddenly the Archduke's car was alongside him and there was a sound like a gunshot.

The Archduke must have been waving as he passed Mehmed Mehmedbasic who had been placed by Ilic at the head of the avenue of assassins, accorded pole position by Ilic, on account perhaps of his being the eldest and, supposedly, the most determined of the assassins.

Mehmedbasic later told a friend that Ilic had advised him not to throw his bomb unless he was certain he had recognized the Archduke, so as not to make a mistake. He could always wait until later, when the car was coming back down Appel Quay from the town hall, if needs be.

But Mehmedbasic then told the historian Albertini that, just as the procession was approaching, a gendarme came and stood behind him. He claimed that he was afraid then to produce the bomb from his belt because he might have been seen by the gendarme and given the whole plot away ... or perhaps he too lost his nerve. This is clearly what Albertini believed: 'In reality, he [Mehmedbasic], like the others, lacked courage and ran off as soon as he heard Cabrinovic's bomb explode.'

A number of witnesses saw Nedjo as he waited by the river. A young lawyer's assistant described looking out of his office window and seeing across the street, standing beside an 'electric pole', a tall young man in dark clothes who, it seemed to the witness, was wearing a black hat. Next to the tall man was 'that crazy Moric' (this was a mute street urchin, Moric Alakalaj, who was often in the company of the students and often the butt of their jokes, an object of amusement). There was no one else near them, but the witness did not pay them any special attention: 'When the first car came we didn't hear anything, but when the second car came we heard a light explosion. When the third automobile came, in which the Heir was riding, facing the Quay, with the late archduchess on his left, I saw that a box was thrown, about 15 centimetres long and five or six centimetres wide. It fell on the shoulders of the Heir, who threw it off with his hand.'

The witness was mistaken, but emphatically believed what he had seen. When he was asked in court if that was right, he said, it was: 'It fell on his shoulders and he bent over and threw it outside with his hand, and the box fell in front of the door to the office and it exploded. That's all.' But it wasn't. That wasn't right at all.

Another witness was standing outside the cabinetmaker's shop, Rupnik's and was just greeting a friend – 'hello' – as the third car passed. 'Just then there was an explosion. People began running. Then I turned around and I saw where the car had stopped and saw a tall, thin man who waved his arms as if he were throwing something. I saw that His Highness stood up in the car and jittered a little. Also I saw the assassin. He turned around, seemed to take something into his mouth and then jumped over the wall. At that moment the bomb exploded and I was hit and wounded in the left leg.'

Some witnesses, including, initially, the Archduke's chauffeur, did not see Nedjo throw anything and believed there had been two gunshots. In fact, the first 'gunshot' was Nedjo striking the bomb against the 'electric pole' – the lamp-post – to prime it. By his own account he had unscrewed the bomb already and kept it hidden in his belt, holding it with his hand the whole time. He had apparently stood next to a gendarme for a while and asked him, as an enthusiastic spectator might, which car was the Archduke's and the gendarme had helpfully identified the third car for him.

All Nedjo could see as the car approached was a 'green cap', as he put it – the peacock feathers in the Archduke's helmet. 'I hit the bomb against the lamp-post. It broke and I threw it.' He said it sounded like a weak shot, as he struck the bomb against the lamp-post.

What he should have done, of course, was count to ten, slowly, and then throw it, but he was too excited to wait so that the bomb, once hurled, still had twelve seconds to go before it exploded.

After he had thrown it he saw 'the late Ferdinand turn towards me and look at me with a cold, inflexible gaze. At that moment the bomb fell on the folded roof of the automobile, bounced off the automobile and fell on the ground. I turned around, took the poison and jumped into the Miljacka.'

He took a double dose of the poison, he said, but it didn't work. He was sick and couldn't eat for several days afterwards, but it didn't kill him. This has invariably been attributed to the fact that the poison was no good in some way, or had been ruined, but I think it more likely the dose that Nedjo took, even the double measure he claimed to have swallowed, was too small. Cyanide works by stopping the body's tissue from taking in oxygen. A fatal dose will have you unconscious within five minutes, perhaps even after a few seconds. The symptoms proceed through nausea and vomiting and falling blood pressure, to convulsions and death, often finally due to cardiac arrest, after about two hours.

A lethal dose is between 150–200 milligrams. In fact it is more dangerously potent as a gas and it was hydrogen cyanide – Zyklon B – that was employed by the Germans in the gas chambers of their death camps during the second world war. For their own death, two Nazi leaders, Goering and Himmler, used potassium cyanide, the form given to the Sarajevo assassins. It was also deployed at Jonestown, Guyana in 1978 during the mass murder/suicide of 909 people in the cult led by the Reverend Jim Jones.

There is no evidence that potassium cyanide degrades or loses effectiveness over time or if kept in a pocket for two weeks. I suspect the doses distributed to the assassins were simply too small to be fatal. This would explain why Nedjo only experienced the symptoms of mild poisoning.

Sitting in the car, both the general and the Archduke believed they had seen two bombs flying towards them. The Archduke told Potiorek immediately afterwards that he had been ready to throw the second object back but did not see where it fell and thought it was lying on the floor inside the car. He did not say anything, he told Potiorek, because he did not want to alarm the Duchess.

Apparently, then, he was sitting there waiting to be blown up.

They must have seen Nedjo's movement, priming the bomb, and mistaken that for a bomb being thrown. In fact, they were saved by the instinctive reactions of the chauffeur who accelerated forward – Potiorek noticed how the car suddenly went fast and then slow – so that the bomb did not fall inside the car or hit the Archduke on the shoulder but hit the folded-down hood, just as Nedjo had seen it, and dropped down onto the road directly into the path of the car behind. The bomb exploded in front of the next car's left rear wheel, making a small crater in the road about twelve inches wide and six inches deep.

The Archduke's car kept moving until the Archduke asked the chauffeur to stop and ordered Count Harrach, sitting beside the driver, to go back and see if anyone was dead or injured.

Sitting in the next car was Erich von Merizzi, the governor's assist-ant, the man who had persuaded the Archduke against ending his trip the night before. Merizzi noticed the explosion and felt a blow on the right side of his head. He was soon told he was bleeding. One of the Duchess's ladies-in-waiting began dabbing at his wound with her handkerchief. A second officer, Count Alexander Boos-Waldeck, was also slightly injured.

Seven spectators suffered minor shrapnel wounds. One woman, watching from her balcony, suffered a perforated eardrum. Even the Duchess had not been spared – she complained of a pain at the base of her neck and her husband looked and saw that she had a slight graze on her shoulder. At least three pieces of shrapnel had hit the car but caused no more than superficial damage.

As they waited, the Archduke said to Potiorek, sitting opposite him on the pull-down seat, 'I thought something like this might happen.'

Harrach came running back to report what he had seen. Another officer on the Archduke's staff ran up and told the car to drive on to the town hall – stopped there in the middle of the road, the royal couple were sitting ducks. 'The fellow must be insane,' said the Archduke, 'let us proceed with our programme.'

Four people chased Nedjo after he had put the poison in his mouth and thrown himself over the wall, dropping some fifteen feet into the shallow water below, where he was lying facing down. A gendarme who had watched him throw the bomb drew his sabre and chased him down into the river, stumbling down the bank at the same time as a Muslim detective. Two local men also jumped down into the river. One of them was a shopkeeper and he heard the detective order Nedjo to raise his hands, but Nedjo said he couldn't. The witness thought the detective was about to kill Nedjo but instead they dragged Nedjo across the river and hauled him out of the water in the park opposite. The other civilian witness was holding Nedjo's shoulder and punched him when he tried to escape. 'Why aren't you going?' said the shop-keeper. 'You're a Serb aren't you?'

'I am,' said Nedjo, 'and a heroic Serb.'

When they reached the police station Nedjo was searched but all they found was the single copy of the *Narod* newspaper.

'Leave me alone,' he said, 'I'll tell you everything.'

'Where did you get the bomb?'

'From our association.'

'From what association?'

'I'll tell you later.'

'Do you have accomplices?'

Nedjo didn't answer.

At the trial he said he was sorry other people had been injured and he had tried to keep away from the crowds. He wished he could say he was not sorry to have participated in the whole affair, 'but this brought with it unanticipated consequences which no one could in any way have foreseen. If I had foreseen it I would have sat on the bomb so that it would have blown me to pieces.'

Back at the Quay a crowd lingered as a photographer took pictures of the scene of the explosion, showing huddles of men, some in fez hats and traditional dress, others in suits and fedoras, in front of a building with a pillared frontage. After standing for some time in the street with a copy of the photograph I was able to identify it, still standing, and still recognizable despite the modifications that had taken place over ninety years, and despite the considerable damage it had suffered, presumably from shellfire during the siege of the 1990s. The house next to it in 1914 had been pulled down since to make way for a short new road that ran into Cumurija Street.

The continuing procession had passed Vaso – who had thrown himself to the ground at the explosion – Popovic, Gavro and Grabez who all did nothing. Some of the crowd began running down Appel Quay towards the town hall, perhaps wondering what would hap-pen next. The first two cars had not stopped and so arrived ahead of schedule, the occupants waiting in some confusion for the royal couple to arrive. Some had heard an explosion – one thought it was a cannon salute.

There was an all-embracing welcoming party – Muslims, Catholics, Serbs who were loyal to the Austrian empire and representatives of the local Jewish community. They were waiting around the red carpet that had been rolled out on the steps of the town hall.

That building was also still there in 2006, but had been badly damaged during the siege and was boarded up. It had become a national archive in later years and a plaque on the outer wall conveyed an angry message, a reminder, as if one were needed, that the oppressed Serbs had become oppressors too. It was written in English, so obviously meant for an international audience:

> On this place Serbian criminals
> In the night of 25th–26th August 1992 set on fire
> National and University's library
> Of Bosnia & Hercegovina
> Over 2 million books, periodicals
> And documents vanished in the flame
>
> Do not forget
> Remember and warn!

The Lord Mayor had a prepared speech which he began immediately the Archduke arrived. 'Your Imperial and Royal Highness, Your Highness! Our hearts are full of happiness on the occasion of the most gracious visit with which your Highnesses have deigned to honour the capital of our land …'

The Archduke was fuming and could no longer keep himself in check. He did not wait for the Lord Mayor to finish but burst forth, 'Herr Bürgermeister, what is the good of your speeches? I come to Sarajevo on a friendly visit and someone throws a bomb at me. This is outrageous.'

The Lord Mayor, by all accounts, seemed flummoxed and not sure what to do. The Duchess leaned into the Archduke and whispered into his ear. They must have been words intended to soothe and calm – no doubt she was practised in this art – as the Archduke was seen to hesitate a moment before saying, 'now you can get on with your speech.'

His words faltered but the Lord Mayor eventually completed his speech: '... our deep gratitude for your Highness's graciousness and fatherly care ... for the youngest jewel in the Holy Imperial Crown, our dear fatherland Bosnia and Hercegovina ...'

As he finished it was the Archduke's turn to make the reply. He looked around for the staff officer who was holding his speech, but he was in the next car and there was another awkward moment, until the car arrived and the officer handed over the speech which was wet with blood from the injured passengers, Merizzi and Boos-Waldeck.

The Archduke fluently added a line about the bombing incident to his prepared text, saying how he had received with special pleasure 'the Lord Mayor's assurances of unshakeable loyalty and attachment to His Royal Highness, our gracious Emperor and King and I thank you Herr Bürgermeister, very heartily for the enthusiastic ovations offered to me and to my wife by the population, all the more as I see in them an expression of their joy at the failure of the attempt at assassination ...'

When he had finished they all went inside for the reception. The Duchess was taken to the first floor for a meeting with the Muslim 'ladies' and their children. The Archduke held court in the lobby and tried to make light of the attempt. 'You mark my words, the chap will probably, in good old Austrian style, be decorated with the Order of Merit instead of being made harmless ... Today we shall get a few more little bullets.'

The Archduke turned to Potiorek and asked if he thought there would be more bombs. In his witness statement Potiorek said he answered that he didn't think so, but that if something like that should be undertaken within a very close distance, despite all security measures it should not be impossible. Others who heard the exchange said he was more reassuring and said, 'go at ease, I accept all responsibility.'

Potiorek said that after this incident the citizens of Sarajevo deserved some punishment, so it would serve them right if they changed the order of the day. The Archduke could now, instead of going to the museum reception, go straight to the Konak where they were due for lunch, or even back to his hotel in Ilidza.

There had been more dramatic discussion among the officers on the Archduke's staff about how best to get him out of the city alive. The Archduke rejected one suggestion that he remain at the town hall until troops could be brought in to clear the streets. He instead said he wanted to go to the hospital and visit Erich von Merizzi who had been taken there to be treated for his head injury.

It was agreed that, rather than turn right at Franz Josef Street as originally planned, which would have taken them into the narrow roads of the city centre, they would go straight back down Appel Quay, taking the long way round to the hospital.

The Archduke dictated a telegram for the emperor, telling him what had happened. He took his aide Baron Morsey to one side and asked him to take the Duchess away separately to safety, either at the Konak or to Ilidza. Morsey collected the Duchess's stole and went upstairs where he told her it was the Archduke's wish that she go with him. As Morsey described it, 'she replied quietly but in a manner which brooked no argument, "As long as the Archduke appears in public today I am not leaving him."' Morsey went back downstairs and told the Archduke. Then his wife reappeared, holding a bouquet of flowers presented to her by a Muslim girl. She said, 'I will go with you to the hospital.'

There is a photograph of the couple leaving the town hall at 10.45am. They are sitting side by side in the back of the car, the Duchess to the right of the Archduke, being watched by a group of dignitaries, some of whom are saluting their goodbyes.

Count Harrach, the owner of the car, had decided not to sit next to the driver but instead to stand on the running board, next to the Archduke, to shield him from any further attacks from the river side of the road as they drove back down the Quay. Harrach was convinced there would be another attempt and refused to move even when the Archduke smiled and asked him to take his seat beside the chauffeur, Lojka. Of course, Harrach's position was limited as it did nothing to protect the royal couple from attacks on the right.

There was only one vehicle ahead of them now, the car containing the Lord Mayor and the police chief, Dr Gerde. Though Gerde knew of the changed route no one, apparently, had briefed the chauffeurs.

They set off once more, passing the first bridge, the Emperor's Bridge where Trifko Grabez said he was standing waiting for them to slow and turn left onto the Bridge to the Konak, wrongly guessing they would go that way. Instead they went straight past him without slowing, intending to pass the second bridge too, the Latin Bridge which also crossed the river to their left. But as they approached the Latin Bridge, the car ahead of them turned right into Franz Josef Street, mistakenly maintaining the original route. The royal chauffeur was also supposed to go straight ahead but he too began to turn right, following the car in front of him.

History has not recorded why this happened. It seems like a mistake – in the confusion after the bomb, the drivers had not been briefed – but some prefer to see it as a conspiracy, a deliberate move to drive the royal couple into the hands of the assassin.

At this precise moment a photograph was taken of their car on Appel Quay. The leaves of a branch are drooping into the foreground and you can see the distant hills above the city; across the Miljacka is the rising minaret and onion dome of one of the mosques. There is a thin crowd of people waving from both sides of the street. You can't hear it, of course, but no doubt some of them are crying Zivio! Long may he live! You can see the wheels of the car just turning slightly to the right, towards Franz Josef Street. This frozen moment is perhaps thirty seconds before the shooting starts.

To the right of where the car would now pass, on the corner site of the junction, with its main entrance on Franz Josef Street was the general store and delicatessen of the Jewish retailer Moritz Schiller. Among other things, Schiller's sold tobacco and alcohol, the latter arranged in an elaborate display in the store window, besides a floor to ceiling hoarding outside the front of the shop, on the corner of the junction, representing a huge bottle of sparkling German wine.

A witness, Milan Drnic, and his wife had retreated into Schiller's doorway after hearing the bomb. Schiller had just walked round with a chair which he had offered to the wife so she could rest. The cars of the royal procession began turning into the street from Appel Quay, passing one after the other. Drnic, whose wife was now sitting down, saw 'His Highness' with his own wife next to him and Drnic raised his hat to greet them, removing his hat from his head, out of respect. At that moment, Drnic noticed a short man on the pavement less than six feet away. The short man was hollow-eyed with long hair and he was holding a Browning pistol.

Drnic put his hat back on and wanted to say something. Look out, perhaps, or stop! But he never got his words out and he never heard the shots. The next thing he heard was a shriek. Then the uproar began and people began beating the hollow-eyed man. Drnic saw a box drop to the floor and was sure it must be a bomb and now he really did shout: 'Watch out and don't step on the bomb!'

Gavro had heard the explosion of Nedjo's bomb and, as he told the trial, 'I knew that it must be one of ours but I didn't know which one.' The mob started to run and Gavro ran a little too, but then he saw the Archduke's car stop and assumed it was all over and the Archduke must be dead. He saw that they had caught Nedjo and thought of getting to him and shooting him dead, then shooting himself, to preserve their secret. Then the cars began moving again and, even though he had still not seen or recognized him, he realized the Archduke must still be alive.

He returned to the Latin Bridge and wondered where to stand. He knew the published route so decided to cross the road and wait in front of Schiller's. As he waited a Young Bosnian, Mihajlo Pusara, came up and said he was looking for a friend, Vargic. Gavro said he hadn't seen him. Just as the royal car approached, Pusara said, 'Do you see how dumb they are?'

At the trial, Gavro said he ignored Pusara as he didn't trust him and believed he might be a spy as he had a relative who was a spy. Gavro was probably trying to save Pusara as it seems unlikely he really believed Pusara was a spy. It had been Pusara who had mailed the initial clipping about the Heir's visit to Nedjo in Belgrade. Indirectly, therefore, Pusara had helped to initiate the plot.

Dedijer describes Pusara as a 'tall, handsome young man' who was a civil servant at the town hall and also a talented actor and singer who had refused a theatrical offer in Belgrade because he wanted to stay in Sarajevo. That morning, Pusara had celebrated Mass at the Serb Orthodox church and had sung in the choir during the Service of Remembrance for the Serbian heroes who had fallen on the field of blackbirds, Kosovo Pole, on 28 June 1389. He had gone straight from the service to Appel Quay and was soon off again to join the Sloga, the Serb choral society which was also celebrating Vidovdan, St Vitus Day. At the Sloga he would discuss the assassination for a while, before the police arrived to arrest him. He would tell his fellow choristers as he was taken away, 'I shall not be long.'

Pusara testified that he stood near Gavro as the Archduke's car approached hearing the shouts, Long Live the Heir! But he didn't notice anything suspicious about Gavro and, so he said, he never even heard the shots.

As the car turned, Potiorek realized the driver's mistake and shouted to him. 'What is this? Stop! You are going the wrong way! We ought to go via Appel Quay!' The car pulled up as the driver prepared to reverse. The car came to a stop directly in front of Gavrilo Princip who was standing on the pavement, maybe six feet at most from the car, closest to the Duchess. Gavro himself said he was 'four or five paces' from the car.

Princip pulled out his pistol from his pocket and raised it. He turned his head away and fired once. He then fired again. Two shots and it was all over.

Within the hour Gavro would be describing the moment to Leo Pfeffer, a member of the Sarajevo judiciary, appointed to investigate what had happened. 'When the car arrived I recognized the Heir Apparent but as I saw a lady sitting next to him I reflected for a moment whether I should shoot or not. At the same moment I was filled with a peculiar feeling and I aimed at the Heir Apparent from the pavement – which was made easier because the car was proceeding slower at that moment. Where I aimed I do not know. But I know that I aimed at the Heir Apparent. I believe that I fired twice, perhaps more, because I was so excited. Whether I hit the victim or not, I cannot tell, because instantly people turned around to hit me.'

At a later hearing, before the trial, he gave a second account saying he had initially meant to throw the bomb which he had in his belt on his left side. 'But because the bomb was screwed closed it would not have been easy for me to open. Also, in so great a crowd it would have been difficult to take it out and throw it. Therefore I drew the revolver instead and raised it against the automobile without aiming. I even turned my head as I shot.

'I let go two shots one after the other, but I am not certain whether I shot twice or more often, because I was very excited. That is also why I did not want to throw the bomb, because the strength for this failed me. Thereupon the crowd began to lynch me. Somebody took the revolver away from me, and the bomb fell out of my belt.'

After firing the two shots, Gavro had turned the gun inwards and was about to shoot himself in the head. A spectator, Ante Velic, standing outside the barbers' shop next to Schiller's saw what he was about to do and, as Velic put it, reached him in one leap and took the revolver away.

In the ensuing chaos Gavro managed to get the cyanide into his mouth and swallow it. But of course this did not work either and, for the time being, he could not be a martyr. He merely began vomiting as he was being dragged to the police station where 'bloody as I was ... they beat me again, in order not to be unavenged'.

Gavro said at the trial he had hoped to kill Potiorek with his second shot and he was not sorry about that. 'I believe I did away with one evil and I thought that was good. In general he [Potiorek] did evil to all things. He is the initiator of the "exceptional measures" and of the high treason trial.'

He was challenged on this: the high treason trial is no kind of evil whatsoever?

> *Gavro*: Those are all consequences from which the people suffer.
> *Prosecutor*: Of what do the sufferings of the people consist?
> *Gavro*: That they are completely impoverished; that they are treated like cattle. The peasant is impoverished. They destroy him completely. I am a villager's son and I know how it is in the villages. Therefore I wanted to take revenge and I am not sorry.

Dedijer cites two sources for a version of events in which a detective saw Gavro raise his gun and was about to stop him, but Milhajlo Pusara instead stopped the detective by kicking him in the knee.

There is no evidence of this in the transcript of the trial and it seems more likely this event is a distorted account of what happened to Smail Spahovic, a 25-year-old Muslim guard who was on duty in Franz Josef Street, standing about ten feet from Gavro and with his back to the road, watching the crowd, as he had been instructed to do. He heard the first shot but could not tell where it came from. He looked left but saw nothing, then he heard the second shot, to his right.

I threw myself toward the spectators and grabbed the assassin's arm. Somebody waited for me and hit me in the stomach. Princip hit me on the head with his revolver. I saw Pusara. I grabbed the assassin's arm, then the officers began to hit Princip with their sabres and I could not pull them away until the company commander arrived and helped me to catch him. We pulled him out to the Appel Quay. I couldn't take him further so I asked Alojz Fordren to take him … My stomach was hurting badly from the blow somebody gave me. Pusara was nearby and should know who hit me.

Spahovic seems to be dropping broad hints that Pusara had been his assailant, but there was another possible culprit, Ferdinand Behr, who had tried to help defend Gavro when, as Behr put it, the crowd wanted to lynch him. He said he had not realized Gavro was the assassin. He too was arrested and dragged to the police station, apparently suspected of being involved in the assassination. He was photographed on the way to the station and the photograph has been reproduced many times in books and articles, claiming to depict the arrest of Gavrilo Princip. But there is no photograph of Gavro's arrest – this photograph shows the arrest of Behr.

The cars behind pulled up behind the Archduke's car and Austrian officers poured from them. Baron Morsey drew his sabre – a ceremonial sword with an unsharpened blade – and lunged at Gavro, striking him twice. A spectator shouted in German, 'do not touch him' and then spoke in Serbian which Morsey could not understand. He struck further blows at Gavro, and, despite shouting 'anyone who touches me will die' he in turn was attacked with several 'powerful' blows which dented his helmet.

Morsey struck at one of his attackers and then, pointing at him with his sabre, shouted to a police officer standing nearby to arrest him. This must have been Ferdinand Behr.

The crowd were shouting at Morsey, 'see that you clear out of here.' In German too! Morsey was outraged at being insulted in his own language.

In the car, Governor Oskar Potiorek had not seen the shots being fired but looked at the crowd and saw Gavro being thrown to the ground and hit with sabres. Potiorek saw that the royal couple, a hands' reach away from him, were still sitting quite peacefully, and was relieved that this attempt too had been unsuccessful. He ordered the driver to back up, intending to continue down Appel Quay to the hospital, but the road was blocked by a crowd so he told the driver to go over the Latin Bridge.

While he was still issuing his instructions the car began to reverse and the Duchess fell forward and to her left, across the Archduke's lap, almost touching Potiorek himself. Potiorek saw now that there was blood at the Archduke's open mouth. Potiorek could see they were exchanging words quietly but could not hear what they were saying. He thought the Duchess was fainting.

Count Harrach, still on the running board, had seen a thin stream of blood spurt from the mouth of His Imperial Highness. Harrach took out his own handkerchief to wipe the blood. The Duchess said, 'In God's name what has happened to you' and then she collapsed, her face resting between the Archduke's knees. Harrach too thought she had fainted. But the Archduke called, 'Sopherl! Sopherl! Don't die! Live for my children.'

Harrach saw the Archduke begin holding his right side and grabbed the collar of the Archduke's tunic to stop him slumping forward. Harrach asked, 'Is something hurting you?'

'That's nothing,' said the Archduke, his face now slightly distorted. He repeated in a fading voice, 'It's nothing, it's nothing, it's nothing, it's nothing, it's nothing, it's nothing.' After six or seven repetitions he choked violently on the blood in his mouth and then, after this convulsive rattle, he was quiet.

It was said to have been one of the most affecting moments during the trial, when Count Harrach's evidence was given in court. Gavro was asked by his own lawyer if he too had been affected. 'Surely', he said, 'you don't think that I'm an animal.'

The car drove quickly across the bridge to the Konak, a journey of less than five minutes. Some doctors ran alongside the car and were on hand to begin immediate treatment. The Duchess was already unconscious, probably dead, as the car arrived. She was lifted from the car by a servant and taken to the first floor and placed on a bed. The Archduke also collapsed as they arrived at the Konak and he too was carried upstairs where he was placed on a chaise longue.

Blood seeped across the Archduke's tunic. Some attempt was made to revive them both, but there was nothing anyone could do. Sophie had died just ahead of her husband. It was impossible to say whether the bullet that struck her had been the first or second shot fired by Gavro.

That bullet had gone directly through the side of the car where she was sitting and hit her in an almost straight line, the entry wound being in her right groin, four centimetres above the haunch bone at the top of her hip. It had torn a six-centimetre opening in her flesh.

The senior doctor and privy councillor who later oversaw the embalming of the royal couple was Dr Ferdinand Fischer, the same doctor who had attended hospital with the injured officer, Merizzi. He testified that the bullet was removed from Sophie's abdomen during the embalming, presumably while some of the internal organs were being removed, and placed in an envelope which was signed and sealed by the physicians who were present.

The Archduke's bullet was lodged in his spine and remained there, as it could not be removed without great damage to the body. It had hit his neck through the right-hand side of his coat collar and severed the jugular vein before entering the spine. The point of entry was a small but irregular tear of just five millimetres. It was four centimetres from his chin and two centimetres from the Archduke's larynx.

Later historians would say that the bumpy, hurried journey to the Konak and the consequent delay in treatment must have hastened the royal couple's demise, but the evidence of the time was that death was unavoidable and no treatment, however immediate, would have prevented it. The cause, in both cases, was given as internal bleeding.

Death was confirmed by 11.30am and soon the bells of all the churches in Sarajevo, of all denominations, began ringing the death toll.

Father Anton Puntigam, the Jesuit priest, arrived at the Konak after hearing of the shootings. Discovering that the royal couple had not received the sacrament of the sick, also known as extreme unction, he went to a nearby church and collected the required oils, then returned to administer the sacrament, allowing the Archduke and the Duchess a final pardon for all their sins, enabling them to leave the world in perfect spiritual health.

That night two Sarajevo artists, Ludmila and Rudolf Valic, a sculptress and a painter respectively, were called from their beds and brought to the Konak to make death masks of the royal couple.

In an interview some 24 years later, Ludmila described the scene

– the Duchess laid out on the governor's own bed and the Archduke in an adjoining room – and could still recall the charms the royal couple had been wearing around their necks. The Duchess had a gold chain with a scapular, a cloth pendant containing small emblems designed to stave off misfortune. The Archduke also had a gold chain, trailing seven amulets in gold and platinum which had been intended to ward off different evils. On the left arm, where his sleeve was rolled up, the sculptress saw a Chinese dragon tattoo.

The death masks can be seen at Artstetten, on display in the public museum there, above the crypt where the two bodies are entombed, side by side in heavy stone sarcophagi.

The solidity and certainty of those eternal stones was in stark contrast to the ephemeral moment of chance outside Moritz Schiller's store that had preceded them in history. Only the flimsiest set of circumstances had created the assassination. After Nedjo had been arrested it was left to Gavro who was alone among the conspirators in his determination to succeed. He could have stood anywhere on the route he believed the Archduke would take but he had, more or less randomly, selected that position outside Schiller's. The Archduke was not meant to be there at all and yet, through incompetence, confusion, error or, implausibly, dark conspiracy, he had not only turned into the road in front of the one committed assassin, Gavro, but had actually pulled to a halt right in front of him. Gavro had barely taken aim, had simply raised his arm in the Archduke's general direction and turned his head away as he fired. The bullets could have gone anywhere, injured anyone or no one, but instead they were both fatal.

Two blind bullseyes, you could say.

Those two almost indiscriminate shots and the haphazard circumstances that led them to their target would shape the hundred years to come and lead directly to the death of millions.

Even so, it would be a brave determinist who tried to argue that the assassination was bound to happen.

19

June 1914 – a Small Group of the Misled

Mehmed Mehmedbasic had run off when he heard Nedjo's bomb. The known details of his escape are sketchy but it appears he got away to Montenegro before the Austrian police had even identified the entire group of assassins. He spent the night of the assassination with some young Muslim men in Sarajevo he knew from the madrasah, the religious school he had attended as a child. These young men were preparing to become imams, while Mehmedbasic had just fled the scene of his participation in an assassination. He left Sarajevo on 30 June wearing a fez and having a genuine travel permit was able to take the train to Hercegovina, crossing the border into Montenegro on 3 July.

The Austrian police eventually asked for him to be arrested and returned to Sarajevo to stand trial. Montenegro was a small kingdom, broadly neutral in its politics but pro-Serb by inclination. Once he arrived there, Mehmedbasic was said to have bragged noisily of his part in the assassination. He had no hesitation in admitting it all to the Montenegrin police. He was jailed and escaped. His jailers may well have allowed him to get away, to avoid having to hand him over. They told the Austrians they no longer knew where he was. In fact, he remained – more quietly now – in Montenegro until November when he made his way to Belgrade and joined the Komite, falling under the wing of Colonel Apis.

Mehmedbasic was the outsider in the group and perhaps he was lucky to get away. During the trial Grabez was asked if there had ever been any discussion between the other conspirators about killing Mehmedbasic if he had succeeded in the assassination. Grabez denied it, but the question must have come from somewhere.

After Cvjetko Popovic's courage had failed him on the corner of

Cumurija Street, he wanted to run home, he said, and started to move away but then returned to hide his bomb and his gun and his cyanide in the basement of the Prosvjeta offices, which were right on Appel Quay, from where they were later recovered. He said he thought his friend Vaso must have thrown the bomb. Ahead of the assassination Popovic had been ready to kill himself afterwards. The idea must have seemed less appealing, in the aftermath, when it was time to act, as he made no attempt at all to commit suicide.

Popovic did not leave Sarajevo until early on Tuesday morning, heading for Zemum where his father and stepmother lived. He had five days of freedom until 3 July when he was summoned to the local police station where an accusation of his involvement in the assassination was read to him. The officer across from him was shocked, apparently, when he said, 'yes, everything is true.'

Trifko Grabez was still near the Emperor's Bridge when he heard the two shots, very clearly, one after the other. It was not long before the news that the Heir was dead began to spread rapidly and Grabez thought he had better get away. He went to the home of an uncle and hid the bomb under the seat in the bathroom and the gun under the roof, then he went back onto the streets and strolled leisurely to the scene of the crime. He spent the next day and night at the home of another uncle in Sarajevo but then returned to his parents' home in Pale where his father thought he must have been arrested. Grabez felt completely calm, he later told the trial, being in Pale. In that place no one would think he was among the assassins.

His girlfriend, Leposava Lalic, a teacher, was also at the house and, as Grabez claimed at the trial, when Lalic said she was going travelling the next day, he decided to leave too, as he would be less conspicuous in a couple. He had a friend in Višegrad, a town on the Serbian border, and thought he would go there. He did not tell his father he was going. The police found his high school certificate in a toilet where he had apparently dropped it, perhaps to conceal his identity. He was arrested anyway, later in the day, as he was travelling without an official permit. His passport (the one Nedjo had used) showed he had come from Serbia on 30 May and this alone aroused suspicions that he was one of the assassins, so he was returned to Sarajevo and put in jail.

After leaving Appel Quay, following the first explosion, Vaso

Cubrilovic went to his pre-arranged rendezvous with Ivo Kranjcevic. By this time Kranjcevic knew the assassination had happened and was anxious, standing there waiting for one of the assassins. When Vaso finally arrived, Kranjcevic immediately saw that he was trembling all over. Vaso gave him his bomb and his gun and they quickly parted. Kranjcevic did not take the weapons home but took them round to the house of some close family friends, where he was admitted by the 'retarded' daughter of the house. He told her he had two old revolvers that didn't work and he wanted to hide them from his father who wanted to donate them to the museum. Kranjcevic wrapped the gun and the bomb in some cloth and hid them in a bureau drawer in the bedroom of the father of the house, Ivan Momcinovic.

It was the afternoon of the assassination and there was a strong anti-Serb mood in Sarajevo, with demonstrations and the first signs of the serious rioting to follow. Kranjcevic and his family and their friends in the house where he had hidden the weapons were all Catholics. They were ostensibly loyal Catholics too. Kranjcevic's father was a retired sergeant in the Austrian Bosnian police force and had been decorated for fighting as a soldier with the Austrians in the 1870s.

Ivan Momcinovic's son-in-law had joined the anti-Serb demonstration but eventually came home and heard about the weapons. He was angry with Kranjcevic and furious with his wife, the sister of the retarded girl, for not stopping him leaving the arms. 'Should I have to go to prison for Kranjcevic?' They looked in the drawer together and saw the weapons. 'I hope lightning strikes him,' said the son-in-law, 'leaving a pistol at a time like this.'

The son-in-law went for a walk, perhaps to calm down, and then called at Kranjcevic's home and asked him, 'What did you do at our place?' Kranjcevic said he had left some old pistols for the children to play with. 'Tell your mother to come and take them away,' the son-in-law told him. And this was what happened. Kranjcevic, not content with implicating an entire household, now involved his mother too.

'Don't you have anything better and smarter to do?' the mother asked her son. 'Are you out of your mind, trying to ruin yourself and all of us?'

It was Tuesday by the time Kranjcevic's mother came to collect the weapons. The son-in-law complained to her, 'Do you want to destroy us?'

Both of Kranjcevic's parents were called to give evidence at the trial, but his mother exercised her right not to testify against her own son. Kranjcevic's father, the retired policeman, was asked to explain how his son had become involved in hiding the weapons that had killed His Royal Highness.

Kranjcevic senior was at a loss to explain his son's behaviour. 'At home he was always good and obedient. He was reliable. He did not smoke. He did not drink. He never stayed away from home overnight … when he was at home he used to concern himself mostly with his school assignments, and in his spare time he read novels. When he was relaxing, he would play the violin or tamburitza or accordion.' He admitted, however, that his son had been taciturn at home and not easy to talk to. For a policeman, he seemed strikingly unaware that his son was a fervent Young Bosnian who believed in Serb nationalism. He could only suggest his son had been misled.

This indeed was the phrase that would be used by the emperor in an imperial manifest published following the assassination: it had been carried out by 'eine kleine Schar irregeleiten' – a small group of the misled.

Nothing to do with the Austrians, of course.

Mrs Kranjcevic removed the weapons and they were then hidden, the bomb in a city park and the gun in the Muslim cemetery, from where they were later retrieved by the police. The three adults of the house where he had hidden the guns were arrested and put on trial too, the son-in-law weeping as he was questioned by detectives about his remote part in the plot.

On Monday, 29 June, the day after the assassination, Vaso Cubrilovic met up with his friends Dragan Kalember and Marko Perin. Kalember had been walking around the town examining the ruins of buildings damaged by the anti-Serb riots. He was with another friend when they met Vaso. The friend looked Vaso up and down, apparently with some contempt, and walked away.

Vaso had been boasting before the assassination of his part in it and now, in the aftermath he jokingly, bizarrely claimed the distinction for himself and said he had fired a shot, maybe even two shots.

Kalember, who was just 16, had been out with his father on the day of the assassination, commemorating St Vitus Day at church before strolling around the Quay and Franz Josef Street. He had heard the shots and immediately turned pale. What is it? said his father. 'Is it Cubrilovic?' wondered Kalember out loud. He had been fearful after that and only calmed down later when he heard that Gavro had been the assassin.

It was Kalember who befriended Nedjo's youngest brother Dusan in later years. According to Dusan's daughter Ranka, her father and his friend were both unhappy at the way that Vaso, in their view, was always talking publicly about the assassination, claiming all the glory and the attention for it, and apparently waiting until all the other conspirators were dead, to do so.

Perhaps Kalember had confused the immature, boastful young Vaso with his adult self and never stopped to consider that he might eventually have grown up and was merely serving history, in discussing what had happened. In fact, Vaso had kept the true story to himself all those years. It was contained in that long letter to his sisters which he had written in 1918, its contents available here for the first time, outside Serbia.

As Vaso pointed out in the letter, no one had ever stopped to consider what the conspirators would do or say if they were caught. They were all fixated on the martyrdom that would be conferred by honourable suicide, with the additional benefit that it would have maintained the secrets of the plot and who was involved. Once the poison had failed to kill Gavro and Nedjo, there was no plan to fall back on and they were all in trouble.

Their first inquisitor was Leo Pfeffer, the relatively junior member of the Sarajevo judiciary assigned, for some reason, to be the investigating judge in the case. You might have thought the head of the district court would take on the role himself, but instead he hurriedly appointed the 37-year-old Pfeffer who was said to be both inexperienced and lacking competence. There had been demands for him to be dismissed as a judge five years earlier, on the grounds of inefficiency. Dedijer describes him, in unlovely terms, as 'a short fat man with a pale, puffy face and yellow, irregular teeth'.

In fairness to the head of the court, Pfeffer was chosen after the bombing but before the shooting, before it had become a double murder of world-shattering significance. And Pfeffer was handily placed. He had been walking on Appel Quay as a spectator, with his daughter, when Nedjo's bomb went off. He had sent the girl home and gone to his office at the town hall but could not get in because of the imperial reception, and had to wait until the royal couple had left to be assassinated.

His office was near the police first aid room and so his first sight of the assassins, before he had been tasked with investigating them, was of Nedjo, sitting on a bench waiting to be treated: 'With his alert lively black eyes he looked around defiantly, and on his lips there was a provocative grin. He had a very white complexion and rosy cheeks and a short black moustache. He was a tall, strong young man.' Pfeffer saw that Nedjo was wearing a black sports cap and this must have labelled him as Pfeffer immediately decided that he was an anarchist.

Within minutes news of the shooting was being shouted out by a detective who rushed into the town hall. Soon after, Pfeffer watched as Gavro was dragged into the building by officers surrounded by a large crowd, some of them wielding their walking sticks to try to beat him. Gavro's head was bleeding and he too needed medical attention – his head was soon swathed in white bandages. Pfeffer wrote later:

The young assassin exhausted by his beating was unable to utter a word. He was undersized, emaciated, sallow, sharp featured. It was difficult to imagine that so frail a looking individual could have committed so serious a deed. Even his clear blue eyes, burning and piercing, but serene, had nothing cruel or criminal in their expression. They spoke of innate intelligence, of steady and harmonious energy. When I told him I was the investigating judge and asked him if he had the strength to speak he answered my questions with perfect clearness in a voice that grew steadily stronger and more assured.

He confessed that already two years earlier he had vowed on the grave of Bogdan Zerajic to avenge the man who had sought the life of General Varesanin. When he learned that the Archduke Franz Ferdinand was to visit Sarajevo, he decided to take his vengeance because he regarded the Heir Apparent as the embodiment of the supreme power which exercised its terrible pressure on the Yugoslavs.

During these first exchanges, neither Gavro nor Pfeffer knew the Archduke and the Duchess were dead. It was only later that the news reached them. That evening at seven o'clock, Gavro was formally charged with murder and said, 'I acknowledge it and do not complain, but I am sorry that I have killed the Duchess of Hohenberg, because I had no intention of killing her.'

There appears to be respect, almost admiration, for Gavro, in Pfeffer's account of his demeanour. It's surprising that Pfeffer sees 'nothing cruel or criminal' in Gavro's serene blue eyes. Most Austrian officials regarded the plotters as sub-human terrorist fanatics.

Although the Austrians knew of only two conspirators, and had not yet made the connection between them, they made a wide number of arrests among associates of Gavro and Nedjo and other known radicals, including Ilic who was arrested at Oprkanj Street that same evening after Gavro disclosed that he had been lodging there, at the home of Ilic's mother.

Otherwise, Gavro had given nothing away of his involvement with others, not even Nedjo, so Pfeffer left Ilic alone at first, having no idea of his importance. When he was searched, Ilic still had the wrap of cyanide in his pocket which had been prepared for use by Grabez. There was plenty of incriminating literature for the police to seize, both at Oprkanj Street and at Nedjo's home. There was a report that 'a whole library of pan-Serb' literature had been found at the home of Gavro's poor brother, Jovo, in Hadzici. The papers were Gavro's, naturally, not his brother's.

Nedjo was questioned by a different judge that afternoon and offered a clear and rather eloquent account of his motivations. It seems apparent from his words that he had risen in stature, since becoming an assassin:

I am an adherent of the radical anarchist idea, which aims at destroying the present system through terrorism in order to bring in the liberal system in its place. Therefore I hate all representatives of the constitutional system – of course, not this or that person as such, but as the bearer of power which oppresses the people. I have educated myself in this spirit through the reading of socialist and anarchist writings and I can say that I have read through almost all the literature of this type that I could get in the Serbo-Croatian language.

Nedjo initially said that no one but him had known about his bomb as he did not dare to trust anyone. But then he admitted his connection with Gavro while trying to suggest that their two attempts were merely a coincidence.

Finally, the following day, Monday, 30 June, Nedjo admitted that he had conspired with Gavro in Belgrade to plan the assassination. The two were brought together in the tactic of 'confrontation' which was part of the Austrian criminal procedures. Gavro, hearing Nedjo's admission, agreed with his account. The name of Ciganovic was given, but he of course was out of reach of the Austrians, in Serbia.

Whether deliberately, or not, the Austrians put considerable pressure on Gavro and Nedjo, placing them in chains in isolated cells at the military prison within the army barracks. From their windows they could see or hear that many local Serbs, peasants, students, businessmen alike, had been arrested and were being held in the prison courtyard, deliberately left without water to suffer in the full glare of the sun. There were beatings too and later some random hangings after the familiar sounds of carpentry had heralded the erection of gallows.

The mood in Sarajevo was virulently anti-Serb, and it is tempting to see in those hours and days after the assassination the origins of the genocidal ethnic violence that would erupt in Bosnia and across the region during the second world war, and again after the break-up of Yugoslavia, towards the end of the century.

Demonstrations against the assassination and the Serb community in general began on the afternoon of Sunday, 28 June but passed off without incident. Even so, the police chief Dr Gerde asked for army support, and two troops of soldiers were marched into the town.

Next morning, early, the demonstrations turned into riots, with shops, businesses, schools and clubs owned by or run for Serbs being ransacked and looted. Rioters stormed through the Serb-owned Hotel Europe, tossing everything they could lay their hands on out of the window, though fortunately not the management, staff or guests. Nedjo's family home and his father's café were targeted. The senior Serb Orthodox priest in Sarajevo, the Metropolitan, received cuts from broken glass as he stood inside his palace watching rioters smashing his windows. Two Serb newspaper offices were ransacked. The inn owned by Kosta Kontos was ransacked, in the belief that he too was a Serb – but in fact he was Greek.

The rioters were predominantly Catholic Croats and Muslims. There was some debate later about the extent to which they had acted spontaneously or been incited by the Austrian authorities or even the Catholic Archbishop Stadler. Stadler may have been among the speakers at the cathedral that morning when a large group arrived. They had earlier carried black-draped flags and pictures of the dead royals to the scene of the assassination, singing the national anthem and cheering, Zivio! Long may he live! before they knelt and prayed and listened to some patriotic speeches. They then went to the cathedral for more prayers and a service and it was after they had left the cathedral that they were sufficiently aroused to go on the rampage, attacking and assaulting many Serbs and their homes and property.

The Times said the mobs seemed to comprise the lowest elements, especially those from the Muslim quarter of the city. Others said they were 'work-shy riff-raff from town and country' or watched as 'the scum of the streets broke into private flats, destroying everything they could lay their hands on and grabbing all the valuables'. A Viennese correspondent also saw 'many very well dressed ladies and gentlemen' among the rioters. Around 50 people, mainly Serbs, were injured but the only fatality was a non-Serb member of a mob, killed by a Serb in self-defence.

The troops were called in at noon and began to clear the streets. Martial law was declared with early closure for inns, coffee shops and hotels and curfews for young people.

Many Serbs did their best to show their own disapproval of the assassins. The Serb Orthodox Bishop called Gavro and Nedjo antichrists. There were substantial contributions to a planned memorial for the royal couple on the corner of Appel Quay and the Latin Bridge, across the road from the assassination.

Gavro and Nedjo must have known of the arrest of those Serbs who were herded into the courtyard of the military prison outside their cells and probably knew all about the riots too. The thought of the suffering they had inflicted on all those innocent Serbs no doubt concentrated their minds as they weighed up whether or not to tell the truth.

When Grabez was brought to the prison he too was questioned but made no admissions. He later claimed he was tortured, though there is confusing evidence on this point as some of his supposed allegations appeared in a letter he was said to have written to his father. But the letter never existed and was a later invention by a writer, apparently designed to undermine the Austrians. On the other hand, Grabez said at the trial, 'I saw that they didn't have the evidence to make a good case against me because they tortured me and if they'd had convincing evidence they wouldn't have done that.'

Grabez said he was mistreated at the police station, and there was evidence that the police had secretly been removing prisoners from the jail at night to interrogate them. He was, he said, immersed in water, among other things. No one else initially complained of torture though, and there was no obvious reason why he would have been singled out.

The precise circumstances in which the whole plot was eventually disclosed are unclear. Almost every account gives a different sequence of events, creating a muddle of timings in relation to who was arrested when and who spoke out first.

One account has Ilic breaking down and thinking only of himself as he tried to save his own neck from the gallows, promising on 1 July to confess everything in return for being spared a death sentence. According to Pfeffer this was 'chiefly because what had been done was against his will and it was visible that Ilic was extremely depressed'. Pfeffer told him the law was generous with those who made confessions and said anyway, his confession was necessary to spare the many innocent people who had been arrested because of his actions.

Ilic then, for the first time gave the bare bones of what had really happened, explaining the roles of Gavro, Nedjo and Grabez. He later named Vaso, Popovic and Mehmedbasic and some of those who had helped to smuggle the weapons from Belgrade.

But Dedijer believes Pfeffer disliked Ilic and favoured Princip, so distorted the story accordingly. He appears to think that Pfeffer invented Ilic's desperate plea and confession on 1 July. In Dedijer's version, for which he claims documentary support, it was Gavro who initiated the full disclosures the following day, 2 July.

As he was being led from the jail, Gavro said, 'I will explain everything in detail and name the guilty, but only so that innocent people do not suffer. For we guilty ones were in any case ready to go to our deaths. I nevertheless request that you confront me briefly before the hearing with Danilo Ilic and Trifko Grabez to whom I want to say only two or three words. Then I will tell you everything. Otherwise I will confess nothing at all, even if you beat me to death.'

In Dedijer's account Gavro was confronted, one after the other, with Grabez and Ilic. He told Grabez, 'confess everything, how we got the bombs, how we travelled and in what society we were, so that just people do not come to harm.'

He told Ilic, 'Since the court has already learned much and so that we can save the innocent it is necessary that you tell everything, among whom you divided the weapons and where the weapons are.'

One writer put the blame on Nedjo but it was the writer, Jevdjevic, the same man who had invented the letter from Grabez to his father, who most criticized Ilic, describing him as 'a cynical man with the physiognomy of a fish' and as someone who liked the good life. According to Jevdjevic, Gavro expressed his regret that everything had been betrayed and even spat in Ilic's face.

It is hard to imagine anyone perceiving the ascetic social revolutionary Ilic as someone who liked the good life. It is no less hard to imagine Gavro spitting in his friend's face. Still, there is good reason to believe Ilic really was to blame.

There was no doubt in Vaso Cubrilovic's mind that Ilic had betrayed them. Vaso was arrested on 3 July in the town of Dubica, the same day as Popovic in Zemun, and they were both delivered back to Sarajevo, where they too went into solitary confinement.

Vaso's unpublished letter was written while he was still in prison, events fresh in his mind. 'Truth be told I believed in Ilic more than in myself and I was absolutely convinced he would not betray me. As far as Princip and Cabrinovic, I wasn't in the least worried about them because they didn't know about us, nor did we know about them. Therefore I only had to worry about Ilic. Even though I learned from Popovic on 30 June that he too [Ilic] had been arrested still I wasn't worried because I held that he would not betray us.

'The main thing is that Ilic, who was at the centre of everything was the first to give in and say everything. As far as he is concerned I still don't understand him. That man, who was so steadfast and sure of himself and who was not involved in such things for the first time – his spirit broke and he betrayed everyone.'

Vaso said Ilic had told him personally how they managed to bring him to such a desperate state that he would betray his friends and colleagues. They had shown him forged letters purporting to be from

Serb magazines that had attacked and criticized him and the other assassins. He had been threatened with a noose. Vaso knew this must be
true as he had been threatened with a noose too, had it brandished in
front of him and been asked if he knew its purpose. 'If they did that to
me, you can imagine what they did to him. In a moment he betrayed
all of us: myself, Popovic, Djukic, Veljko and Misko.'

Ilic told Vaso that Pfeffer had given him his solemn word and his
oath that he would be released if he admitted everything. 'That poor
fellow hoped until the last moment they would show mercy on him.
As far as I can tell he bore the worst of it. They mistreated him, made
false promises, arrested his mother and in general used every means
possible to learn as much as they could from him.'

Vaso had once asked Ilic why he betrayed them and he replied,
'because I was an ass.' He regretted the whole thing, wrote Vaso, but
even so he had still only given away a tiny proportion of everything
he knew and Vaso believed he had been unjustly smeared as a traitor
and was really as much a patriot as any of them and it was not his fault
that more was asked of him than he could bear.

In his letter Vaso commented on the immaturity of all the young
men and this too was noted by the investigating judge Pfeffer, who
described them as 'youths, almost boys still, callow, hesitant, not
grasping the seriousness of the judicial inquiry'. They were so naive
that 'they involuntarily talked and disclosed things which were not
asked of them'. It really was a miracle, said Pfeffer, 'that with young
men still so raw and irresponsible nothing leaked out beforehand of
the preparations for the outrage. Each of them regarded himself as a
hero, but not one of them had had the courage to fire.'

Vaso wrote that when he was first arrested he assumed it must be
to do with the Yugoslav students organization or slandering German
businesses, with which he had recently been involved. He was so
shocked when the police asked him instead where he had left the bomb
that, in his confusion, he admitted he had given it to Kranjcevic.

He was interrogated for the whole night, he said the officials came
one after the other from nine at night until four in the morning when
he was taken to the local prison and left to sleep on the concrete hallway because they feared for his safety in a cell with other prisoners.
Then an officer came along screaming and swearing at him, hitting
him on the arms and legs with a metal stick to get him up, so that

he could be put in a carriage for the journey to the military prison in Sarajevo where he would spend the next four months, with the others.

Vaso described the constant violence and abuse he and the others had suffered, making it clear there was physical and psychological torture – a Polish warder who had behaved like 'a rabid dog', missing no opportunity to strike them from behind. Soldiers were permanently stationed at their cell doors, watching them, and would kick the door and scream like animals if they so much as turned their backs while reading. The prisoners were given no walks or periods of association but realized their cups were being mixed up and swapped around when drinks were distributed by their jailers, so they devised a way of communicating by writing in code on the bases of the cups, and later created a second code of communication deploying knocks on the cell walls to pass messages between them.

Vaso described the system in detail in his letter, explaining that each letter had a place on a grid, and was denoted by the number of knocks for its position, one for the row across the grid and the other knock for the downward column. 'A' was at position 1,1 so that it was signalled by one knock for the row, then one knock for the column. They each had their own call sign too, so that they could indicate whom they wished to speak to.

On one occasion, Nedjo was trying to contact Ilic but there was no answer. Nedjo guessed that Ilic had hanged himself and began to spread the news with his knocks. Gavro replied, 'he was such a good friend.' Then, after a few hours, Ilic woke up – he had only been sleeping. In his relief Gavro joked, 'Okay, if you did not hang yourself Svabe will do it for you.' Svabe was the Serbs' nickname for Austrians and Germans. 'We became so adept at this', wrote Vaso, 'that I was able for example to hear our late brother on the second floor tell Cabrinovic on the first floor that he had received a ham sandwich, while I was on the ground floor.'

The late brother – Vaso was writing in 1918 – was of course Veljko Cubrilovic from Priboj, who had taken Gavro and Grabez to the Kerovic zadruga and sent them on to his friend Misko Jovanovic, the cinema owner in Tuzla. Both men were rounded up after Ilic's disclosures. Unlike the young conspirators, these two and many of the peasants whom Gavro and Grabez had relied on during their journey with the weapons from Belgrade to Sarajevo, had wives and children. Jakov Milovic, who had helped deliver them to Veljko, was a poor widower, with four children alone at home after his arrest.

Veljko could have escaped – he must have known his arrest was coming – but said, 'what would my peasants have thought of me if I had fled and left them alone in those trying days?' It was later apparent that both Veljko and Misko (among others) felt betrayed by Danilo Ilic.

Veljko wrote a series of letters to his wife Jovanka after his arrest, often addressing them to his 'two female heads', a Serbian expression, meaning his wife and daughter. Nada, his newborn child, was then ten months old and at the beginning of a long life that was coming to a close in the autumn of 2006 when I met her in Belgrade, not long after her 93rd birthday.

Nada showed me those letters which were often flooded with passion and the agony of separation. She was too young to recall the moment of his arrest, their last parting, as Veljko recalled it in this letter of 7 October 1914, after more than three months in prison.

My dear two female heads,

My thoughts are swarming, there are thousands upon thousands of thoughts running like electricity through my mind but I can't sort them out because the feeling that I haven't seen you for so long, and my desire for the two of you has overtaken everything else, and so if this letter is a bit confused and despondent the reason: my longing for you two.

Our separation in Priboj was very difficult for me. That moment when I kissed Nada's nightgown, and she looked at me through her sleepy eyes, and that painful cry of yours in front of Milanovic's house: 'They don't let us live. They're taking us to slaughter like lambs' is constantly on my mind and before my eyes. Those moments bring forth tears in my eyes.

Over the past ninety days I've recounted our life together countless times, especially since Nada was born. My dear, our beautiful and free lives were made up of the smallest details we didn't even notice. If they would now let me, just once, walk down the hall, those ten to twenty metres, I would consider that happiness and a privilege.

My dear there is not one day, not one hour in the day when I'm not thinking of you. I'm embarrassed to admit, but not a day has passed that I haven't wept over my fate. Hope has weakened in me. Just the thought of being separated from you for many years kills forbearance in me, and it is as awful as death.

But the desire for life – and I've now realized how much I love life, because you two are what give my life meaning, and my life is not bitter even in the prosaic sense – the desire for life, freedom, overcomes and lessens my sadness.

If they don't hang me.

Austria declared war on Serbia exactly one month after the assassination, on 28 July 1914. The prisoners' greater need to share information about events in the outside world prompted Nedjo to devise a new system of communicating in writing by scratching on the underside of their metal plates with their spoons. As with the mugs, so the plates would be jumbled by the jailers and redistributed. The prisoners called these their newspapers and gave them individual names. Nedjo's was The Bowl, Grabez had The Bomb and Gavro called his The Woodpecker, using it to write and share some poetry, which echoed the heroic tradition of Serb verse:

> Time goes slowly and
> There is nothing new –
> Today everything is like yesterday,
> And tomorrow will bring the same –
> But I will always remember
> The just words of the fallen falcon Zerajic:
>
> 'He who wants to live, has to die
> He who is ready to die, will live forever.'

He expressed his frustration at being trapped in jail, unable to join the fight against the Austrians:

> Instead of being on the battlefields,
> Where the war trumpets are blown;

> Here we are in the dungeons,
> Listening to the jingling of chains.

Not all the prisoners were so high-minded. While Gavro expressed his soul, Djukic and Popovic played tic tac toe with knocks on the wall.

By 28 September the Austrians were ready to make formal indictments against 25 people who would be tried together over the assassination. Evidently, they were each given a copy of the indictment, and then had it taken away again for amendment.

The first draft described how 'the Almighty saved His Imperial and Royal Highness the Archduke Franz Ferdinand, by not permitting the bomb to explode in his car', but then 'with the Almighty's will the bullets hit their target'. The phrases caused considerable amusement among the prisoners. One of their 'newspapers' declared, 'the chief accused ought to be the Almighty, and we should all be released at once, because we are innocent according to the indictment.'

There had been similar levity when they were brought from their cells and gathered together for the first time so that Pfeffer could read the charges. They all but ignored Pfeffer and chatted and joked among themselves. Pfeffer told them their fate was at stake and they should stop behaving like children. Though, of course, some of them were children.

Gavro said, 'Please understand us sir. We see each other after a long time. What you are reading is well known to us, and we also know what we have to expect.'

When Pfeffer explained, as a formality, that they had the right to appeal against the charges, only Nedjo showed some interest. The war was going on, he said, and nobody knew what would happen tomorrow. Pfeffer asked him if he expected to be acquitted and said, even before the war was over 14 Cabrinovices would be hanged. 'That will make the position of the hangman even worse,' said Nedjo. The others wanted to get the trial over with as soon as possible, so he agreed not to pursue the right of appeal.

During their conversations at this hearing, Gavro said he planned to try to protect the peasants and others who had played a part in the smuggling of the weapons, such as the Kerovic family, by testifying that he had threatened them with violence and forced them to take part.

Austrian law did not permit the death sentence to be passed on anyone under 20, so there was a significant division between the younger and older conspirators, with Gavro sitting right between them, a mistaken entry of his birth record exposing him to the risk of execution. His actual age at the time of the assassination was 19 years and 11 months but the mistaken entry in the civil register back at Grahovo had given him a date of birth of 13 June 1894, which would have made him 20.

Ivo Kranjcevic later recorded that while 'the other young conspirators agreed to behave calmly, not to use any sharp expressions, in order not to make the situation of the older conspirators, who were faced with the death penalty, more difficult', Gavro had said he would not be submissive and would speak his mind openly. 'He was the only one aware that one day public opinion would judge their statements and therefore he regarded it as his duty to behave bravely.'

20

A Timely Reckoning

Even as it came creaking and shuddering to its end, the Habsburg empire was still clinging to its desperate notions of propriety and protocol, its place in the world above everyone else's place, even the dead Archduke's wife. Even as world conflagration beckoned, the Habsburg court was busily devising posthumous humiliations it could inflict on poor Franz and his Sopherl, and their children.

In life, the Archduke had already been only too well aware that the body of his 'morganatic' wife could never be buried beside him at the imperial vault in the church of the Capuchins in Vienna so he had built the crypt at their castle, Artstetten, and left instructions in his will that they should be interred there, side by side. Alas, he had left no instruction for the eventuality of their sudden joint demise so it was left to the Court Chamberlain, Prince Montenuovo, to uphold the imperial honour.

In his plan there would have been a lying in state and a proper imperial funeral, but for the Archduke only. He had suggested the Duchess's body could be 'left at the station' in Vienna. Others had insisted there must be a joint service, so it had been downgraded from an imperial ceremony, and all the heads of state had been uninvited and asked merely to send their ambassadors instead for a private service that would be brief and simple. The strain of receiving foreign royalty would be too great for the emperor, it was said.

The bodies were returned to Austria by retracing the same route the Archduke had taken on his way to Bosnia. There was no state procession for them on arrival in Vienna. Instead they arrived at night and were taken by horse-drawn hearses to the small Hofburg chapel where the service would be held the next day.

The Archduke's coffin was bigger than his wife's and raised eighteen inches higher on the dais. While his was covered in symbols of his rank and imperial status hers bore just a black fan and a pair of white gloves which might have signified a noblewoman or a lady-in-waiting – a hint, perhaps, of her own status at the time she had met her husband. Or perhaps not: 'Their presence here was not necessarily ... an offensive token of Sophie's former station,' wrote Gordon Brook-Shepherd, a Habsburg sympathizer, in his biography of the Archduke.

A large queue had formed by eight o'clock the next morning, when the chapel doors were opened so that well-wishers among the Viennese public could pay their last respects. There was still a large queue four hours later when the chapel doors closed. Visiting time was over.

The service itself began at four that afternoon and was over by four-fifteen. Some of the family members there complained it had been a 'third-class funeral' and showed their respect for the couple by walking behind their hearses as the bodies were taken to the railway station for the journey to Artstetten. Here, apparently, as the coffins were being loaded onto the train, the Court Chamberlain said to the Archduke's private aide, 'Now my job is done. From here on it's your private affair.'

It was a difficult journey back, especially the night crossing of the Danube on a raft-like ferry during a violent storm on the choppy river. The horses almost bolted at a fissure of lightning and were only narrowly restrained from racing the coffins into the river.

Here at Artstetten there was one more service before the interment in front of hundreds of guests. Many who were expected did not come, however – the Court Chamberlain back in Vienna had arranged an official court requiem for the exact same time. Of course, as Brook-Shepherd is quick to point out, this may not have been an act of spite: 'It might have been a formal gesture of piety.'

In a sense these events, governed essentially by miserable expressions of self-importance and petty snobbery, only served to emphasize that it was time for a much needed change to the old world order, and an end to empires. All those people at that funeral, except perhaps the couple's three young children, had a great deal more to worry about than the size of the Archduke's coffin.

Ironically, the Archduke had been an urgent advocate of caution and non-aggression against Serbia during the crisis following the annexation in 1908. Offered the role of Commander in Chief for the expected military conflict to come, he had instead said that any 'impetuous action' would be disastrous and asked officials to 'please restrain' his own warmongering chief of staff Conrad.

Now, with news coming through to Vienna of Pfeffer's inquiries, the idea that 'the trail leads to Belgrade' made some kind of military response inevitable. In the hours following the interment, on 4 July, Conrad was once again advocating aggression, and this time there was no Archduke to encourage restraint. Conrad wanted immediate mobilization of the troops and argued that if the country did not act against Serbia, Austria would lose all prestige in the Balkans and her status as one of the Great Powers would be fatally undermined. Conrad had the full support of the Bosnian governor, Potiorek, who was quick to point out that he had been making the case for war against Serbia for two years.

The Hungarian leader Count Tisza said there was, as yet, no conclusive proof of official Serbian involvement in the assassination and so the justification for declaring war was dubious, at best. Such a move would be an appalling blunder and result in a wider European war.

Tisza's reluctance applied the brakes to the Austrian government, especially the Foreign Minister, Berchtold, who had been ready to attack without warning but now told Conrad his idea of instant mobilization was out of the question. He retained the initiative, however, saying to Tisza that if Austria failed to act it would be seen as a sign of weakness.

Berchtold wanted to be sure of German support and Kaiser Wilhelm was ready to oblige. He too had encouraged restraint in the past but, after the assassination of his dear friend and ally the Archduke he sent a message to the Austrian emperor offering full support, even 'in the event of action against Serbia giving rise to serious European complications'. If, as seemed likely, Russia entered a war on the side of Serbia, Germany would stand next to the Habsburgs.

Having given this broad guarantee – 'the blank cheque' – over lunch, the Kaiser alerted various senior military officials of his decision and then returned to his yacht for a cruise up the coast of Scandinavia.

Serbia was carrying out its own propaganda campaign, trying to reassure its allies that it was 'absurd' to think it had played a part in the assassination. How could Serbia be responsible for those 'demented children' of Austrian territory – Bosnia – who had carried out the attack?

Austria was desperate for some snippet that might counter Serbian claims, but the only information from Sarajevo, mainly in bulletins from Potiorek, was contradictory and confusing.

With German support, Berchtold could move closer to an attack. He told a meeting of ministers that Austria should 'get ahead of her enemies by a timely reckoning with Serbia'. Finally, he elected to present Serbia with a Note, the response to which would either justify a war or push Serbia to a severe diplomatic defeat. The emperor was informed of this compromise measure. He, apparently, had no appetite for war and approved of the Note, apparently seeing it as a means of bringing Serbia under 'practical control'.

Such a document needed unambiguous evidence, however, which was just not forthcoming from Sarajevo. Vienna decided to send an official there, in the hope that he could deliver the compelling facts of Serbia's role in the assassination that had so far eluded Potiorek. The special emissary was Friedrich von Wiesner who arrived in Sarajevo on 1 July and barely slept for 48 hours as he sat up reading the papers, though never bothering to interview the conspirators himself. On 13 July, he telegraphed to Vienna, 'there is nothing to indicate or even give rise to the suspicion that the Serbian Government was involved in the organization of the attack or the provision of the weapons for it. On the contrary there is far more to indicate that this is out of the question.'

It took ten more days to prepare the Note and, apparently ignoring the lack of evidence, Berchtold took an increasingly hostile position. He sent the emperor a memo saying the content of the Note was likely to force the Serbians to reject it, making war probable. It would be accompanied by an ultimatum, insisting on unconditional acceptance of all the demands within 48 hours.

The Note now became a matter of great secrecy, in order not to alert either Serbia or its potential allies. Some ministers were sent on leave, to suggest nothing was about to happen. The final agreement on the wording took place at a secret meeting at Berchtold's home, four days before delivery of the Note which was carefully timed for six o'clock in the evening of 23 July.

The timing meant it would not be known about by the Russian

Tsar or the French President who were meeting that afternoon in St Petersburg. The Serbian prime minister was out of town too and his deputy complained the deadline was too short. The Austrian minister in Belgrade, Baron Giesl, said that in the age of railways, telegrams and telephones the prime minister was hardly out of contact and could soon be back in the capital. The deputy refused to take the Note from the Baron's hand, so he placed it on the desk of the deputy and walked out.

The Note made ten demands in all, and was so stringent it amounted to a declaration of war. When it was read by Foreign Secretary Sir Edward Grey in London the following morning he observed that it was 'the most formidable document I have ever seen addressed by one state to another that was independent'.

The demands, in brief, were,

1. To suppress all publications inciting hatred of Austria-Hungary
2. To dissolve the Narodna Odbrana and all other similar societies
3. To eliminate anti-imperial propaganda from the Serbian education system
4. To dismiss anyone guilty of spreading such propaganda
5. To accept the collaboration of the empire in suppressing this subversive activity
6. To begin a judicial inquiry into the murder and allow the empire to participate in the inquiry
7. To arrest Major Tankosic and Milan Ciganovic
8. To stop border officials smuggling arms and explosives and dismiss those involved in the murder
9. To explain the 'unjustifiable' language used by Serbian officials after the murder
10. To notify Vienna without delay that the above measures had been carried out.

Serbia's reply, at two minutes to the deadline, 5.58pm, 25 July, conceded all except demand 6. Allowing Austrian officials into a judicial inquiry in Serbia would be a violation of both its constitution and its criminal law. There was an additional problem with demand

7 as Ciganovic had been granted a month's sick leave from his post at the Serbian State Railway on 1 July and had since disappeared. He was the only tangible link between the conspirators and the state and there was suspicion that the Serbian government had encouraged him to make himself scarce.

The Austrian Minister in Belgrade was no longer in Belgrade at the deadline. He and his staff were already on the train to Vienna, where minds must have already been made up.

War was declared on 28 July. 'If the monarchy must perish,' said the emperor, 'let it at least perish decently.' Apparently a war that would kill millions was at least decent.

Russia mobilized its troops along both the Austrian-Hungarian and German borders. Germany asked it to withdraw and, receiving no answer, declared war on Russia on 1 August. This automatically brought in France, who had shared a dual alliance with Russia for two decades, as Germany of course knew. In a pre-emptive strike, Germany declared war on France on 3 August.

Britain might almost have kept neutral but for Germany's invasion of Belgium, trying to outflank the French. Britain could not be seen to support the violation of Belgian neutrality, so it declared war on Germany on 4 August. Austria formally declared war on Russia on 6 August, so fatally stretching itself over two fronts.

Ten days later, General Potiorek would be in Serbia leading approximately 200,000 troops against 180,000 Serbian soldiers at the Battle of Cer, resulting in the first of a succession of Austrian defeats. His elevation to Field Marshal would not help much at the Battle of Kolubara in December which would lead to even greater losses and further retreat.

By the end of 1914, after only four months of war, Potiorek had presided over losses of around 227,000 men. He had claimed, 'I was spared at Sarajevo so that I may die avenging it.' Instead many others died while he was left to face the ignominy of being relieved of his command.

21

We Are Not Criminals

Being preoccupied on the military front, Potiorek was among those who advocated delaying the trial of the Sarajevo conspirators until after the conclusion of the war, whenever that might be. He and the Austrian finance minister Leon von Bilinski both felt the same way, until Berchtold, the foreign minister, pointed out the trial's broader ramifications. The trial needed to be seen to justify the action against Serbia and if they waited until afterwards Austria would be criticized, if it won the war, for only dispensing justice when it was sure of victory or, if it lost, a punitive sentence would seem like an act of revenge and place Austria under pressure from its victorious opponents.

Pfeffer had never managed to make a conclusive link with the Serbian government but he had effectively pieced together most of the intricacies of the plot, and the plotters. No doubt, the Austrians would have liked to have put Ciganovic and Tankosic in the dock too but they were somewhere in Serbia, fighting the Austrians. They were still largely unaware of Colonel Apis and The Black Hand.

Instead the Austrians suspected Narodna Odbrana of being implicated and also believed there might have been a conspiracy among Freemasons. The Archduke himself had often expressed a deep mistrust of Freemasonry, for its secretive, anti-Catholic, anti-imperial beliefs. Both Narodna Odbrana and the Freemasons would be themes of inquiry at the trial.

There were 25 defendants in all, not literally in the dock, but lined up in rows of chairs at the front of the makeshift courtroom within the military barracks where they had been imprisoned since their arrests. There are photographs of them sitting with their arms folded, their heads shaved, wearing jackets and even three-piece suits over collarless shirts. They are flanked by armed soldiers but do not appear to be in chains, though in one other photograph I have seen, of the defendants being led across open ground to the court, they all appear to be shackled to each other.

Only Mehmed Mehmedbasic was missing from the court. The main group of six defendants were Gavrilo Princip, aged 19; Nedeljko Cabrinovic, 19; Trifko Grabez, 18; Vaso Cubrilovic, 17; Cvjetko Popovic, 16; and Danilo Ilic, 24. Then there was Ivo Kranjcevic, 19, who had hidden Vaso's weapons; Lazar Djukic, 18, who had introduced Ilic to Vaso; Veljko Cubrilovic, aged 28, the schoolteacher from Priboj who had taken Gavro and Grabez to the Kerovic zadruga; Mitar Kerovic, 65, and his sons, Jovo, age unknown, Nedjo aged 28, Blagoje, who thought he was 34 and Cvijan Stjepanovic, who thought he was about 37, who had driven the cart to Tuzla with Nedjo. Misko Jovanovic, 36, had kept the weapons at his apartment in Tuzla until they were collected by Ilic. Then there were the student friends of Vaso who had been told in advance about the assassination: Branko Zagorac, 18; Marko Perin, 17; Nikola Forkapic, 19 and Dragan Kalember, 16.

The other peasants who had smuggled the weapons were also there: Mico Micic, 26, who had been at Isakovic's island and gone to fetch Jakov Milovic, 43, who in turn had taken Gavro and Grabez to Obren Milosevic, 38.

Finally there were the three members of the household where Kranjcevic had left Vaso's bomb and gun: Ivan Momcinovic, aged 67, his son-in-law Franjo Sadilo, aged 40 and Franjo's wife, Angela Sadilo, 31, who was the only woman in the trial.

Sixteen of the defendants were Serb Orthodox, four were Catholic and the others gave no religion.

While the young students at the core of the conspiracy, along with Danilo Ilic, had been steeped in revolutionary politics and immersed in the campaign of agitation and terror through rebellion and assassination, the majority of the other defendants were older, with families and, in many cases, no more than patriotic Serbs who had been ready, or felt obliged, to play their part. Some could not read or write and were not even sure how old they were. Now they had been dragged out of their lives and communities and faced execution or, at the very least, long sentences in prison.

Vaso, in his unpublished letter, described the horrible experiences of the two helpful peasants, Mico Micic who had liked a swig of brandy and dancing with young women, and Jakov Milovic, the smuggler and occasional courier for Narodna Odbrana. They had been arrested more or less together and held for four days with no food at a military prison outside Sarajevo. The soldiers had been beating every prisoner in the jail but especially those two, when the soldiers discovered they were part of the assassination conspiracy. They had locked them in a special room and an officer had brought in two soldiers who beat them so terribly that Milovic would eventually die from his improperly treated injuries.

Milovic had actually fled to safety in Serbia but had been forced to return home by the leader of the Narodna Odbrana in Sabac, Boza Milanovic. 'Let them hang you, when you didn't want to prevent it,' Milanovic had told Milovic. A clear signal that the national defence organization had wanted no part of an assassination.

No one had ever given him a change of clothes so that for four months, including the duration of the trial, he wore the same blood-stained shirt and underpants.

Micic, said Vaso, had lost his mind and was especially troubled that he had betrayed Milovic by saying too much during the interrogation. When they were brought to Sarajevo he opened his veins to commit suicide and was only narrowly saved. If saved was the right word. He had tried to commit suicide a second time, jumping from a second-floor window of the prison, only to land on another prisoner who broke his fall.

Vaso sat next to Micic throughout the trial and said he was 'beside himself' (presumably with anxiety and distress) the whole time and afterwards was so traumatized he could not remember anything that had happened. In addition he was in constant pain from the injuries to his chest and ribs caused by the beatings.

In prison after the trial Micic could speak of nothing but the assassination and obviously annoyed the other prisoners. Vaso said he got very angry with all those people in the prison who called him an idiot or an ass and so on. 'They don't realize that he is the unhappiest among us because he is overly honest and too good. He has confided in me a number of times that everyone in here despises him and calls him a fool and how difficult that is on him.'

Vaso had done his best to console Micic but Micic had found little solace when he had tried to share his troubles with the priest during confession. The priest had cut him off: 'Pray to God, pray to God for the forgiveness of sins, but I don't want to know anything about that.' Vaso said, 'you can't imagine how desperate he looked when he told me about that.'

Evidently, some sins were too great for the Catholic Church. Vaso was not a believer and would never dream of receiving communion or going to confession: 'but if I practised such things I would not go to confession before such a shameless person, not even if the salvation of my soul depended on it.'

As I understand it – and even in the transcript this is not entirely clear – the defendants were all accused of either high treason or being an accessory to high treason. No one was accused outright of murder.

It was explained by Will Owings, the American academic who had been responsible for the English translation of the complete trial – 530 pages – that was made in the mid-1980s: 'An Archduke had been killed; someone had to hang.' But Austrian law would not permit anyone under the age of 20 to be executed. Only the key conspirators – the ones who had gone out with the guns and bombs – could realistically be charged with murder and they were too young to hang. The others could be charged with being accessories to the murder, but that was not a capital crime. On the other hand, being an accessory to high treason was a capital crime so there was a good chance that some defendants could be convicted and then executed, under that offence. You could only be an accessory to high treason, if others had first been convicted of high treason.

There was no jury, not in the sense of the defendants being judged by twelve of their randomly selected peers, but the president of the court, also known as the presiding judge, Luis von Curinaldi, was sitting with two fellow judges who were described as the jury, Bogdan Naumowicz and Mayer Hoffman. Curinaldi must have been affected by the trial as according to Dedijer he went to live in a monastery afterwards and became a friar.

Lawyers had been assigned to all of the 25 defendants, in groups, so that Dr Max Feldbauer represented Gavro and three others. Gavro told him at the start, 'Do not pay any attention to my defence, con-

centrate all your efforts on the defence of the other three; try to save
their necks and study their cases more thoroughly. If you waste your
time on my defence this will be at the expense of the other three. You
could help them, because they are innocent, while I, in any case, am
ready to face the worst.'

The most energetic of the defence lawyers was Dr Rudolf Cistler
who represented Vaso and Veljko Cubrilovic as well as Ivo Kranjcevic
and Nedjo Kerovic. Like all the lawyers he was appointed by the state,
but some of them acted like state prosecutors in their conduct of the
defence. That was certainly not true of Cistler, who smuggled letters
and other items in and out of prison for Veljko and his wife and was so
determined in his defence during the trial, elaborating on a particularly imaginative strategy, that the Austrians later started proceedings
against him and he was banished from Sarajevo. Both Vaso and Veljko
were full of praise for their counsel, though all his effort made no
difference to the outcome.

Veljko and Jovanka began exchanging letters in late July, some days
after his arrest. There were not many letters – just nine sent by him
and nine sent by her in reply. Jovanka had been forced to leave the
teachers' cottage in Priboj after Veljko's arrest and had gone to stay
with her sister-in-law in Sarajevo, to be close to her husband.

> 24 July 1914, Sarajevo
>
> Dear Jovanka and Stako [Veljko's sister],
>   I was extremely happy to hear that you came with Nada.
> When I found out my soul felt lighter. Let me know to whom
> you left the house and whether Branko [Veljko's older brother]
> came. Dear Jovanka, buy me a pair of leather slippers and send
> them to me as soon as possible. For now, I can do nothing
> more than to wish you and our daughter good health. My
> regards to all of ours ... and your husband gives you and our
> Nada [their only daughter, born ten months earlier] a big hug
> and kiss.
>   Veljko.

*

19 September 1914, Sarajevo

My Dear Veljko,

I want to let you know that Nada and I are, thank God, healthy and well. I will be staying with our child and Jelenka [their relative] a while longer. I can also let you know that God is going to bless us once more with a child. I believe I'm in my fourth month of pregnancy. Don't worry about us, only let God give you health and good things. I pray for this day and night. Send me a few words to put me at peace. We all love you and kiss you, especially your,

Jovanka and Nada.

This was the first time that Jovanka had told her husband of her second pregnancy. In 2006, Nada told me that Jovanka had lost the baby in the second trimester, because of the terrible stress of the trial and the aftermath. Jovanka had never told Veljko the pregnancy was lost and Nada believed this was a good thing as he had died believing he had left a second child about to be born.

30 September 1914, Sarajevo

My Dear Veljko,

As soon as the charges were announced we looked for a lawyer and we wanted Mr Cisler [sic], which the court coincidentally gave you. If the defence succeeds, as we hope, we have decided to give the [Cubrilovic family] home and land in Gradiska as payment and, in addition, whatever else we can scrape together. I'm sure he [Cistler] won't complain. I've requested permission to visit you a number of times but they've rejected me each time, and now they've promised that we will be able to see each other again after the main arguments in the case have been presented. I will also ask permission to bring Nada. She began to walk just before Krstovdan [a church holiday]. She's healthy, restless and very dear. We send you warm greetings ... and we especially send you kisses.

Jovanka and Nada.

*

3 October 1914, Sarajevo

[This letter, from Veljko to Jovanka, abridged]

As Dr Cisler [sic] isn't around, I felt like writing you again. Let me describe my dwellings. The cell is 4.5 metres long, 2 metres wide. There's a square 1 metre window with iron bars, a door with a small grid through which the guard often peeks to see what I'm doing. Along the wall there's an iron bed that is fixed to the floor, and on the bed a mattress filled with hay and a pillow with hay stuffed hard, two sheets and a blanket (yesterday we received another blanket) and next to the bed in the corner a waste paper bin. By the north wall I have a chair and table, and on the table a tin plate and a cup. In the north wall there is a built-in furnace that is shut with a special key. Above the bed there are iron shelves. On the window there are covers which are shut every evening. When you imagine in that cell Nada's father in chains, in a winter coat with a hat on his head, ever hungry, grumpy and nervous, well then you'll have a good picture of me when I'm in the cell. Add to this an annoying and rude guard who's always just outside my door ... For the picture to be complete imagine the 'beshlisha' as they call the keyholder, who you are well served to address as 'herr corporal' or simply 'sir', while he is some miserable Polish sod who gives orders and addresses you as 'you'. In short, I want to see a man and exchange a few words. It cannot be worse in Zenica [the prison where he hoped to serve out his sentence]. We also have some pleasures. We can communicate with one another by knocking. Today, via Cabrinovic, I asked Vasa [Vaso] whether he was cold and whether he had a coat. I sent him my overcoat ...

If the guard notices however he immediately fines you with a fast – no food – but we take no notice of this. I haven't fasted yet but Cabrinovic has fasted twice. We had two (internal) newspapers 'Hour' and 'Chains' but the censors confiscated them and fined the editor with a fast and stopped them from coming out. We communicated by writing with our shoelaces on cups. They have moved us around twice. Every day passes monotonously and in boredom. I cross my cell regularly 2,000 times, which is 8km. My shoes and slippers are in tatters. Really, if you could send me some nice books.

Once the main court argument is over we shall be moved to another prison and, if they do not hang me, I shall serve my time somewhere in Hungary or Austria. We are all scared of that. If only I could serve time in Zenica, you could get a teaching position there.

Vaso has no undergarments. Get some together for him. You can't imagine how much I look forward to seeing you and Nada. If I can only get out alive we'll push forward somehow … Vaso just asked what's new. We heard that the Serbs are in Semizovac and that Tankosic died. There's a lot more to say but I have no more paper. I hug you and kiss you all, especially you and Nada, with much love, Veljko … I hold that Priboj belongs to Duk Vuk Vojin. Menu: Breakfast: Stew. Lunch: Stew with 4-6 bites of meal, 80-100 grains of rice or paprikash after which you don't have to wash the cups. Dinner: black coffee, or stew (if it's 'gershla' it's good) along with half kilo of bread.

Veljko.

Major Tankosic was still alive at this point. In fact he outlived Veljko but was shot and wounded during fighting a year later, in October 1915. He died of his wounds some days later.

I have been unable to identify Duk Vuk Vojin or establish why Veljko thinks Priboj belongs to him. I suspect it is a patriotic cry that Priboj, in Bosnia, is really Serbian.

The trial was scheduled to begin on 12 October …

6 October 1914, Sarajevo

My dear Jovanka,

My defence attorney Dr Cisler [sic] has arrived. I'm glad you've 'found' him. I'm alive and healthy. Please send: pair of shoes, size 43, socks, soap and something nice to eat, but not much. I miss all of you and god willing we will see each other. I think of you day and night and dream with you. We haven't seen each other for 90 long days. Let everything be all right and to me, let come what may. I love you and hug you countless times. The Dr [Cistler] will tell you the rest. I love you and hug you.

Veljko.

*

7 October 1914

My Dear Veljko,

Today I got that slip of paper from Dr Cisler [sic] and was so happy after many long days to read a few tender words written by your dear hand. I'm writing this at Staka's and will rush to send you the few things you've asked for via the defence attorney. Have you received the socks, slippers and undergarments that I sent by way of the district court? My dear Veljko, we shall soon see each other, and I'm not sure whether it's from joy or sadness that I fear that day. Our Nada is healthy and dear, smart, and she goes around the room teetering on her little fat legs. She is just like you. I've already written that I'm pregnant again. It's the fourth month now. My dear, be brave, don't let your spirits be down. Be healthy and brave. We all love you and we send you kisses, your Jovanka, Nada and Jelenka.

I send my brother much love, sister Vida

I send my brother much love, sister Staka.

In his last letter before the trial began, sent on the same day that Jovanka was writing to him, as above, Veljko referred to the distress of his arrest, as described earlier. It was a long, painful letter, which continued ...

7 October 1914, Sarajevo

My dear two female heads ...

Your new blessed state (pregnancy) thrills me. Take care of yourself dear, God may give me a replacement, an angry avenger. If it's a son, send him to the Royal Army, like the old saying, 'bear a son and send him to the army. Serbia will not rest.'

My ordinary imagination has betrayed me. I created a picture about what I would have to pass. The perspective is bleak. In the best case we will be separated for at least five years and in the worst case, death. But enough about that. It will be as it must. There is no such horrible fate out of which man will not exit, nor such misfortune which man will not survive.

And you, Joko [Jovanka], you write nothing of how you live, what you're doing, whether you have money … what did the people of Priboj say when I was arrested? What did you do with the bacon, dry meat and brandy? I often think of the rich offerings in our humble home. The food is poor here. They don't allow us to get more. I forgot to tell you to send handkerchiefs, a spoon, a needle and thread. Make me a sour strudel and send it along, if they allow it in, or perhaps milk bread.

In any case I am alive and well, but once in a while my stomach gives me trouble. Write me about what Nada does now. Does she know how to say 'daddy'? What do her aunts say about her? Get her picture taken and send it along secretly. They confiscated the other one. Send it along by way of Dr Cisler [sic]. He is a beautiful man. Write me about [everyone] especially Nada … All of you should hug and kiss each other in my place. I'll be with you in thought. I kiss all of you, especially the two of you, my women heads.

Nada's father, Veljko.

There was just time for Jovanka to make a brief, practical reply before the trial. This was their last letter for a month. By the time their correspondence resumed his fate had been decided.

10 October 1914, Sarajevo

Dear Veljko,

I'm sending you shoes size 43, 3 pairs of warm socks, soap and a comb which you requested through the defence lawyer. Let me know if you have clean shirts, undergarments and you still have a winter coat and overcoat. Be healthy, from all of us who love you.

Kisses from your,
Jovanka.

The trial opened on 12 October 1914 at 8.10am, with the 25 defend-ants being summoned, one after the other, and then the charges were read and then all the accused except Nedjo were sent back to jail and his hearing began. He was the first as he was the first to be arrested. According to Dedijer, 22 of the accused were charged with high treason and first degree murder, and three were charged with complicity in the murder. To some extent this contradicts the version of Owings, the translator of the trial transcript.

When he was writing his book in the 1960s, Dedijer was working with an earlier and incomplete version of the transcript. It might be hard to imagine now, but for decades the transcript and the various copies that surrounded it were treated like a political 'hot potato'.

There had been two official stenographers at the court along with a third who worked for the Catholic newspaper *Hrvatski Dnevnik* and five or six reporters, whose accounts were subject to censorship by the Bosnian government at the time. According to Owings the original 1914 transcription went from Sarajevo to Vienna, then much later to Belgrade and, during world war two, returned to Vienna. A copy of the transcription, which had apparently been made at the time, was found in 1925 in Belgrade and reached Sarajevo after world war two. The original 1914 copy went missing after it had been worked on by some German-Austrian historians during world war two. They had tried to make propaganda out of the transcript, seeking evidence of Serbian government involvement. This copy has never been found since.

The two stenographers kept their notes and after one died the other took both sets of notes and tried to reproduce a complete record which he was about to publish until prevented by the Yugoslav government, by chance in the same year as the so-called 'Belgrade copy of 1925' was found.

Meanwhile, a version had been published in 1918 under the name Pharos, which is widely thought to be a pseudonym for the Jesuit priest Father Anton Puntigam who had sat through the trial as one of the privileged few invited guests. Apparently he would curl his legs under his seat as the defendants walked by so they would not touch him as they passed.

Unsurprisingly, if he is Pharos, his account was considered incomplete and biased – aimed at implicating both the Serbian government and the Freemasons. The same was true of a French version published in 1930 by Mousset, who even added in bits of evidence he had made up himself while ignoring other aspects that either didn't suit him or were too difficult to translate.

The best version until 1980 was the transcript assembled for publication in Serbo-Croat in 1954 by Vojislav Bogicevic, the director of the archives in Sarajevo. The basis for his copy was a later version based on the original stenographers' personal notes and the Mousset edition. Owings drew everything together for the first time and picked his way through the omissions and additions. He was helped by two American-based Serb academics who have since died. He too had met Vaso Cubrilovic and Cvjetko Popovic. He admitted that he was endlessly fascinated by how easy it was to get those two and the others to take part. All you had to do was say, would you like to participate in an assassination and Popovic, without hesitation, said *yes*!

There was a public 'gallery' but it was not actually open to the public, except those who had been injured by Nedjo's bomb, whom the judge invited to sit and listen, and those who had been given special invitations. There were only two Serbs and as Sabor moderates, social democrats, they would have been greeted with contempt by the conspirators.

The judge seemed almost offended when Nedjo was trying to remember a detail and said he wished he could get some help but 'since the hearing is secret there are no people here who would know the situation better'. 'The hearing isn't secret,' said the judge. 'I don't see the journalists of the opposition newspapers,' said Nedjo. 'You consider it to be public only when the opposition is here?'

Owings is dismissive of the significance of Father Anton Puntigam and says he was 'frequently though inaccurately referred to as the confessor of the Archduke'. It's true that, since he was mostly based in Sarajevo or nearby, Puntigam could not have seen much of the Archduke, but he does seem to have had a royal role as a keen imperialist, giving talks and even meeting Nedjo, after inviting two anti-Austrians to his room for coffee to discuss their different philosophies. He would meet Nedjo again, after the trial, which he sat through as one of the specially invited guests – a further indicator of his influence.

He had also been called, or went of his own accord, to the Konak to perform the last sacrament after the assassination and, most intriguingly, was later given permission by the royal couple's children to take care of a number of artefacts, including all four pistols that had been used.

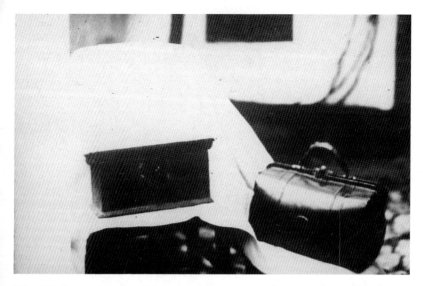

The Gladstone bag in which the weapons were kept, as the police found it at the home of Danilo Ilic. (Muzej Sarajeva)

One of four guns used by the plotters. Three are on display at the military museum in Vienna. One is missing. (Heeresgeschichtliches Museum im Arsenal)

One of the bombs, with the screw cap that must be removed before priming. (Muzej Sarajeva)

The scene on Appel Quay, moments after Nedjo's bomb had exploded.
(Muzej Sarajeva)

Nedjo threw himself into the river, after the bombing, but survived and
was arrested. (Getty Images)

The Archduke and the Duchess leaving the town hall in Sarajevo, on the way to their assassination. (Muzej Sarajeva)

The wheels of their car turn to the right as the driver makes the fatal error seconds before the shooting. (Muzej Sarajeva)

Ort der Katastrophe

The scene outside Moritz Schillers' delicatessen after the assassination. Princip had been standing close to the entrance. (Schloss Artstetten)

The bodies of the Archduke and the Duchess lying in state.
(Muzej Sarajeva)

(from the left) Grabez, Cabrinovic, Ilic and Princip on their way to court. (Muzej Sarajeva)

There were 25 defendants at the trial. Princip is at the front, centre. (Muzej Sarajeva)

Anti-Serbian riots
broke out in Sarajevo
after the assassination.
(Muzej Sarajeva)

The only known
photograph of Dr
Martin Pappenheim,
who interviewed
Princip in prison in
1916.

Dr Zdravko Antonic, the Belgrade historian with the author outside the school building in Priboj where Veljko had once taught.

Nada Cubrilovic, the newborn daughter of Veljko in 1914, aged 92 when the author met her in 2006.

Ranka Cabrinovic, the niece of Nedjo, at her apartment in Sarajevo in 2006.

The 'forgotten' chapel in the Christian cemetery of St Mark's in modern Sarajevo.

The memorial to the 'heroes of Vidovdan'.

Puntigam's diaries are tucked away in the vaults of the Jesuit archive in Vienna, where for many years the guns and other artefacts were kept too. The Jesuits are immeasurably secretive and apparently got so bored with my calls and emails and letters and those of my German-speaking colleague, that they eventually took to ignoring us altogether. I tried and failed to get permission to see Puntigam's diaries.

An American Jesuit who had written a biography of Puntigam now insists that Puntigam was not Pharos at all, not the author of the infamously inadequate transcript. He may be right – he alone has had some access to Jesuit archives – but he is a solitary voice in history, in holding that belief. Still, the American Jesuit Father Leo Nicol claims to have found proof of Pharos's real identity at a Jesuit archive in Zagreb. It was Father Franz Hammerl, says Nicol, who shared Puntigam's view that the Freemasons were to blame.

In fact, according to Nicol, Puntigam later began to draw away from the idea of a Freemason conspiracy behind the assassination. He realized it had been he who introduced Freemasons into the trial when he asked Nedjo's lawyer to ask Nedjo about it, in court. He had the chance to ask Nedjo himself, after the trial, if Freemasons had been involved and Nedjo said, no, it was all nationalists.

If this had been a British court the defendants would have been asked to confirm or deny their guilt: 'how do you plead, guilty or not guilty?' Because the British judicial system is adversarial the prosecution would have presented the case against the defendants, using witnesses to demonstrate what had happened. Then the defendants might have given evidence and, if so, would have been cross-examined on their evidence by the prosecution.

Here, as in much of contemporary Europe, the system was more inquisitorial than adversarial, and intended to establish the facts, so it was neither a trial of two halves – prosecution and defence – nor a question of hostile or aggressive cross-examination, though some of the questioning was certainly belligerent, as indeed were some of the responses. Instead, the defendants were called one by one and questioned by the presiding judge, usually following a chronological sequence.

The defendants were not asked to enter pleas but instead invited to say whether or not they considered or felt themselves to be guilty.

The fact of two murders, and the conspiracy that led to them, was undeniable, but the motives of the perpetrators, their conviction in their own just cause, clouded the truth. Did 500 years of oppression justify the cold-blooded killings? Were the Austrians answerable for the sins of the Turks who had preceded them? Were Gavrilo and his fellow conspirators heroes of national liberation? Or were they victims of their own national mythology and misplaced pride? Common terrorists? Those issues haunted the trial, even if the outcome was always inevitable.

> *Presiding judge*: Call Gavrilo Princip.
> [He is brought in]
> *Pr*: Do you consider yourself guilty?
> *Gavro*: I am not a criminal, because I destroyed that which was evil. I think that I am good.
> *Pr*: And what about her? [The Duchess]
> *Gavro*: I did not wish to kill her, I killed her accidentally.
> *Pr*: So you don't consider yourself guilty then?
> *Gavro*: No.
> *Pr*: Then tell us in detail from the beginning how you developed your ideas of killing the Heir Apparent. To begin, what schools did you attend?

At other moments, when perhaps the truth was beginning to get muddied or obscured, the court would bring two or more of the defendants together for a 'confrontation', as in this exchange involving Gavro and Nedjo. Sometimes, the unintended result was that the truth became further blurred.

> *Presiding judge*: Cabrinovic, your friend Princip says that you, who were of the same opinion as he, wished to unify the South Slavs into one state?
> *Gavro*: That was my opinion.
> *Nedjo*: Those were our ideas. Yugoslavia was my ideal.
> *Pr*: Princip, you were the instigator of the assassination?
> *Gavro*: I talked with him in the Zirovni Vejenac [Green Acorn] about the assassination, but he decided on the assassination himself.

Pr: Cabrinovic, you said explicitly, when you received the note …

Nedjo: I received an anonymous note. However, Princip insists …

Pr: That he was already in agreement with you?

Nedjo: I don't remember.

Gavro: I know positively.

Nedjo: Princip insists that the idea of the assassination came to him before I showed him the clipping from the newspaper.

Pr: He says that he decided before.

Nedjo: There was often talk of an assassination among us, but I don't remember the final decision.

Gavro: The final decision fell at the time when we received the newspaper clipping. Before that I thought of the assassination for myself.

Pr: Do you know anything about Zerajic?

Gavro: He was my first model. At night I used to go to his grave and vow that I would do the same as he.

Nedjo: I did the same thing when I came to Sarajevo. I carved his name on the grave.

Gavro: The grave was neglected and we put it in order.

The spirit of Zerajic and the young men's desire to follow him into martyrdom had been a potent influence on the assassination and so inevitably permeated the trial too. When, at a late point in the proceedings various documents were being entered into the trial, the secretary of the court was obliged to give a truncated account of the pamphlet 'The Death of a Hero' in which the author Gacinovic had celebrated the heroic death of Zerajic. Only the introduction was read and the presiding judge then asked, are there any comments?

'May Zerajic rest in peace!' called Gavro. 'That's enough.'

The judge stopped the trial and called an adjournment. When he returned he warned Gavro that he would be excluded if he 'should interfere with the hearing again in this way'. Gavro said, 'if it isn't allowed, then it isn't allowed, but that's my opinion.'

Gavro must have sat and listened attentively to the trial as he was always interjecting and making comments. He seemed very alert to what was happening and became a dominant figure among the defendants, as if he possessed some natural authority and leadership, which perhaps he did, as a result of becoming the assassin of the man often referred to reverentially in court (though not by the defendants) as 'the late lamented Heir'.

While the authorities seemed oblivious to the existence of The Black Hand they were highly suspicious of the role of Narodna Odbrana and of the Freemasons and frequently tried to introduce them into the trial with questions and references, while constantly trying to make a link to the Serbian government.

When it was suggested the defendants were exaggerating the role of the Bosnian Serbs, Nedjo challenged the statement, saying Bosnians were in all the guerrilla bands and Major Tankosic used to boast that his band consisted entirely of Bosnians. Then Nedjo said, 'Nobody could know about the assassination but Ciganovic, Tankosic and one of Tankosic's friends. Nobody else knew about it because if they had known they could have denounced it.'

Was this reference to a friend of Tankosic a slip of the tongue, a reference to Colonel Apis? It was late on Saturday afternoon, after six long days of evidence. The judge, no fool, immediately asked, 'Who was that friend of Tankosic's you mentioned?'

Nedjo became evasive. 'A former officer. I don't know his name.'

Here came Gavro, offering a fresh distraction: 'That was a former officer. And a theology student knew about it too.' The theology student was Djuro Sarac, who had helped to prepare the assassination back in Belgrade and was later sent by Apis to try and call it off.

The judges still wanted to know about that friend of Tankosic. Nedjo said he was a mysterious person and he didn't know his name. Gavro interjected with the name Kazimirovic. 'When Ciganovic talked to me about those Freemasons, he said that he would speak with Vojo Tankosic and this man. But I begged him and tried to dissuade him from telling it and making it known to everybody and then he said that that man was reliable. I said I wouldn't participate if everyone else knew about it and he said that that man was dependable and a good friend and that his name was Kazimirovic.'

The week ended here but the trial resumed early on Monday morning with the judges on the trail of the Freemasons. Gavro and Nedjo must have spent some time that weekend knocking on cell walls in communication. Perhaps they had decided to give the trial what it wanted and describe a Freemason plot, to disguise the part played by The Black Hand.

The first questions that Monday were about the identity of the friend. The court had already heard from Nedjo that Ciganovic and Tankosic were Freemasons. Nedjo had refused to say whether he was himself a Mason. Now he said that while they waited in Belgrade for the arms, Ciganovic told him the delay had arisen because the friend, Kazimirovic, was out of the country, travelling. He came back the night before the arms were finally delivered.

'At that time,' said Nedjo, 'Ciganovic told me the Freemasons had condemned the Heir to death two years before.'

The presiding judge suggested Nedjo was telling them fairy tales. No, said Nedjo, it was the simple truth. 'And a hundred times more true than all your documents about the Narodna Odbrana.'

> *The judge*: 'You said yourself that you first asked the
> Narodna Odbrana for weapons and now you come out with the
> Freemasons.'
> *Nedjo*: 'I thought that you knew more about the Freemasons.
> They asked me and they said I was bragging there that I was
> a Freemason. I said nothing about that, nor did I have any
> intention of talking about that. The only thing I can confirm
> is that we did not have any connection with the Narodna
> Odbrana.'

Court officials had by now identified that friend as Dr Radovan Kazimirovic, a schoolteacher and occasional contributor to a Christian journal. The court was puzzled that he should be a theologian and a Freemason, since the Freemasons were atheists. 'They penetrated into all groups,' said Nedjo, conspiratorially, 'and in all groups worked for their own ends.'

Gavro was asked what he knew about this Kazimirovic. Nedjo had said he was about 40 years old. Gavro said he was about 28 and had studied to be a priest in Russia before persuading Djuro Sarac not to be ordained. 'I know that he is a close friend of Tankosic. I know that Ciganovic told me about the Freemasons. I told him that I didn't want to become acquainted with him and that it was ridiculous to draw in others from outside.'

Dedijer cites trial evidence that Nedjo described Kazimirovic as the chief of a Masonic Lodge but this does not appear in Owings' transcript and I suspect Dedijer may have been relying on falsified testimony from the Jesuits' version of the trial.

He tracks the first allegation of Masonic involvement to the London journal *John Bull*, owned and edited by Horatio Bottomley, the father of all unscrupulous reporters, notorious for his sensationalistic, unreliable journalism. The allegations were repeated occasionally after the trial, most zealously by a retired German officer who was successfully sued for libel by German Masons, after claiming they too had been involved in the plot. In a sign of things to come, the officer, Erich Ludendorff also claimed that Gavro was a Jew, on the grounds that his name was Gabriel, in English. He identified Colonel Apis as a Mason too, with links to that other enemy of Germany, the British secret service.

The Nazis later said the same thing, accusing Princip of being a Jew and a Freemason. In 1941 Hitler would say the assassination of the Archduke had been the work of the British intelligence service. According to Dedijer, the Jesuit, Father Puntigam 'tried to stir up old prejudices against the Freemasons and Jews as instigators of the French Revolution in 1789 and all the other revolutions in Europe'. On reading this I wondered if this could be some explanation for the secrecy of the Vienna Jesuits. Was it possible they did not want Puntigam's diaries published because they were anti-Semitic? Anti-Semitism was still a very sensitive theme in Vienna.

Perhaps Tankosic and Ciganovic and even Apis were Freemasons. But this does not alter the overwhelming evidence that the students themselves initiated the plan for the assassination and went to those Serbian officers to ask for weapons. It seems to have suited the officers to help, albeit after some weeks of delay and indecision, perhaps while they tried to work out what to do for the best.

It seems likely that Princip and the others benefited from the ongoing struggle between military and civil forces in Serbia and the recent triumphs in the Balkan wars, which may have given the army some confidence that it could take on Austria and regain Bosnia.

In this context, shadowy military forces such as The Black Hand seem much more likely to have been involved than the Freemasons. The suggestion that Apis changed his mind at the eleventh hour and sent Sarac to try to stop the assassination also fits this version of events: that the assassination was the work of radicalized, idealistic student terrorists assisted – but not directed – by a small group of power-hungry individual army officers in Belgrade.

When the defendants were invited to address the court at the end of the trial, only Nedjo took the opportunity to explain himself and his fellow conspirators. 'I would like to present to you in a clear way those circumstances which influenced us before the assassination and I request that you listen to me carefully.'

Reporters in court said that his voice cracked with emotion and his eyes filled with tears as he spoke, his jumbled thoughts gradually producing a coherent argument:

We did not hate Austria, but Austria, after she had occupied Bosnia 33 years ago, did not take care of things, she did not solve the agrarian question ... We love our people. Nine tenths of our people are farm workers. They scream, live in misery, they have no schools, no culture. It hurt us. We felt the anguish of our people. We did not hate the Habsburg dynasty.

Although I nourished anarchistic ideas, although I hated everything, never in a single thought was I against His Highness Franz Josef. The only thing I did not like was that he received 60,000 crowns per day. We did not plan this assassination of Franz Ferdinand. We admitted that this idea did not arise in our minds. In the society in which we lived there was always talk of assassination. We read newspapers which praised the assassination carried out by Jukic and Zerajic. We thought that noble people were capable of assassination.

We did not think of an assassination of the late Franz Ferdinand because we did not believe that there were such people among us, and we thought that our situation would never improve. We thought that assassinations directed against the mamelukes in the Assembly, against Nastic, were needed more.

But the people we lived among talked about Franz Ferdinand, they regarded him as an enemy of the Slavs. We heard of him that he was an enemy of the Slavs. Nobody told us directly 'go kill him' but in that milieu we came to that idea.

His final words seemed at first like a last plea for mercy, in the hope of saving himself. But it was clear in the end that they were a genuine expression of his feelings:

> There is still something else I would like to say. Although Princip plays the hero, although all of us play the hero, nevertheless we are very sorry, because we did not know in the first place that the late Franz Ferdinand was the father of a family. We were deeply touched by the words which he said to his late wife, 'Sophie, stay here, live for our children.'
>
> Think what you like of us but we are not criminals. For myself and in the name of my comrades I beg that the children of the late Heir Apparent forgive us; and you render whatever verdict you like. We are not evildoers, we are honest people, honourable, idealistic, we wanted to do good, we loved our people, we will die for our ideals.

He was said to be openly weeping as he sat down, leaning forward with his head bowed. Many others in court – even one of the judges – were also said to be crying.

Dedijer has Gavro immediately leaping to his feet and saying Nedjo was not authorized to speak in his name – implying, in other words, that he was not seeking forgiveness. But this dramatic moment is missing in the most recent, most complete transcript.

Gavro does speak, but in more measured terms, saying, 'If they want to impute that someone else was the instigator, then I must say that that is not true. The idea grew in us, so we carried out the assassination. We loved our people. I do not want to make any other statement in my defence.'

His own lawyer Max Feldbauer had already offered a somewhat unconvincing defence on behalf of Gavro, a client who, as the lawyer said in his statement in court, had consistently rejected any defence or defender.

All Feldbauer could do was blame others and appeal to the prejudices of the judges in saying that Gavro was deliberately trying to take all the blame himself when he had really been 'nothing but the blind instrument of some politicians in Belgrade'.

As Gavro's advocate, Feldbauer could apparently say anything he liked, unchallenged and with no evidence to support it. He claimed that Gavro had been greatly affected by the negligence of his parents during his upbringing. Apparently, it was 'well known that our farm labourers do not care very much for their sons, for their behaviour and for their upbringing once they are sent to school ... therefore I blame the parents as much as the secondary schools.'

Feldbauer also had to address the question of Gavro's age as evidence had been produced in court that he was actually just turned 20 and, as such, liable to be hanged if convicted. The Austrians were desperate to see him executed.

Feldbauer pointed to the contradictions of the two records of his birth – the actual birth register, which gave him a date of birth of 13 July 1894, making him 19 at the time of the assassination as opposed to the 'residence record' which gave the date of birth as 13 June 1894, making him 20. Even Gavro's mother seemed unsure in a statement produced in court, but Feldbauer could point to a third proof – a registry completed by the priest, which supported the birth date as 13 July.

It had been the Cubrilovic brothers' lawyer, Cistler, who created the real drama in court, effectively advancing the argument that not one of the defendants had a case to answer.

Cistler had none of the patriotic hesitation expressed by Nedjo's lawyer, who seemed reluctant to be a defender at all, and sounded more like a prosecutor as he told the court how difficult it was for him, as a Croat, to represent Serbs who had dug the grave of the late Heir, on whom Croatians had pinned their greatest hopes.

In his own speech, Cistler cleverly established a broader scene for the trial while 'the flame of an international war is blazing' and everywhere 'smoke whirls, everywhere the roar of cannons and the chatter of machine guns resounds. We listen to this clang of weaponry close at hand, and see the countless wounded.' This was literally true as Serbian troops were advancing into Bosnia and the fighting could be heard from Sarajevo.

Cistler said everyone was 'boiling with revenge and hatred' against the conspirators, but the court could not be swayed by the mob or the sounds of war and could only reach a judgement based in law. He said the deaths of the Heir and his wife might be called assassination but, legally, were nothing but murder.

He began to consider the historial context for high treason and was told by the presiding judge to stick to the subject and not get carried away with political excursions. Cistler said the hearing had already heard plenty about Serbian nationalism and propaganda. The judge warned Cistler that if he carried on the judge would cut him off and take legal action against him.

Cistler said he would proceed to the legal aspect of the case, but really he continued to make his own case, arguing that Austria had never formally completed its annexation of Bosnia & Hercegovina and, in law, they were still in the hands of the Sultan and Turkey. If they were not Austrian territory then there could be no crime of high treason against Austria.

After trying several times to stop Cistler, the presiding judge called a recess and returned with a reprimand on the grounds that Cistler had insulted Austrian legislation and threatened to make him stand down from the trial if he persevered with the argument. Cistler bravely declared himself against capital punishment, describing it as 'a barbarous institution, an inhuman institution' which, he wrongly claimed, was rejected by all contemporary systems of law and was either not practised or mitigated by amnesty.

'We should not forget', said Cistler, 'that this is a historic trial and that the eyes of the whole world are turned on this most honourable court, and that everyone is waiting patiently for the justice which will be meted out from this bench.

'Future generations and history will speak about this trial. Therefore the verdict must not be cruel, must be just, so that it will constitute an illustrious page in the annals of criminal jurisprudence before the judgement of civilization and the future which we shall meet.'

The judges took five days to reach their verdicts, which were given on 28 October 1914. The judges wore black caps as they delivered the sentences. Altogether nine of the 25 defendants were acquitted: Jovo and Blagoje Kerovic, Nikola Forkapic, Dragan Kalember, the suicidal Mico Micic, Obren Milosevic and the trio in the house where Vaso's gun had been hidden: Ivo Momcinovic and Franjo and Angela Sadilo. The prosecutor appealed the acquittals of four of them, asking instead that Obren Milosevic and Micic be executed. Luckily for them, the appeal was denied, though, confusingly, Vaso's 1918 letter to his sisters says 'Micic is here now and told me about it himself ...' Perhaps he was further detained because of his suicide attempts. There is no way, now, of establishing why he was still in prison in 1918 when he had been acquitted at the trial.

Gavro, Nedjo and Grabez were each sentenced to 20 years' 'penal servitude', Vaso received 16 years and Popovic 13 years. All of them would have their sentence 'intensified by solitary confinement in a dark cell on 28 June each year.' In addition, Gavro's sentence would be further intensified by 'one day of fasting each month'.

Both Lazar Djukic and Ivo Kranjcevic were given ten-year sentences. Stjepanovic, who had driven the cart to Tuzla with Nedjo Kerovic, received seven years; Branko Zagorac and Marko Perin who knew of the plot in advance but did not report it were given three years each.

As head of the Kerovic zadruga, old Mitar was sentenced to life imprisonment. His son Nedjo who had wept and choked in court while giving evidence was sentenced to be hanged, along with the smuggler Jakov Milovic. Both of their sentences were commuted, to 20 years for Kerovic and life imprisonment for Milovic.

Danilo Ilic, Veljko Cubrilovic and Misko Jovanovic from Tuzla were sentenced to be hanged and were not granted any reprieve or amnesty.

The conspirators were returned to prison after the verdicts, where the Jesuit priest Father Anton Puntigam came to Nedjo's cell, apparently carrying with him a letter of blanket forgiveness from the Archduke's children, on the grounds that he had repented and expressed his regret for the killing of their mother and father. The children had acted on Puntigam's recommendation in writing the letter, after he had heard Nedjo's sentiments of remorse at the trial. It was said that as he handed over the letter Puntigam gave Nedjo the benefit of a lengthy sermon while Nedjo was so surprised and confused that he barely spoke.

22

It's All Over

Two days after sentencing, the two youngest conspirators, Vaso Cubrilovic and Cvjetko Popovic, aged 17 and 16 respectively, were escorted from Sarajevo in chains and taken by train to the prison at Zenica, 70 kilometres north of the Bosnian capital. Troops and bystanders cursed them as they passed through stations along the route.

As Vaso wrote to his sisters, the conspirators learned not to respond to the baiting and abuse of guards and others because it only let them in for harsher punishment. Ostensibly, the Austrians were sticklers for the rule book, but in reality the rules could be freely interpreted. For example, according to the regulations, prisoners were only supposed to be held in solitary confinement for three months, but the prison director could extend the punishment if the prisoner misbehaved. In all, said Vaso, he and Popovic and the others who later joined them (those who lasted that long) were kept in solitary for three years and three months.

The second group that came to Zenica were Lazar Djukic, Branko Zagorac, Mitar and Nedjo Kerovic, Jakov Milovic and Cvijan Stjepanovic. They were subject to quiet spite and rigid discipline. On exercise they had to keep their heads down and not look at anyone else and had to keep some distance from the others so they could not communicate; they were not allowed to attend church services; their rooms were stripped out once a week in case they were hiding anything. Vaso was stopped from sending letters for six months, when he was 'caught' trying to send a letter which said simply that his brother, Veljko, was bearing up well, in spite of his sentence.

Even if they were ill they would be denied proper treatment and could not get access to the infirmary. Mitar Kerovic, the oldest of the convicted men, was among the worst affected as he could barely walk and would get abused and cursed by the guards during exercise. Jakov Milovic's health declined rapidly following his earlier beatings which had left him with untreated injuries that had been covered all during the trial by the bloody clothes he was wearing at the time. He was prevented from going to the infirmary. The doctors told him to lie during inspections and say there was nothing seriously wrong with him.

Some things stood out, wrote Vaso, but most of the time he did not recall the details because prison life 'was monotonous and sad and the only thing I remember was the encroaching boredom'. That's how it is for all prisoners, he wrote. 'A person only remembers the first moments and then everything runs together like a dark fog that surrounds a person for the entire time.'

As the Austrians struggled in their war against Serbia they became nervous about keeping the prisoners in Bosnian territory where they might be treated more sympathetically, perhaps even allowed to escape by sympathizers among their fellow countrymen who were guarding them. Bosnia itself could be vulnerable to counter-attack.

When the Serbian army regained control of Belgrade in mid-December 1914, and Potiorek was relieved of his command, the Austrians decided to move all the prisoners out of Bosnia. Some were sent to Theresienstadt in Bohemia (now the Czech Republic); others went to the military prison at Mollersdorf. Marko Perin, who had teased Vaso on the streets of Sarajevo – 'here's the one who thinks he's going to kill the Heir!' – went alone to another prison in Bohemia, perhaps because he was already seriously ill. He died later that December.

Vaso described the long overland journey by wagon from Zenica through Hungary to Mollersdorf, not far from Vienna. The guards took no chances. The prisoners were all tied together, then tied further in pairs, then tied by their feet to the benches where they sat. The guards got angry when they couldn't buy any beer and took it out on the prisoners. At various stops they drew a crowd as the guards told people who the prisoners were. Members of the public screamed abuse at them, especially in Hungary. Vaso would never forget the Hungarians. 'There is no ruder nor more foolish people than them.' They were not allowed to talk to each other during the journey.

While three of them, Lazar Djukic, Cvijan Stjepanovic and Ivo Kranjcevic went on to Theresienstadt, the others – Vaso, Popovic, father and son Kerovic and poor Jakov Milovic – arrived at Mollersdorf and immediately went into solitary confinement cells which Vaso described as being like shacks, beneath the prison factory. The open windows of the cells faced winds that could knock over chimneys and guardhouses. They were just three metres long and 1.75 metres wide so that Vaso would get dizzy turning from the walls, trying to exercise. There was no lighting and the bars across the windows so thick that even in the middle of the day the light was bad and Vaso's eyesight was permanently damaged. There was no heat, except from a fire in the hall, and if it rained the walls and the floor would be soaked and take up to two weeks to dry out.

Food was limited, especially when the 'common gang of thieves' running the prison stole the prisoners' rations, or the money they used to buy food. At one stage, they went six weeks with no bread and no evening meal. 'What we went through cannot be described,' Vaso wrote, as they tried to survive on a morning cup of soup and a half-litre of soup at noon with half a litre of cabbage or potato salad and nothing else then until the next morning. They began to receive bread every five days but it went mouldy within 24 hours so had to be eaten straightaway. 'It was most awful at night when you couldn't eat from hunger and stomach pains.'

When the winter set in they all began to lose their health. Denied the prison hospital, Milovic lay in his cold, damp cell while an abcess the size of a closed fist formed on his rib cage, where soldiers had kicked him until his ribs were broken. He was finally allowed into hospital for two days where doctors drained the pus from the wound and sent him back bandaged to the cell where his wound again filled with pus and his spine bent from the pain and discomfort. After he had moaned night and day for a month the others complained but still he was not transferred to the hospital. Vaso was told that the prison governor could not move him without the direct permission of the Austrian war ministry. The governor's orders were to keep the conspirators separate from the rest of the prison population at all times.

Milovic died from his injuries in April 1916 and was followed a few days later by Nedjo Kerovic who had also been left untreated despite complaining several times of stomach pains. In the end, he could no longer walk and was told he had an infection in his intestines. He was admitted to hospital but had only been there a week when he choked on his own blood and died. His father, Mitar, also suffered from a stomach complaint. He died in September 1916.

Vaso said, 'Milovic was without doubt killed by the guards and commanders, while the Kerovices died from hunger and boredom. You can imagine yourselves what it was like in that box without anything to do and without conversation and with one loaf of bread every five days. As peasants they were used to movement, conversation, not to mention good food in large portions, such that the bread they received was what they would normally eat in the mornings with their broth. Naturally, all that had to lead to catastrophe.'

It sounded almost as if Nedjo had died of a broken heart, wrenched from his home and family, no doubt full of regret for his involvement with the conspiracy that had caused such havoc in his life. He often told Vaso how he had been crying in the night, thinking of his wife and children. Vaso was too young to have a family of his own and said, without empathy, that Nedjo's tears did not help but actually made things worse.

Mitar Kerovic had asked Vaso to write letters for him, once a quarter, sending detailed instructions back to his zadruga for care of their land and livelihood over the season ahead. He was allowed to see a Serbian Orthodox priest before his death and afterwards Vaso asked the priest what Mitar had talked about: 'He only asked if it was true that Serbia had been conquered.'

As teenagers, Vaso and Popovic were better equipped to withstand the harsh conditions of their imprisonment. Popovic would later say he could get books from the prison library and was even able to talk to other prisoners. But Vaso recalled how Popovic became ill, firstly with a chest infection, then diagnosed with tuberculosis and later with rheumatism. Vaso himself had never been seriously ill, but he too had struggled during the winter, waking up with a frozen water bucket in his cell, his hands and ears swollen and covered in sores so that he could hardly use his hands to wash or do anything.

He tried to walk in his cell but the hunger and the giddying turns made his head spin and he would stand and lean against his bed, not moving for perhaps two hours, just standing there in a dream-like state. Vaso said conditions improved after the Russian Revolution in 1917 when he and Popovic were put in a cell together and many of the guards, especially the Czechs but also many of the Germans, began to treat them with greater consideration. Then, with the war turning against the Austrians, they had been returned to Zenica, back into solitary, for the last days of their imprisonment.

Those two were released in late 1918, miraculously with long lives ahead of them.

Vaso's brother Veljko Cubrilovic appealed against his death sentence and waited many weeks for the judgement of the high court. Meanwhile, in their letters, he and his wife, Jovanka did their best to reassure each other and urge each other to keep their spirits up. Jovanka and their daughter Nada had been forced to return to Priboj but could not actually live in their former home the teachers' cottage as it had been impounded and locked by the authorities. Jovanka stayed with the priest, but was able to get access to the cottage and retrieve some possessions, seeing at the same time, what a mess the place was, after the police searches. Priboj was a shadow of its former self, disrupted by the events surrounding the assassination – searches, arrests, increasing tensions – and also the war, which had caused many to move away from the area.

In November Jovanka was writing to Veljko, 'I live isolated. I don't go anywhere nor do I see anyone, but I do notice that people recall you fondly ... We are healthy and Nada is so much your daughter, rambunctious and every day she looks more like you. I show her your picture and ask, "where is dad". She kisses you. Sometimes I take her out on the hill above our house and ask her where dad is, and she says "dad" in her little voice. She runs at full speed. She knows how to say a few words and she immediately understands things after she is told once.'

Many of the letters were simply practical exchanges about their lives, as if they were trying to ignore the enormity of Veljko's fate, while quietly praying for a successful appeal. In one letter, in late 1914, Jovanka wrote, 'I hope that the mercy of God will not allow the horrible sentence you've received to be carried out and I have faith in God that he will bring you back to us alive and well ... my dear have patience and watch your health and God will bring us good things, everything will be overcome.'

Just before Christmas, Jovanka moved back to Bosanska Gradiska, Veljko's family home, the place where he had been raised.

Everything seems familiar. Whenever I see a child running down the street I think of you and your stories about childhood. When I see people speaking in an animated tone here, once again I see you. And that's our fate, that our little Nada breathes the same air her father once breathed. Our little Nada is, thanks be to God, healthy. She was ill in Priboj and lost some weight but she has now regained it. She's progressing very well. She grasps things quickly.

Auntie is teaching her the same silly things that you would teach her. When I ask her where daddy is she spreads her arms wide and says, 'he gone, he gone.' My God, she is so cute.

I often look at the home where you brought me to your mother for the first time and I remember how everything once was and how much things have changed. I now live only from memories and hope, because the present is so difficult.

And now our dear father we wish you a merry Christmas and pray to God that we may be together next year in health and happiness. Don't let it be difficult for you, without us; remember that this year there are many, many thousands of dads who will not spend Christmas with their children.

*

14 January 1915

Dear Jovanka,

I'm very happy that you are with our dear Nada in Gradiska … I'm alive and well. I'm expecting the final decision about my fate at any moment. The high court has confirmed the sentence. My spirit is fresh and I will try to keep that freshness even in the worst of events … Do not worry about me. Let you two be alive and healthy and may you two be well. I will drink from the bitter cup that Providence has ordered in stoic peace. I lived as a man, and that is also how I want to die. I do not fear the future, no matter how cruel it may be. I wish you a Happy New Year

and I wish you progress and hope to see you soon. If you can
receive a pass, come to see me ... Dad loves dear Nada and you.
  Veljko

As the following letter from Jovanka seems to indicate, she was able
to visit Veljko, but was denied the chance of one final visit. This next
letter was written five days before he was hanged:

                                        27 January 1915, Sarajevo
My Dear Sweetheart,
  I thought we would be able to see each other again, before
I leave, but we did not receive permission as we really have
received permission quite a few times. Ljubica and I are leaving
tomorrow. I miss our dear little Nada. I asked the district
court about the money you have there, and it will be given
to you. Veljko, don't miss food, but get as much as you can,
and when you spend the money, ask Staka, she will give it to
you. I'm sending you a warm wool cap, fine wool socks and 3
handkerchiefs. Whatever else you need, write to me or Staka,
don't suffer for a lack of something. Watch your health, which
is dear to all of us, and don't lose patience. God will provide
what is good.
  Always remember that you are not the only one who is
suffering because millions are suffering. I'm sorry that we
couldn't see each other again to say goodbye, and to see you in
better spirits than you were yesterday. See if you can move your
mattress farther from the window and always sleep in flannels.
  If God gives health, I will ask for a travel pass every now
and again to visit you, and if the weather allows, I'll bring
Nada. Jelenka told me briefly that they are fine and that Nada
kisses dad. I can hardly wait to go back to my child, but it's
also difficult to go away from you, but you also know that my
thoughts are always with you. I pray to God that He gives you
strength and health, that you persevere through everything and
that you once again return to me and your child in health, who
love you endlessly and kiss you warmly.
  Jovanka

At the bottom of this letter, when it was later returned to Jovanka, Veljko had written: 'With God, my dear wife, with God, my dear child, 2 February 1915 on Wednesday at 5:00 in the morning. I kiss your faces and send you countless kisses. May the Lord Christ comfort you.' These were literally the last hours before he was taken to the scaffold.

31 January 1915, Sarajevo

I received your dear letter. I'm sorry that we could not see each other once more before your departure, but I'm happy that you delighted our little Nada. I've received all the things you sent me. Thank you! My poor spirit the last time you saw me was due to a cold and excitement. I repeat once again, my dear, not to worry about me. Whatever the final decision be, I am prepared for everything. Just watch for yourself and our dear child. I am scared for you. Now that you're in Gradiska, write me about her. Visit my aunts. In any event, I am healthy and well. Write me as often as you can because your letters make me very happy. Write to me at length about Nada. My regards to everyone, and you Jelenka and Nada, your father loves you very much,

Veljko

*

2 February 1915

To my Daughter Nada
When she turns 15 years old
My dear only Child,

By the time you read this letter, a good many years will have passed. From a tiny seed there will be a beautiful blossom. From my little Nada, whose picture I'm looking at now, there will develop a mature young woman. Your father already sees you as a grown young woman, full of humility, that most beautiful adornment of young women: quiet and calm, collected and intelligent. My dear, your father could not leave you with anything except for an honest and unsullied name. He remained indebted to you, but he leaves his great love and untarnished name. You have already grown and can understand those turbulent times in which your father lived, and if you understand them you will forgive your father.

Love and respect your mother, my friend in life. She will sacrifice much for you. She will be your father and mother. From you, my dear, your father expects purity of heart and high thoughts. Be noble! Love the people from whose roots you have sprung. There, that is everything that your father has to leave you as an inheritance; for the rest, merciful God will take care, who provides for everyone, and without whose thoughts nothing exists. My only child, I love you in these last hours of life, my thoughts are directed to you and your mother.

Your father,
Veljko

Dear Jovanka, save this letter and give it to our Nada when she can understand it, and you be the faithful interpreter of my thoughts, feelings and wishes. May God give you a long life.

Your father loves you

*

                                   Dated: 2 February 1915
To my dear brothers Milorad, Branko and Vaso
To my sweet sisters Staka, Lepa and Vida

That difficult hour has arrived, when your eldest brother must drink from that bitter cup that Providence has determined. Your brother dies with a lightness of soul because he understands that he is falling as a victim of turbulent times and crises, which the entire world is experiencing. Peractum est [It's all over].

My dear ones, in these last hours I am reliving the sweet moments of our childhood, and a picture of our parents is before me. I will say hello to our parents and tell them that their children live as people (meaning honourably), and that they preserve that good voice and name which they left us as an inheritance.

Dear brothers, do not forget me, your eldest brother. Do not grieve for me. Be as you should, honourable as people and as Serbs. That is what our father left you as an inheritance and that is what I leave you as well. My sisters, there is no greater happiness than sisters, but do not weep for me, because your brother lived and died as a man.

Recollections of childhood are dear, brotherly and sisterly feelings are strong, because they are bonded in blood and the same recollections, the same wishes. Our mother and father wanted a firstborn son and so I hurry off to send them greetings and to kiss their hand.

My dear Lepa, you are a mother and have two children. Tell them that uncle is very sorry that he never saw them and took them on his lap. Feed the little hawks with care.

Give my warmest to my brothers-in-law, I love them. I leave you my fatherless Nada and Jovanka entrusted to you. Love them in the same way that I loved you and love you. Take whatever you want of my things by which to remember me. I love all six of you and send uncountable brotherly kisses.

Your brother
Veljko

My Dear Stako, ask the court to give you my remains and bury me. Let it be known where my grave is. Let Nada and my Jovanka, when they come to Sarajevo, pray to God at my grave for Him to be merciful and for them to be happy and to advance.

With love for his sis and childhood friend, brother Veljko. Give my regards to Dr Katica. Thank her for the attention she gave to our Vida.

*

2 February 1915, Sarajevo

To my dear Jovanka, my friend for life

By the time you receive these lines, my soul will be flying above you and our little one Nada. Your Veljko will leave this 'valley of tears' and he has nothing to leave you, my dear, nor to our dear daughter aside from unfathomable love for you. I regret that I cannot look into your face and the face of our child in these last hours, but love, my last thought will be with you, my dearest.

Do not grieve too much and don't be sad! It had to be this way. The Lord's ways are mysterious. Before me on the table are your and Nada's picture, I kiss you and an inner voice whispers: after my tragedy, happiness and God's blessing will follow you. Be joyous, and time will heal this difficult wound.

My dear, I know life and I forsee that you will walk bravely through it, that you will pass thorny paths on which you will face obstacles. But love, if the path is too thorny so that it would not suit you to manoeuvre it alone, my dear, find a friend who will understand you as I've understood you, and join forces in life with him. I forgive you! You deserve to be happy. Forgive me dear, if these thoughts and words insult you. A great and unusual love resonates in them. You understand me ...

Veljko left his guards some money for them to have a drink in his memory. A priest, a friend from Priboj who was also in prison with Veljko in Sarajevo later wrote to Jovanka to describe her husband's courage:

As he was being given last rites on the platform, alongside Danilo Ilic and his old friend Misko Jovanovic, Veljko asked the priest to tell his wife and daughter that he was thinking of them at the end. He was very cooperative with the executioner and, when ordered to take off his coat also removed his collar and tie so that it would be easier to fit the noose. He was smiling the whole time and as the noose went on, he said: 'Long live the Serbian people! Long live the Serbian army! Long live King Petar!'

Another priest who was there painted a picture of a bright winter's morning with the snow-capped peaks of the mountains around them clearly visible. There was a platoon of soldiers with fixed bayonets on their rifles on parade in the courtyard of the military prison where the scaffold had been built. They were led by an officer in white gloves who ordered the drum roll to start as soon as the three men reached the scaffold. The executioner himself, an Austrian, Alois Seifried, also left an account, saying that the men's chains had been removed in their cells and they walked unaided to the gallows led by the priest reciting prayers. They were composed and fully aware of what was going on and listened quietly as the verdict was read. Then the first one stepped forward. This was Veljko, says the executioner, but he describes him as short, and Veljko was actually rather tall so this point is confusing.

But then it must have been Veljko as the executioner said that he had offered to help him unbutton his shirt and loosen his tie, because Veljko was fumbling with his fingers, and Veljko had calmly said, 'I'll do it.' The second man – Misko – was calm and the third man, Danilo Ilic who, according to the executioner, had the greatest guilt on his soul was serene.

One of them, the executioner could not afterwards remember which one, said, 'please don't torment me for long' and the executioner had said, 'don't worry I am a master in my trade it will all be over in a second.'

The executioner recalled hearing their shouts. 'I heard that better than anyone else because the drums were rolling all the time. They expressed themselves very strongly against Austria. As an Austrian loyal to my own sovereign I can assure you that I never met such brave, calm delinquents in all my experience.'

According to Vaso, both Misko Jovanovic and his brother Veljko refused to say goodbye to Ilic on the scaffold, apparently blaming him for the betrayal that led to their arrest and execution.

'I don't blame nor do I support the fact that the late Veljko and Misko did not wish to say farewell to him before their deaths,' wrote Vaso, 'because I know from my own experience that there are moments in life that require the utmost energy of the soul to remain in balance.'

Telegram, Sarajevo to Vienna, signed Chief, Administration, No. 1439: 'Trial sentence against Veljko Cubrilovic, Misko Jovanovic and Danilo Ilic executed today between 9 and 10am without incident.'

Veljko's last letters to his family were not given to Jovanka but sent to the district judge, Dr Josip Horvat, at the town were Jovanka was living, Bosanska Gradiska. The judge read the letters and wrote back to the higher court in Sarajevo proposing that they should be destroyed. 'It would be a sorry state of affairs if the authorities of our monarchy

were to allow a child in a crib [Nada] to be told that a man who committed the crime of grand treason and who was subsequently hanged,
that such a man was leaving an "untarnished name".'

In Sarajevo the court spent some time analysing the letters before
reaching the conclusion that Judge Horvat was right. In the meantime
a court clerk had copied the letters and retained the copies when the
originals were destroyed. They were passed to the director of a bank
in Sarajevo who gave them to Vaso after the war, who passed them to
Jovanka.

The Austrians' intentions were constantly being subverted. They
proposed burying the bodies of the three hanged men secretly so that
their graves could not become a point of pilgrimage like the grave of
Zerajic. As the chief of police wrote: 'their graves will be decorated
with flowers every night as if they were martyrs and heroes.'

Burial took place during the night of the following day, 3 February.
No one knew where until some time later when an artist was walking
around the suburbs of the city looking for locations from which to
paint landscapes. A village peasant told him how one of his sons had
watched some city policemen on the night of 3 February 1915 as they
dug graves below the mill where he was standing. After the policemen
had gone the villagers had put fresh basil and flowers on the grave.

The artist was actually a professor at the Teachers' College. He had
taught painting to Danilo Ilic so knew all about him and immediately
guessed it was his grave, the grave of all three hanged men, that the
peasant's son had watched being dug. He told the authorities after the
war and the bodies were recovered and reburied in the cemetery in
Sarajevo where they were eventually reunited at the memorial for all
the conspirators and their helpers.

When I met her in Belgrade in the autumn of 2006 Nada, who was
then aged 93, told me some family members had visited the Sarajevo
cemetery quite recently and had been disappointed to find the memorial to her father and his fellow plotters looking run down and uncared
for, the ground around it strewn with empty alcohol bottles and other
rubbish. It was a sign of the times – Sarajevo was now a predominantly
Muslim city. No one cared about – and many would have been openly
hostile to – the Serb Orthodox cemetery of St Mark.

Nada had indeed been given the letter on her fifteenth birthday, in September 1928. Her mother had never exactly hidden the story of Veljko's life from Nada, but had only become more open about it as Nada became older and could comprehend the meaning of her father's death. Nada had never felt angry or disappointed with her father for leaving her, she told me. He was a Yugoslav hero and both his wife and his daughter had been immeasurably proud of him.

Jovanka had dressed in mourning clothes for many years after her husband's death, wearing a black dress and black coat even when she returned to teaching. It seemed to Nada that this had continued for the duration of her childhood. Jovanka had never remarried. She had been a feminist, said Nada, and had always spoken of Veljko as a tender, ideal husband. Nada said she was proud that her parents had both been freedom fighters and that Jovanka had remained a fighter all her life, always driven by the ideals of her youth which she had shared with Veljko.

They had lived in Belgrade later where Nada had studied law and met and married a lawyer and had two daughters of her own, one now an architect in Paris and the other a professor of mathematics in Belgrade. The daughter in Paris had two daughters of her own. The daughter in Belgrade had one son and had named him Veljko, after his great-grandfather.

There was a family gathering every year on 2 February to remember the execution. Nada would light a candle in memory of her father's sacrifice and special food would be cooked, roasted meats or pies, as part of the celebration. On that day they could recall Veljko's words in court, when he told the judges he had married for love and been happy.

23

A Living Corpse

In 1941, Croatian fascists were fighting Serbian troops in Bosnia and wreaked havoc in the small town of Priboj where they burned down the teachers' cottage that nearly 30 years earlier had been the home of Veljko and Jovanka Cubrilovic and their newborn daughter Nada.

In that same year, the Nazis set out to make a 'model' concentration camp in Czechoslovakia, a propaganda exercise in which they could show they had created a town for the Jews, at Theresienstadt, north of Prague, also known as Terezin. They dressed it up for both a documentary film of their own making and then a visit from the International Red Cross, who failed to notice its true, murderous intent. On the arched entrance to this town was the slogan 'Arbeit macht frei' – 'work will set you free' – which the Nazis posted at numerous other camps in their empire of death.

Terezin had a small and a large fortress. The small fortress had been used as a prison and the large fortress as a garrison town for a few thousand people. After 1941 it became a ghetto for Jews from Czechoslovakia and all over Europe. It is thought that up to 200,000 passed through there, many on their way to death camps further east. As many as 60,000 people were kept here at any one time in sub-human conditions of overcrowding, illness and starvation. It was not a death camp, in the sense that people were not systematically exterminated there. Still some 35,000 died, their corpses efficiently cremated in ovens.

Terezin is now known in the Czech Republic as the National Suffering Memorial to commemorate all the Czech victims of the Nazis during the second world war. Visitors are often surprised to discover Terezin's earlier notoriety, as the place where Gavrilo

Princip and some of his fellow conspirators were imprisoned in the small fortress. You can still see the bare rooms where Princip was kept, and imagine the scratched verse on the wall where he inscribed these words: 'Our ghost will walk through Vienna, and roam through the palace, frightening the Lords.'

The two fortresses had originally been constructed in the eighteenth century to repel invaders, their outer walls over four feet thick. But they had never been used for their intended purpose and, instead of keeping people out, and had been co-opted to hold prisoners in cells built into the walls.

Gavro, Nedjo and Grabez had been the first of the conspirators to arrive there, in December 1914, after an eight-day journey overland by train which, according to Vaso, was so harsh they had nearly died of starvation. They were kept in a special prison coach, with blinds drawn, each of them chained to their seats.

They passed through Vienna en route to Bohemia (the former name for the Czech Republic) where they had to change trains and were confronted by a large crowd held back by police and troops as they bayed for the three young men to be lynched and shot.

One of the guards on the journey claimed afterwards he had told them of recent Austrian successes in the war against Serbia and Gravo had said, 'Serbia may be invaded but not conquered; Serbia will one day create Yugoslavia, mother of all south Slavs.' The guard asked Gavro if he was sorry he was going to leave his bones in jail. Gavro waved his hand dismissively. He had counted on that, he said. But why had he killed a woman, the Duchess? His answer, according to the guard, was that he had no wish to kill a mother, it just happened. A bullet does not go precisely where one wishes and they were sitting close to each other. 'It was the Archduke's mistake for he wanted to subjugate and destroy the whole of our people and all Slavs.'

The trio were joined at Terezin by Lazar Djukic – the leader of the young group of Young Bosnians – Ivo Kranjcevic who had taken Vaso's weapons after the shooting and Cvijan Stjepanovic, the driver of the cart to Tuzla.

Kranjcevic and Stjepanovic were the only ones who got out alive, eventually rejoining Vaso and Popovic in Zenica. The officers who escorted them were subsequently put on trial to face allegations that they had fraternized with the prisoners during the journey. Stjepanovic's brother was in the Austrian army medical corps and at an earlier stage put in a request for transfer to Terezin to care for his sibling.

Djukic suffered a psychosis of some form, believing he was being poisoned and talking nonsensically, which was just as well as he started to claim he knew of an old plot to assassinate the emperor and the authorities took this seriously for a while and Kranjcevic was summoned to a confrontation with Djukic where he denied all knowledge of the plot (which in fact he had been involved in). Apparently, Djukic looked like skin and bones by now and had a festering wound in his right eye which, Kranjcevic said, made him painful to look at.

Djukic was sent to a psychiatric ward in Prague where he died in May 1917 (according to Vaso, or March 1917 according to Dedijer). He was buried secretly and his grave has never been found.

There was an inspection of Theresienstadt, in early 1917, following 37 deaths among inmates at the prison during the previous year. The inspection counted 866 prisoners, of which 21 were ill and 24 were in the prison hospital.

Although there was no evidence of informal cruelty or abuse at Terezin and the rules were strictly followed, those rules were so unforgiving that it was no wonder the prisoners suffered. There were extra rules for the political prisoners from Sarajevo, so that when the other inmates had their chains removed because the food rations were depleted by the war, the young Sarajevo plotters remained in their chains. The rules stated that the shackles should weigh at least ten kilograms, or 22 pounds.

Kranjcevic explained how they caused him to contract rheumatism. 'The first winter I left my shackles outside my bed. The chain thus sucked the warmth from my body, and in the morning I was frozen stiff and had great difficulty standing up ... The second winter I realized that I should bring the chain into bed and warm it with my hands, so that it remained warm all night and did not lead my heat away. But I realized this rather late ...'

By the winter of 1916 Trifko Grabez was also facing a drastic decline in his health. According to Vaso he had been taken to hospital complaining of stomach pains but was returned to his cell and died the following morning. His cause of death was never discovered or disclosed and Vaso believed Grabez had killed himself, as he had tried to commit suicide once before, while they were still held at the military prison in Sarajevo.

A significant proportion of the plotters expressed suicidal thoughts or even actions. They may, of course, have simply been trying to regain control of their fate, take control away from the Austrians and live out their intentions to become suicide martyrs. Perhaps too, as the Great War intensified and losses in tens and hundreds of thousands were reported, the plotters were overwhelmed by the enormity of their act and its effect on the world. Killers, or politicians who perpetrate acts that lead to deaths, are often said to have blood on their hands, as if it might easily wash off. Here, by now, these young men were drowning in oceans of blood.

Kranjcevic saw Grabez on the eve of his death and found him weak and exhausted, unable to eat or sit up or stand. Kranjcevic tried to reassure Grabez that he didn't look so bad and told him they had both suffered from stomach troubles and hopefully they would meet again, if they could find a friendly guard who might allow it. 'But next morning Grabez was found dead in his cell.' According to Kranjcevic he died from general exhaustion and chronic starvation.

The prisoners were not allowed visitors. There was a report that the brother of one of them had travelled from his home in Bosnia to try and see his sibling at Terezin, but had been refused and sent home again. The brother was unidentified but it could well have been Gavro's brother Jovo, from the Bosnian town of Hadzici.

The family of Nedjo Cabrinovic were preoccupied with their own misery. His father Vaso had been arrested and the rest of the family expelled from Sarajevo, both their home and the restaurant attacked and ransacked by anti-Serb rioters.

Nedjo's surviving niece Ranka, seemingly one of the last Serbs still living in Sarajevo by 2006, told me how Nedjo's mother gathered everyone together and took them by train to Trebinje, the home of her husband's brother and his two sons. Nedjo's father had looked after the sons and seen to their education in Sarajevo, where one had become a butcher, so it was reasonable to assume the Trebinje Cabrinovices would not turn them away. But when the mother knocked on the door with her children Vaso's brother shut the door in her face, according to Ranka, saying they could no longer have anything to do with them.

The Trebinje Cabrinovices changed their name to escape the notoriety of association with Nedjo and were ever after known as the Listic family. Ranka was told they acted that way because their butcher's business had just won an Austrian army contract to supply the local barracks with meat.

The mother went back to the station and was sitting there trying to decide where to go next when a friend of her husband's appeared. He took them in for three months until the police came, when they were all removed to an internment camp where some of the children contracted dysentery and were taken away; the family was broken up and never happily reunited.

Nedjo's mother died during the Great War and his father Vaso later returned to Sarajevo and remarried but was unhappy and embittered and used to drink and talk of suicide. There was some suggestion he had actually tried to kill himself, but when a report of this appeared in a newspaper, Nedjo's sister Vukosava wrote in to deny it.

Vaso Cabrinovic died in 1938, in his mid-seventies. His second wife had not been kind to the children and they dispersed following their father's death, though all of them, said Ranka, remained proud of Nedjo, despite the suffering his actions had caused. Ranka's father Dusan was the youngest of the Cabrinovic children, only four years old at the time of the assassination. He lived in Sarajevo until his death in the mid-1990s. Not long before he died he was wounded by a Serb shell which penetrated his apartment and injured his foot.

None of them had ever seen Nedjo again, after his arrest, but Vukosava did later receive second-hand information from a young Austrian soldier, Franz Werfel, who had seen her brother in late 1915 while on duty at Terezin. Werfel had been invited by his corporal to 'see something' on the closed ward of Hospital Number 13 in the fortress town. That something was Nedjo who was in the hospital suffering from advanced tuberculosis, his lymph glands swollen and his overall condition so pitiful that he could not keep his legs from shaking while he was sitting. He had been destroyed by cold, hunger and isolation.

Werfel was apparently horrified that Nedjo had just been pronounced fit enough to return to his cell and continue his sentence as to Werfel the truth was the opposite. He noted the appalling joke that the doctors believed Nedjo posed a danger of escape. In fact, it appears that the doctors had concluded his condition was incurable and there was nothing more they could do for him.

In an article published in 1924, Werfel wrote, 'I now detect a white, indescribably ethereal form clinging with a phosphorescent hand to the iron bedstead. It seems to be clothed in spectral white linen wound tightly around it. But it does not give the impression of a shrouded skeleton – no, of a tremulous, pale vision, an insubstantial, hovering vapour in the air – as if a disembodied spirit was about to dissipate in the unnatural yellow luminescence that filled the room.

'Chabrinovitch, supporting his hand upon the bed, made motions with his feet like those of a man trying to step into his slippers standing up. His emaciated knees touched each other. His limbs trembled violently as in some nervous crisis.'

It seemed to Werfel that Nedjo offered a striking contrast to his guards who were rude and aggressive where Nedjo was elegant and gentle; a tragic figure almost saintly in his martyrdom. Werfel could not forget that Nedjo was just 20 years old and wondered whether the assassins were really murderers.

In addition to the article, Werfel wrote a letter to Vukosava, Nedjo's sister, describing the meeting in the same sympathetic terms. Werfel was Jewish, born in Bohemia, and later faced charges of high treason himself because of his outspoken support for pacifism. He met and fell in love with the widow of the composer Gustav Mahler, who divorced her second husband to be with Werfel. They were living in Austria at the time of the Anschluss in 1938, when Austria was annexed to Nazi Germany (just as Austria had annexed Bosnia 30 years earlier). Werfel moved to California where he died in 1945 after a long career as a writer.

Nedjo lay in his cell for a few more weeks and died on 27 January 1916. The police authorities in Sarajevo later wrote asking for Nedjo's body to be exhumed and the skull removed and sent to them. It would have joined the skull of the martyr Zerajic, which was in the possession of the Sarajevo chief of detectives who occasionally used it as an inkpot or as an instrument of psychological terror during interrogation. The Austrians had been interested in the theory that criminals could be recognized by the malformed shapes of their heads. In Nedjo's case the theory remained untested as permission to cut off his head was withheld and his body was intact when it was exhumed in 1920.

At the time of Nedjo's death Gavro was also becoming seriously ill and was still being held in chains, in solitary confinement, more than 18 months after his arrest. It must have been about this time that he had tried to take his own life, using a towel to hang himself. Perhaps Nedjo's death was the trigger for this attempted suicide.

This no doubt only increased the authorities' determination to keep him bound and isolated. He described the suicide attempt a few weeks later, on 19 February 1916 during the first of four visits from the psychiatrist Dr Martin Pappenheim who had been serving since the beginning of the war as an army physician. He had not long since been rotated out of combat at the Russian front to the garrison town of Leitmeritz in Bohemia, close to Terezin. Like many other medics with an interest in the burgeoning science of psychiatry he had taken a particular interest in cases of 'shellshock' and other 'abnormal' conditions he encountered.

By the time he met Gavro for the first time, Pappenheim had actually been working in Terezin for four months, so one wonders why he had not seen him earlier. There is no way of knowing. When I began my research there was next to no information in existence about Pappenheim.

He took sparing notes of his meetings with Gavro and apparently had no thought of publishing them himself until the 1920s when a Vienna-based journalist introduced him to Ratko Parezanin, a Young Bosnian survivor who was based in Vienna as a cultural attaché for the Yugoslav government.

According to Parezanin, Pappenheim's wife did not want him to publish the notes but he agreed and gave the original notes to Parezanin who transcribed them. They were published first in German and then in 1927 in the American journal, *Current History*, under the headline 'Confessions of the Assassin Whose Deed Led to the World War'. The text was said to be an exact copy of the notes Pappenheim had made.

I invested considerable effort in trying to trace Pappenheim's notes and some biographical information about him. He was the only person who had ever interviewed Gavrilo Princip and made a contemporaneous note of his own words.

Pappenheim had a daughter still living in New York. She was 96 on 22 May 2007. Else Pappenheim had also qualified in medicine and specialized in psychiatry. She was by now in poor health but her husband, Stephen Frishauf, a retired attorney, could speak to her and for her on the telephone and in email. 'Else has no idea why the interviews [with Princip] ended,' Stephen wrote crisply in one email, 'after all she was only six years old at the time.'

Pappenheim had been born in 1881 in Bratislava (as it is now called) and studied medicine in Vienna, specializing in psychiatry and neurology. His daughter Else had been born in Salzburg and her parents had divorced at the end of the war, while she was still a child. She had seen little of her father and, it was apparent, there was some disappointment at his absence from her life. But she could say with confidence that Pappenheim never spoke about his patients at home, prominent or not, so there was never any mention of his talks with Gavro.

After the war Pappenheim had been stricken by the influenza epidemic and was given a medical discharge to Vienna. He married the doctor who had treated him and set up private practice in Vienna as a psychiatrist, before becoming Professor of Neuro-Psychiatry at the Municipal Hospital in Lainz. He had also become active in politics as a Social Democrat until the mid-1930s when, while he was attending a conference overseas, his party was crushed by violent action from the opposition. He was warned not to return and went to live in Tel Aviv in what was then still Palestine, where he took a third partner and had a second surviving child (a third child, born to his second wife, died in infancy).

Pappenheim's papers, I established, were with him in Palestine but after his death in 1943-4 they were either destroyed or given away by his third partner. She died over 30 years ago and their daughter Nira died in the 1980s. His notes had disappeared and could not be traced. Else had only seen him once after he emigrated. Soon after, in 1938, she had emigrated in the opposite direction, to New York. As her husband Stephen wrote, Else's father had been 'a remote figure in Else's life; he left more bitter than pleasant memories in her'.

There is one existing photograph of Pappenheim, taken many years after his interviews with Gavro, a grainy image from Tel Aviv in which he is perched on a balcony rail and looks every inch the Viennese head-shrinker with his thick-rimmed, round glasses and his swept-back tufts of thinning hair.

He must have been a good and patient listener, catching his subject at vulnerable, lonely moments at the end of his brief life, as Gavro's uncompromising character, his troubled soul and, finally, his growing despair shine through these halting notes, as they flit back and forth between the first person and the third person.

The notes begin: 'Prison. 19 II 16 [the date of interview] 27 VII 1894 [Gavro's date of birth]. Here since 5 XII 1914. The whole time in solitary confinement. Three days ago, chains off. Father a peasant, but occupies himself with enterprises. Father a quiet man, does not drink. Father lives in Grahovo, Bosnia. No diseases in the family.'

If Gavro's chains had only been removed three days earlier, on 16 February 1916, he must have been permanently shackled for most if not all of the previous 19½ months, since his arrest. According to one account, he was chained by both hands to the wall of his darkened cell, where he could do nothing but sit and think or sleep.

Gavro outlined his past for Pappenheim, while still maintaining his typical reserve: 'Always "excellent student" up to the fifth class. Then fell in love. Began to have ideals … The love for the girl did not vanish but he never wrote her. Relates that he knew her in the fourth class; ideal love, never kissed; in this connection will reveal no more of himself.'

It was very hard in solitary confinement, he told Pappenheim, without books, with absolutely nothing to read and intercourse with nobody. He had always been accustomed to reading and was now suffering most from not having anything to read. He was sleeping only four hours a night and dreaming a great deal. They were beautiful dreams, not uneasy, about life and about love.

When he was awake he thought about everything, particularly about conditions in his own country: 'He had heard something about the war. He had heard a tragic thing, that Serbia no longer exists. His life is in general painful, now that Serbia no longer exists. It goes hard with my people.'

It was true that the Serbian army had been routed and forced to flee Serbian soil during a massed attack by over 400,000 troops from Bulgaria, Germany and Austria-Hungary. Still, over 100,000 troops had regrouped and would soon join the allied forces led by Britain and France as they pushed for victory, which would pave the way for the new kingdom of Yugoslavia, the fulfilment of Gavro's dream.

Gavro told Pappenhein that he believed the world war would have started anyway, irrespective of the assassination. He had acted as a man of ideals wanting to revenge his people. His motives were revenge and love. All the young men felt the same.

He admitted the suicide attempt a month ago, when he had tried to hang himself with a towel. It would be stupid to have hope, he said. He already had wounds on the breast and on his arm (Pappenheim called it a 'fungus'). A life like Pappenheim's seemed impossible to Gavro. At the time of the suicide attempt it was about midnight and he could not eat and was in bad spirits. 'And on a sudden came the idea to hang himself. If he had the opportunity he would do it.' Gavro thought of his parents and everyone from his old life, but heard nothing of them. He confessed longing but said such a longing must exist in everybody.

Prison Hospital, 12 V 1916 [the second interview, nearly three months after the first].

He recognizes me immediately and shows pleasure at seeing me. Since 7 IV here in hospital. Always nervous. Is hungry, does not get enough to eat. Loneliness. Gets no air and sun here; in the fortress took walks. He has no longer any hope for his life. There is nothing for him to hope for. Life is lost. In former days was a student, had ideals. Everything that was bound up with his ideals is all destroyed.

My Serbian people.

Hopes that something may turn for the better but is sceptical … Thought that if Austria were thrown into difficulties then a revolution would come. But for such a revolution one must prepare the ground, work up feeling. Nothing happened. By assassination this spirit might be prepared.

There already had been attempts at assassinations before. The perpetrators were like heroes to our young people. He had no thought of becoming a hero. He wanted merely to die for his idea. Before the assassination he had read an article of Kropotkin about what we can do in case of a worldwide social revolution. Studied, talked about it. Was convinced it was possible …

For two months now has heard nothing more of events. But it

is all indifferent to him, on account of his illness and the misfortune of his people. Has sacrificed his life for the people. Could not believe that such a World War could break out as a result of an act like his. They did indeed think such a World War might break out, but not at that moment.

Pappenheim gave Gavro a pen and some paper and invited him to write something about the social revolution. As he began to write Gavro said it was the first time in two years that he had held a pen in his hand: 'On a certain occasion we spoke among comrades on a question Kropotkin had put in Welfare For All – What will the anarchists do in case of a social revolution? We all took this more for a phrase of an old revolutionist than that he had seriously thought such a revolution possible at this time. But we nevertheless debated over this revolution and nearly all admitted that such a revolution was possible, but according to our conviction that previously in all Europe there must be created between peoples ...' Gavro stopped here, saying he was feeling ill. His thoughts were already (a word or phrase was missed here: 'confused', perhaps, or 'gone from his head'). He complained that he was feeling very nervous, presumably meaning anxious or agitated.

Pappenheim distracted Gavro with some questions, asking him if he believed the assassination had been a service. 'Cannot believe that the World War was a consequence of the assassination; cannot feel himself responsible for the catastrophe; therefore cannot say if it was a service. But fears he did it in vain ...'

He must have calmed down as he then resumed writing, adding a further 15 lines to the ten he had already written, continuing the theme of social change and nationalism. He stopped often to reflect and complained that the process was difficult. He was still writing 15 minutes later as the interview came to an end.

'18 V 1916' [the third interview, six days after the second].

'Wound worse, discharging very freely. Looking miserable. Suicide by any sure means is impossible. "Wait to the end." Resigned, but not really very sad.'

Pappenheim asked Gavro what he thought about, and he said that sometimes he was in a philosophical mood, sometimes poetical, sometimes quite prosaic. He thought about the human soul. What was the essential in human life, was it instinct or will, or spirit? What moves man?

Gavro said that many people who had spoken with him thought he was a child, that he must have been inspired by others. But this was only because he cannot express himself sufficiently and was not, he claimed, generally gifted as a talker. He had always been a reader, always alone, not usually engaging in debates.

He began a narrative of events leading up to the assassination, describing his friendship with Ilic, Cabrinovic and Grabez and how Ciganovic had come to be involved and Major Tankosic had not been told of the plot until the last moment when the conspirators were already mentally prepared.

During all this time, he said, he had still been able to read and study quietly and build a library of books. 'Books for me signify life,' he said and that was why it was so hard now, without them. If only he could have something to read for two or three days he could then think more clearly and express himself better. He did not speak to anybody for a month then, when Pappenheim came, he wanted to speak about ideas and about dominating thoughts.

'Now comprehends that a revolution especially in the military state of Austria is of no use. What he now thinks the right thing he would not say. Has no desire to speak on the matter. It makes him unquiet to speak about it. When he thinks by himself everything is clear, but when he speaks with anybody, then he becomes uncertain.'

The fourth and final interview took place on 5 June 1916. There were no first-person words of Gavro this time, just this brief note: 'When permission has come, arm is to be amputated. His usual resigned disposition.'

I would like to know why these interviews ended at this point, with such a terse sign-off. According to Pappenheim's daughter and son-in-law, Else and Stephen Frishauf, he remained at Leitmeritz near Terezin until late in the war when he contracted the flu and returned to Vienna. If he was still there, why did the visits stop? And why such a spare record of the fourth and final interview? Did Pappenheim say or do something that upset and/or alienated Gavro? Was he too ill to talk or was it that Pappenheim became ill or did the authorities terminate their meetings? There is no one left alive who can tell us and no record that might shed some light on these events of almost a century past.

Gavro had nearly two years to live – he was left behind at Terezin a year later when the other prisoners were returned to Zenica – and there is no reliable record that he had any other visitors, though he certainly spent some time in the company of doctors and others who were involved in his treatment.

An aide to the Archduke later wrote in his memoirs about a meeting with an Austrian army officer who claimed he had seen Gavro in prison and listened to his sobbing confession that he had been forced to carry out the assassination after being put into a 'fanatical state of intoxication' in which he believed that 'the elimination of the Austro-Hungarian successor to the throne would ease the oppression of the fatherland and free it from the yoke of subjugation'.

Others said this account could not be accurate because Gavro had remained unrepentant to the end and when challenged once by an Austrian army general had told him that the empire was doomed and would lose the war. Which was all in fact true.

These remarks were echoed by one of the doctors who treated him in the prison hospital, Dr Marsch who talked to Gavro and never heard him express any regret or desire for forgiveness. By the time the interviews with Pappenheim were ending, in the summer of 1916, Gavro was already a living corpse, according to Dr Marsch. His body was wasted to the bone and he had several tuberculosis ulcers as large as a hand. There was no doubt, in the doctor's mind, that Gavro had been carrying the disease before his arrest.

Tuberculosis is usually thought of as pulmonary, a disease of the lungs, but in fact it can spread into different areas of the body, including the bones and joints and the skin, as appears to have happened to Gavro, the disease eating away at his elbow joint and causing the outbreak of suppurating ulcers on his chest and elsewhere.

The doctor said that Gavro received the same treatment in hospital as any Austrian soldier might have received, except that he was treated as a dangerous prisoner who might escape, which the doctor said was entirely unnecessary as he could barely walk more than 200 metres. Still there was one soldier with a fixed bayonet in his room, two outside the door and two more walking back and forth outside the window.

Although he had been given strict orders not to talk to Gavro, the doctor did speak to him, noting the solemn earnestness on his face and how his eyes, sunken in their sockets, had lost the fire and brightness of youth, but flared briefly when Gavro spoke about the liberation of his people. He had grown a long beard over the two years in prison, but when it was shaved away the doctor saw an intelligent, young face full of expression. Still, the doctor could see that Gavro had given in to his inevitable fate; earthly life was finished for him and he anticipated his early end. Gavro spoke about his family and his 'short' life without ever mentioning The Black Hand or anyone in it.

'The slim frail body showed the typical tubercular appearance ... his chest was covered with tubercular ulcers of hand size and full of pus. The disease had destroyed the elbow joint of his left arm to such an extent that the lower part of this limb had to be connected with the upper part by a silver wire. Why the doctors were forbidden to amputate the lower part of the arm, which had become completely useless, I am unable to explain to this day.'

Gavro routinely went every 48 hours for his wounds to be re-dressed. His wounds were so extensive that the whole of his upper torso had to be covered, using more bandages than would serve five soldiers.

He was apparently shown some kindness by a Jewish doctor who was actually an inmate after being sentenced for issuing false health certificates to help Czechs avoid military service. The doctor would bring Gavro a piece of chocolate or something similar which he had received from home. But kindness ended when the doctor killed himself, after hearing that his fiancé had died.

The prison guards were predominantly Czech and many of them also came to admire Gavro and treat him with some sympathy and consideration, especially keeping him informed of the changing pace of events as the Great War entered its final phase.

Gavro's arm was eventually amputated, but this can have done little or nothing to alleviate the misery of his final months, which must have seemed like an eternity in the midst of all that suffering and isolation.

According to the records, Gavro died of tuberculosis of the bones at 6.30am on 28 April 1918 in room 33 of Hospital Number 13. He was three months short of his 24th birthday.

The prison authorities ordered five prison guards to take Gavro's body that night to a nearby Catholic cemetery for secret burial. The guards were led by the deputy commander of the Terezin garrison, a young Czech officer, Frantisek Lebl. He had overseen the earlier burials of Nedjo and Grabez, in unmarked plots at the same cemetery. Lebl had secretly noted the locations.

When he arrived with Gavro's coffin he found that Gavro would be sharing the plot with a young delinquent who had died. And, in a further calculated insult, the grave had been dug already in the middle of the path where he would be forever trampled on by visitors. They lowered the coffin into the hole and replaced the earth. That night Lebl made a sketch of the cemetery, marking the site of the grave. He sent the map to his father, in case he should be returned to the front and killed. But he survived the war and went straight to the cemetery where he placed a Czech flag on Gavro's grave.

24

The Terrorist – the Hero

The first memorial to the assassination was raised in honour of the Archduke and the Duchess. It was a tall monument, rising 14 metres into the air, and was put up in 1917 by the Austrians, on the corner of Appel Quay and the Latin Bridge, just across the road from the scene of the assassination.

The monument did not last long. It was pulled down two years later, in 1919, after the end of the Great War, when Bosnia was no longer an annexe of the Austrian empire (indeed, there was no longer an empire to be annexed to) but was instead integrated into the new Kingdom of Serbs, Croats and Slovenes. It was not until 1929 that the country was formally renamed Yugoslavia (Land of the South Slavs), after King Alexander had dissolved parliament and proclaimed a Royal Dictatorship.

This arrangement only served to alienate the Croats, sowing the seeds for discontent and violence in the future decades. It led directly to the launch of an underground Croat organization with fascist leanings, Utasa. They were implicated in the assassination of the Yugoslav King Alexander in 1934. His brother Paul became Prince Regent.

While the royal dictatorship pursued repressive measures to keep its kingdom together, the Communist party was growing in influence, with the Soviet Union both a useful model for its unifying capabilities, and an important means of support.

Josip Broz, who adopted the nickname Tito, had been an early member of the Russian Communist party and emerged as a new leader of the Yugoslav Communists in 1939. He called for armed resistance in 1941 when the Prince Regent Paul decided to align the country with the Nazis. The Prince was deposed by a combined military-

Communist action so the Nazis invaded, after bombing Belgrade, and the capital was soon occupied by German troops.

The country was chopped up and divided among the Nazis and their allies, the Italians, the Bulgarians and the Utasa fascists who took charge of a combined state of Croatia and Bosnia & Hercegovina, pursuing a genocidal policy of racial purification, during which around 750,000 Serbs, Jews and Roma were exterminated.

Yugoslav resistance came from two fronts – the Chetniks who supported the royal family of the new King Petar, now in exile in London and the Partisans, who were the Communists, led by Tito. Later in the war the Partisans were supported by the Soviet Red Army and by the British. They had regained control of the country by 1945, after the deaths of over one and a half million Yugoslav people.

The Communists won elections in 1945 and created a socialist federation of Yugoslav states, comprising Serbia, Croatia, Bosnia-Hercegovina, Macedonia, Slovania and Montenegro. Kosovo, in the south of Serbia, became an autonomous region of the state of Serbia.

Tito severed links with the Soviet Union in the late 1940s, as he disapproved of Stalin's hard-line tactics. Though Tito practised his own repressive measures his was generally regarded as a more benign version of state socialism, his great achievement being to combine the diverse states and ethnic groups in a long period of relative stability and prosperity.

Hoping to avoid a future dictatorship, Tito prepared for his death by establishing a power-sharing model, where the presidency would revolve annually from one state to the next but after his death in 1980 there was a gradual decline into regional tensions, with increasing debt from international loans, high unemployment and growing inflation. Western tourism was the only significant benefit during the eighties. The Croats were fed up with Serb dominance in the federation, Slovenia wanted economic independence, and there were difficulties in Kosovo where the Albanian majority wanted full independence, not just autonomy within the state.

Fighting began modestly with a brief battle of independence fought and won by the Slovenians in 1991. Croatia soon followed but here there were echoes of the old Utasa, with the emergence of a new right-wing nationalist movement that wanted to sweep the Serbs from the country. Even a UN peacekeeping force could not protect the

200,000 Serbs who had been burned out of their homes or fled in fear to Serbia by 1995.

There was an even greater conflict in Bosnia & Hercegovina with its more or less balanced population of Catholic Croats, Serbs and Bosniak Muslims. The Catholics and the Muslims wanted to leave the control of Belgrade while the Serbs wanted to remain. There was three-way fighting in this region – including the siege of Sarajevo – for three years from 1992 until the Dayton Peace Accord of 1995. The agreement enshrined the division of the region along ethnic lines, with the autonomous Serb region of Republika Srpska on the one side, and the remaining territory of Bosnia & Hercegovina, now dominated by Bosniak Muslims, while allowing for a joint assembly shared by Croats, Bosniaks and Serbs.

Shortly before the agreement was made, in July 1995 some 8,000 Bosniaks were killed by Srpska army soldiers in the town of Srebrenica, even though it had been designated a United Nations safe area. The killings were said to be the biggest single act of murder since the second world war. Altogether some 100,000 people of all ethnic groups died during fighting in Bosnia & Hercegovina. In addition some half-million non-Serbs were said to have been forced to leave their homes in Republika Srpska, as part of the widespread 'ethnic cleansing' that went on.

Footage of the massacre at Srebrenica was played in court when four former Serb soldiers were convicted, in April 2007, of taking part in the killings. They were tried by the war crimes tribunal set up by the United Nations in The Hague, Holland, to prosecute cases arising from the conflict in the former Yugoslavia.

The biggest single defendant at The Hague had been the former Yugoslav president Slobodan Milosevic who faced 66 counts of war crimes, including overseeing acts of murder and violence in Bosnia. The main charges against him related to Kosovo, the autonomous region in what was left of Yugoslavia by the late 1990s. He had sent in troops to stop an uprising led by the Kosovo Liberation Army, which was fighting for independence on behalf of the Kosovo Albanians.

Milosevic refused to withdraw his troops, despite international pressure, and when he boycotted peace talks in Paris in March 1999, the allied forces of NATO launched airstrikes on Belgrade. The bombing went on until June when Milosevic finally accepted a peace plan.

His troops left as Russian peacekeeping troops went in to Kosovo, followed soon after by NATO forces.

Milosevic was arrested in 2001, after standing down from the presidency in the face of mass demonstrations against him on the streets of Belgrade. His trial began in February 2002 and was still going four years later in March 2006, when he was found dead in his cell.

Milosevic and other Serb leaders accused of war crimes, such as Radovan Karadzic, the former president of Republika Srpska and Ratko Mladic, who had commanded the Bosnian Serb Army, were characterized as ultra-nationalists only interested in the welfare and prospects of the Serbs and brutally, sometimes savagely indifferent to the lives of others from the wider ethnic communities. At the time of writing Mladic is still a fugitive, but Karadzic was arrested in Belgrade in July 2008 and now faces a war crimes tribunal at the Hague.

Where perhaps Gavrilo and the others in 1914 had stood for equality and freedom from oppression, the late-twentieth-century Serb leaders stood for ethnic superiority and repression. No doubt, the reasons are complex as Dr Antonic with his books about the genocidal conduct of the Croat fascists during world war two could testify.

As their heroic songs and poetry suggested, the Serbs had known defeat and subjugation for 500 years and more since that June day in 1389 on Kosovo Fields. For a brief moment in history, from the 1950s until his death in 1980, Tito's Yugoslavia, the unified federation of socialist states, had been the nation's triumph, the embodiment of the dreams of the Sarajevo conspirators.

Gavro, I think, would have been proud of that achievement, just as Yugoslavia, in those days, was proud of Gavro. The first memorial to his actions was unveiled in a ceremony on 2 February 1930 on the wall of the delicatessen, above the spot where he had stood and fired. The black marble plaque was mounted high on the wall: 'Here in this historic place, on St Vitus Day, the 28th of June, 1914, Gavrilo Princip proclaimed freedom.'

It was a religious ceremony presided over by the Orthodox Archbishop in the presence of relatives of Veljko, Misko and Grabez. The secretary of Narodna Odbrana called to the crowd to sing hymns to the 'hero' Princip.

Vaso Cubrilovic observed to the writer Luigi Albertini that, 'the

Serbs carry on a hero-cult and today with the name Milos Obilic they bracket that of Gavrilo Princip: the former stands for Serb heroism in the tragedy of Kosovo Polje, the latter for Serb heroism in the final liberation.' Songs and poems were written about Gavro, just as they had been about Obilic. The Latin Bridge had been renamed the Princip Bridge. Later in 1930 a road in Theresienstadt was renamed Principova Aley, in his memory.

Many people in Europe, especially those of the old empires, were offended by the tone of the plaque on the wall and the general mood of celebration, the cult of heroism, that went with it. Winston Churchill wrote in his book *The Unknown War: The Eastern Front* that, 'Princip died in prison, and a monument erected in recent years by his fellow-countrymen records his infamy and their own.'

For Churchill, and many others, Gavro was not so much a freedom fighter as a terrorist who had resorted to a terrible act of violence, the killing of two people, one of them a woman – the mother of three young children – in pursuit of his political aims.

Later still, a set of footprints was cemented into the pavement beneath the plaque. They had no historical significance in the sense that no one could say precisely where Gavro had been standing or in what position his feet had been, but they served as a further tribute to his act.

In the 1950s the old delicatessen was opened as a Young Bosnian museum with displays of artefacts and old photographs, centred around Gavro. The museum remained there until the beginning of the war in 1992 when it immediately closed and many of the exhibits were placed in a container in storage for safekeeping.

I was told it was a common habit for the besieged citizens of Sarajevo to spit at the footprints or the plaque, or both, as they walked past, during the years of war in the mid-1990s. The footprints were hacked at too and were eventually removed and have since been re-made. The original marble plaque seems to have disappeared. There is a story that it too was hacked out and tossed into the Miljacka, but I could find no evidence for this. The fate of the plaque may be a Sarajevan urban myth.

The long-standing curator, Bajro Gec, died in 2006 not long before the museum was due to reopen. His successor, Mirsad Avdic, had restructured the museum to tell the broader story of Sarajevo under

Austrian rule, so that it was no longer simply a celebration of the assassination, and not so insensitive to the current population.

Avdic had lost track of some of the exhibits, in the chaos that was the legacy of the siege and the fighting. He was unaware of some letters from the conspirators which I had read about as being part of the original collection. He had a pair of trousers which Gavro had supposedly worn to school and a bag, which was alleged to have been Gavro's too. He was not sure about the bag as there was no provenance.

Once the war started, he said, the museum staff had been ordered to guard the building and the exhibits. The building had never taken a direct hit from the endless shelling, though the glass windows had been blown out. Just walking in the street outside the building had been hazardous in those years so packing up the exhibits and removing them had been an act of bravery by his predecessors. Even so, in reviewing the material, Avdic had realized what a poor collection it was. He said he had looked everywhere – if he'd found so much as a recipe Gavro once wrote out he would have included it.

He said that even immediately after the Great War, Gavro had not been celebrated by the new kingdom of Yugoslavia. There was no wish then to glorify an act of terrorism, not until later. But even then, the assassination had always been kept in Sarajevo and never taken to the centre, to Belgrade and celebrated there. In Avdic's view Gavro had never become a national hero.

This had changed to some extent after the Communists came to power and he could be seen as a symbol of revolutionary drive, an icon of liberation. The assassination was constantly being re-evaluated. The act was reviled by the Austrians, ignored at first by the Serbian kingdom after the Great War, then came the plaque, the footprints, the renaming of the bridge for Princip, the opening of the museum of Young Bosnia, the lionizing of Gavro by the Communists.

Then the break-up of Yugoslavia, the descent into ethnic conflict, Gavro once again condemned as a Serb terrorist. The museum closed, the footprints and the plaque disappeared or destroyed, the bridge renamed as the Latin Bridge.

A new plaque has gone up since the war, a very neutrally worded affair, in English and Serbian, 'From this place on 28 June 1914 Gavrilo Princip assassinated the heir to the Austro-Hungarian throne Franz

Ferdinand and his wife Sofia.' Now the museum had reopened, albeit in a different guise, and Gavro's reputation is shifting once more.

But, as Avdic said, any revival around Gavro would always be problematic as non-Serbs simply couldn't identify with him. According to Avdic he was not a pan-Yugoslavian, he was a Serb. I thought Gavro would have been disappointed to hear Avdic say that. After all, Gavro had believed in a unified south Slav state and all of Bosnia had suffered under the Austrians so all of Bosnia had stood to benefit from the assassination.

Still, when we walked across the 'Latin' Bridge to the long row of taxis on the cab rank and began to ask them to take us to the Princip memorial at the Orthodox cemetery, it was soon apparent that the Bosniak majority had no time for and little interest in Gavro. From their blank looks and some overt expressions of hostility it was apparent that the wounds of the recent war were still raw and would not be forgotten anytime soon.

An earlier writer describing a visit to the museum some 20 years ago had reported seeing Gavro's mother's black apron and her working tools in one corner of the display. Avdic no longer had these items, but he did remember hearing how Gavro's mother had died just before the second world war. She was said to have lived her last years in extremes of poverty and had been seen begging in the community around her former home in Grahovo. There could be no doubt, if this was true, that it was a direct result of her son's actions.

Princip was lucky he had not lived to hear this. It is hard to imagine he would have thought his mother's misery an acceptable sacrifice.

25

Serial Numbers

In Austria, even now, the Archduke's life is celebrated, his death mourned, his killers regarded as terrorists and puppets of the Serbian government.

The Graf and Stift car in which the Archduke and the Duchess were travelling is the centrepiece of the exhibition devoted to the assassination at the museum of military history, the Heeresgeschichtliches, in Vienna. There too is his bloodstained jacket, the chaise longue on which he was laid after he had expired and many other artefacts and photographs.

The museum had a stroke of luck in 2004 when it was approached by the Viennese Jesuits with a remarkable offer. It transpired that the four guns carried by the conspirators, including the gun Gavro had used to shoot the royal couple, had been in the Jesuits' possession more or less since the assassination. How widely it was known the Jesuits had the guns is not entirely clear. As I've mentioned before, the Jesuits did not wish to talk to me.

It appears that Father Anton Puntigam had been given the guns after the assassination in 1914 by the newly orphaned Hohenberg children, along with some other artefacts. Perhaps the children, or their representatives, appreciated Puntigam's role with their parents, especially Sophie, who had been interested in an orphanage in Sarajevo, which had also involved Puntigam. Then too, it seems that the children had considered the guns to be macabre objects which they had no interest in keeping for themselves.

So Puntigam had taken the guns and other items on the understanding that he would somehow use them to promote or create a memorial to the royal couple. The other items included some bullets, the bloodstained shirt the Archduke had been wearing beneath his jacket, the dried posy of flowers the Duchess had been carrying, tucked into the belt at her waist and also fragments of her gloves and her shoes. Apparently, in an Austrian tradition, the Duchess's gloves and shoes had been cut up after her death and distributed among her ladies-in-waiting and others, as souvenirs.

According to the director of the military museum in Vienna, Dr Christian Ortner, Father Puntigam had gone around for a while giving talks about the Archduke and the Duchess at which he would brandish the guns and other items. Perhaps because they had considered this bad taste, the Hohenbergs had asked him to stop and, thereafter, following his return to Vienna, the guns and other items were kept in a store at the Jesuits' Vienna headquarters.

They had not been stored very well. The guns were so rusty when Dr Ortner first saw them that he could tell they had not been kept oiled and might even have been stored in damp cloth. The Jesuits had also become concerned about the deterioration of the bloody shirt as blood, apparently, does not store well in normal storeroom conditions.

The Jesuits were not ready to give up ownership altogether of the weapons but were willing to offer them to the museum on permanent loan. The current generation of Hohenbergs also gave their permission. Dr Ortner knew that, even now, the Hohenbergs did not like drawing salacious or sensational attention to the death of their grandparents.

When the chaise longue had come up for auction, from a private collection, in the mid-1990s there was a risk of it being bought by bidders in Britain or the United States. Everyone involved had agreed it ought to remain in Austria so a ban had been imposed on its sale outside the country, but still a substantial sum was needed to prevent it going to a private collector. The museum had been contacted by several noble families who wanted to stop the chaise longue going abroad and, in the end, it was these families, not the Hohenbergs who provided the funds the museum used to win the bid.

The museum had recently been challenged over its ownership of the Graf and Stift car. The car had belonged to Count Harrach and his descendants had asked for it back. But Harrach had wanted nothing to do with the car after the killings, and had given it to the emperor, Franz Josef, who had offered it as a gift to the military museum. There was paperwork to prove the chain so the Harrach family's action failed in court.

The guns were handed over in a ceremony at the museum in 2004. Dr Ortner immediately suspected that one was a fake. He did not tell the Jesuits, but examined the fourth gun carefully and realized that one of the five digits on the serial number had been changed. There was no doubt in Ortner's mind that, at some point in the previous 90 years, someone had switched the pistol, under the Jesuits' noses, so to speak, substituting a fake and stealing the real one for themselves. Not used to looking at the guns, the Jesuits had continued to count four and been satisfied. As Ortner said, the 9mm Browning pistol was a common enough weapon widely used by the Serbian military.

There was some publicity following the handing-over ceremony, and though Ortner had not told anyone, not even the Jesuits, about the substituted gun, he had a call from a lawyer who claimed to represent the man in possession of the weapon that had killed the Archduke. Ortner thought this might solve the mystery and was keen to see the gun for himself. The lawyer brought it to the museum and when Ortner examined it he saw that here too an extra zero had been added into the number sequence. This made the number match the missing weapon, but it was clear another number underneath had been erased to make room for the zero. Ortner opened the pistol and looked on the lock where the number was also printed and there it was the same, one digit erased and a zero added in. He gave the gun back to the lawyer. Thanks, but no thanks.

Soon after, a Bavarian gun collector came forward claiming he too had the gun that had killed the Archduke. Ortner spoke to the collector on the phone and asked him to read out the serial number. This time it was the wrong number.

To date, says Ortner, he is aware of five collectors who believed they had the Princip gun. It is, he says, just like after the second world war when the cap worn by Hitler was sold 200 times. Who knows how many ex-Serbian army Brownings were sold as the gun used in the assassination.

Ortner refuses to disclose the serial number of the missing gun. He claims there is a mystery over which gun Gavro actually used, as some official documents cite one number and another document, from the police in Sarajevo, cites a different number. He said he had the documents and would show them to me but he then could not find them.

So far as I have been able to establish, there is no mystery about which weapon Gavro used as he clearly identified the weapon during evidence at the trial. It was 19075. The serial numbers of the other three weapons were 19074, 19120 and 19126. Ortner is right to keep his secret and I have no idea which weapon is actually missing. One of the four, is all I can say. Maybe it's 'the' pistol – 19075 – or maybe not.

The bullets the Jesuits gave Ortner turned out to have been manufactured in 1924, so it looks as though these too had been swapped for the real thing at some point in the past. If I was being flippant, I would say the Freemasons were to blame but, in all the circumstances, that's a line of levity I ought to keep to myself.

26

Back to Sarajevo

When I met Ranka Cabrinovic in Sarajevo, in the autumn of 2006, she gave me a copy of a pamphlet which had been published in the early 1920s, in Serbo-Croat. It turned out to be an eloquent piece of reportage, describing the events of 1920 when the bodies of Gavro and his fellow conspirators had been brought back to Sarajevo and reburied together in St Mark's cemetery. The pamphlet was called 'From Terezin to Sarajevo' by S.T. Zakula and it described how the plan to bring back the bodies had originated in Hadzici, the home town of Gavro's brother Jovo, in the first half of 1919, when a committee had been formed. This was the official title of the committee: 'The Committee for the Return of Gavrilo Princip's Remains and for Raising A Monument In His Honour'.

The people on the committee had begun raising funds to pursue their aim but then, early the following year, a new committee was formed and this one was called, 'The Committee for the Transport of the Vidovdan Heroes'.

This new organization wanted to bring back all the bodies, not just Gavro's. By now, only the remains of Lazar Djukic had not been found, and never would be found. The whereabouts of all the others were known. The new committee arose out of the Sokol organization, the Slavic social network that promoted sport and fitness as well as traditional culture. There was to be a Sokol gathering that June, on Vidovdan, in Czechoslovakia, their first since the Great War, and it provided an ideal opportunity to bring back the dead heroes.

The new committee was joined by the members of the old committee, and new membership was restricted to those who had suffered under or been persecuted by the old Austrian regime. 'This was to prevent people from joining the committee to prove, after the fact, how patriotic they were,' wrote the pamphleteer.

Thanks to Frantisek Lebl, the Czech prison officer at Terezin, the bodies of Gavro, Nedjo and Grabez had already been located and exhumed and reburied temporarily in the family plot of a local civic leader. An organization called the Yugoslav Academic Youth had helped with these arrangements, under its own leader, Branko Cubrilovic, the brother of Veljko and Vaso.

On 1 July 1920 everyone gathered in Prague – committee members, Sokol members, Academic Youth members – and together took the train to Terezin. As they stopped at stations along the way they handed out leaflets thanking the Czechs for keeping the remains and honouring their bodies. The corpses of the three men who had died at the other prison, Mollersdorf, had been disinterred and brought through Austria to Terezin, thanks to the co-operation of Austria's new socialist government.

A temporary podium had been created by the cemetery wall, draped with cloth and decorated with candelabra. There were six metal coffins on the podium and they were guarded by six Czech Sokol members holding bare swords in their hands: Jakov Milovic, Nedjo and Mitar Kerovic, Gavro, Nedjo and Grabez were the six men in the coffins.

After an afternoon of speeches and a visit to the cells at Terezin the party returned to the cemetery where thousands of local people had gathered to accompany the coffins on carts to the railway station where they were loaded onto a special carriage decorated with flowers. The Czech guards gave their swords to their Serb Sokol counterparts, just in case there was any trouble going through Austria, which there wasn't.

The train stopped at Bosanska Brod in Bosnia and the carriage remained there for a few days while the other five bodies from Sarajevo were exhumed and put on display at the Judicial Palace in Sarajevo. This was the three who were hanged, Danilo Ilic, Misko Jovanovic and Veljko Cubrilovic, then Marko Perin and finally Bogdan Zerajic, the martyr the conspirators had all worshipped before the assassination.

Evidently, the committee had arranged for the six bodies in the metal coffins to be carried over the last part of the train journey to Sarajevo on a goods wagon, but officials of the transport workers' union had complained: 'If the deceased tyrant could be transported out of Bosnia in a luxury car, why couldn't the deceased heroes be transported in the same manner?' A special train was prepared and left at night, passing slowly from one station to the next, with choirs at one stop and silent crowds at another waiting in the dawn and still more crowds gathering at stations through the morning as the train continued to Sarajevo, arriving in the mid-afternoon.

The coffins were transferred to a tram for the journey to the Judicial Palace. The pamphleteer described a roar like thunder as the tram pulled up and the crowd cheered, 'glory to the Vidovdan heroes'. The eleven coffins were now together and were carried in a procession past the site of the assassination, by Princip's Bridge, and on to the cemetery, where a large plot had been prepared. The coffins were lowered one by one, allowing Gavro's a slight elevation in deference to his prominence as the assassin.

In later years a chapel would be built at the site and their names inscribed in an arched plaque of black marble. The chapel is still there today, albeit no longer quite enjoying the cultural prominence of old. A small service of remembrance continues to be held there every year on Vidovdan, 28 June.

Only one relative among all the conspirators had gone out to Terezin to take part in the 1920 ceremony to bring the bodies home and that was Vukosava Cabrinovic, the beautiful sister of Nedjo, whom Gavro had once loved or been attracted to and had made the subject of his youthful expressions of romantic yearning.

Vukosava had been at the cemetery in Terezin where a service had been held before the podium with the six metal coffins. The pamphleteer said he had experienced many moving moments in his life that shook his nerves, especially during the dark years of the World War, but he had never experienced, nor would he ever experience, a moment as powerful as that when he approached the draped podium with the six coffins, inside which rested the remains of those whose courage so amazed him from the moment he first learned of their act and which could not be compared to anything in history. 'The image of that event is so seared in my memory that even today, in moments when I recall that event, all of the nerves in my body seem to tremble. An unconquerable and nearly unbearable feeling of pain and sadness, but also pride, runs through my entire being like an electric current.

Burning shocks ran through my legs, my breath fell short, while my heart wanted to burst through my red Sokol shirt.'

The crowd stood in silence before the podium. 'That holy and profound silence was filled with an empathy for all the tragic history from Vidovdan 1914 to the end of the horrible war and the pride of victory cheers in 1918 to this freedom that shines in full splendour on the lands of Czechoslovakia and Yugoslavia. Everyone controlled their emotions as best they could. But then the sobs of Nedeljko's sister cut through the air like a knife.'

27

The Lost Chapel

We left Belgrade early on the Monday morning, heading out of the city on the Zagreb highway, the 'brotherhood and unity road' which had been built by President Tito during the heyday of Communist Yugoslavia in 1948. I had checked out of the Hotel Serbia and was waiting in the lobby when Dr Antonic came to collect me. He could not speak English and I could not speak Serbian but we smiled at each other meaningfully and waiting for Alex, the researcher and translator, to arrive.

Antonic led me to his car, a red Toyota Corolla of some years' vintage and I saw that there was someone else sitting in the back; his wife I recognized from supper at his home the night before. Was she coming with us for the ride to Sarajevo? I had no idea and no way of finding out, until Alex appeared.

It was Alex Todorovic who had found the professor in Belgrade, after we had discovered the existence of Veljko Cubrilovic's still living daughter, Nada. Zdravko Antonic, now in his 70s, was a historian, specializing in Balkan history. He had been to school in Priboj – his uncle had been taught by Veljko – and he had known Vaso for much of his adult life. He had met Jovanka a couple of times and, 15 years ago, had published two books of his own, in Serbia, in Serbian, about the Cubrilovic family.

According to Antonic, Vaso Cubrilovic had been in poor health for much of his life and had twice been rejected for military service. Yet he had lived on to the age of 93 and it was only six months before his death in 1990 that he invited Antonic to go through his papers, wherein he discovered the 36-page letter Vaso had written to his family from prison in 1918, describing the whole assassination plot of four years earlier.

Vaso had often spoken of the assassination but rarely in any detail. He had kept the 36-page letter private for 72 years and its contents, full of bitterness and betrayal, were still unknown outside the modest Serbian academic audience of Antonic's own work.

As the youngest of ten children, said Antonic, Vaso had spent his whole life being looked after. He had risen to an important position as an academic in Belgrade and had been a founder member and secretary of the Serbian Culture Club in 1937. He had delivered a 'memorandum' there in March that year which had ensured him a second seat of controversy in history.

Taking the title and theme 'The Expulsion of the Albanians' the memo's first line was, 'The problem of the Albanians in our national and state life did not arise yesterday.' The memo disapproved of the Albanians' 'intractable character' and proposed the mass resettlement of tens of thousands of them from Kosovo in the south of Serbia back to Albania and to Turkey.

There were various means proposed for achieving this end, including harassing their religious leaders and deliberately inciting riots which could be bloodily suppressed. And then, 'There remains one more means, which Serbia employed with great practical effect after 1878, that is, by secretly burning down villages and city quarters.' When Germany was expelling thousands of Jews and the Soviet Union resettling large numbers across the Union, Vaso wrote, the forced resettlement of a few thousand Albanians was hardly likely to start a world war.

It was this that gave rise to the legend of Vaso Cubrilovic as the architect of 'ethnic cleansing', a practice adopted so ruthlessly by Serbia and its neighbours during the Balkan wars after the break-up of Yugoslavia, around the time of Vaso's death in 1990.

I asked Dr Antonic what he thought about Vaso's memorandum but he was uncharacteristically non-committal. No villages had been burned back then, he said, and the policies were not as radical sounding then as they might seem now. Vaso had not supported ethnic cleansing in later life, especially during the era of Slobodan Milosevic, who had been president of Serbia from 1989 onwards and had eventually faced charges of war crimes, including genocide, for his own practices of ethnic cleansing.

Vaso had briefly risen to become minister of agriculture under

Tito, in 1947–8, though the irony was that many people thought he had got the job by mistake as Tito had said, get me Cubrilovic, and he had apparently wanted Vaso's brother Branko, but someone had summoned Vaso instead, so that by the time he was appointed it was too late to correct the error. In any event, his ministerial career had been over before two years had passed.

Coming to power at the end of the second world war after fierce fighting against the Nazis and their fascist allies in Croatia, the Utasa, Josip Broz Tito had targeted fascist collaborators, imprisoning and then executing thousands of intellectuals. Among those he seized was Vaso's fellow conspirator from June 1914, Cvjetko Popovic, by this time the director of a teacher training school, placing him high on Tito's hit list. Vaso had risked his own safety by writing a long letter to Tito's interior minister, testifying to Popovic's patriotism and decency. Popovic had been spared, though his own brother had been executed.

Nor was Vaso excused suffering, as his only son Milos had in the words of Dr Antonic, 'gone crazy' in 1945 after being involved in fierce fighting as a teenage soldier on the side of Tito's Partisans against the fascists. Vaso's son had spent much of the rest of his life in locked wards in psychiatric hospital and, said Antonic, he had seen Vaso weep many times for his son's pain. The son had died a few years before Vaso. It was always a tragedy, said Antonic, when a father buries his own son.

Alex finally arrived and I discovered that the professor's wife was being dropped at the bus stop, on her way to work as a nurse. The three of us who remained, Antonic, Alex and myself, set off along the dead-straight, blacktop highway in his red Toyota. We hoped to retrace the journey Gavro and the others had taken, smuggling the weapons from Belgrade to Sarajevo in May 1914, helped by Veljko and the peasants along the way. We stopped for our first drink, a brandy, at about 9.30, not long it seemed after we had set off. As he pulled away from the kerb, following the brandy, the doctor failed to notice a passing car that squealed as it turned sharply to avoid us, while the driver beeped long and hard on his horn. I hoped I would get to see Sarajevo.

We stopped for lunch later at a roadside restaurant where a lamb had been turning on a spit. The lamb was served in chunks on a plate in the centre of the table with bread and side salad. Alex told me the doctor had said to him last night that he was nervous about driving to Sarajevo in his car with its distinctive Belgrade number plates. Evidently, he had never made such a journey before and was anxious about becoming the object of Bosnian Muslim anger as there was still great enmity and hatred between many people on both sides.

After two or three hours we crossed the border out of Serbia and into Bosnia & Hercegovina, first entering the Bosnian Serb region known as Republika Srpska, the Serb Republic, a breakaway state formed by Serbians in 1992, after the collapse of Yugoslavia. This secession had been resisted by the main body of Bosnia, the Federation of Bosnia & Hercegovina, which was predominantly Muslim, or Bosniak, as the majority of Bosnian Muslims now preferred to be known.

During the ensuing Bosnian War there had been three years of three-way fighting between the Serbians, Bosniaks and Croatians. In 1991 there had been nearly half a million Muslims in the Srpska region. By 1996 there were only 30,000 left. Likewise, it was said there were little more than 20,000 Serbs left in the whole of the rest of Bosnia.

We stopped suddenly at a junction by a brook just outside Priboj. This, said Antonic, was the place where Veljko had been riding with the priest when the peasants appeared with the students hidden behind them. The road winding away from us up the hill led to the Kerovic family home. We stopped a passer-by and, sure enough, he knew the great-grandson of old Mitar who still lived there. The passer-by said the history was still talked about.

In Priboj we drove up through a settlement and found the schoolhouse, now empty, where Veljko and Jovanka had taught. The teachers' cottage beside it was gone – it had been torched and razed by Croatian fascists in 1941, while the new teachers were inside it, said Antonic, though fortunately they had fled, unharmed.

The professor showed me a copy of one of his other books in which he had documented the Croatian fascists' atrocities committed against Serbia and Bosnia & Hercegovina in 1941.

Yugoslavia had initially allied itself with the Nazis, at the start of the second world war, but then changed its mind following a coup, which prompted a joint invasion by German and Italian forces. Yugoslavia was broken up and Croatia and Bosnia & Hercegovina had been united to become a Nazi puppet state under the Utasa fascists who embarked on their own programme of racial purification which led to the extermination of 750,000 people, mostly Serbs but also Jews and Roma, while entire villages and rural communities were razed. The main road through Sarajevo had been known for a while as Adolf Hitler Street. The fascists had been resisted both by Tito's Partisans and by Yugoslav royalists, the Chetniks who had fought each other too, at the same time.

There had been fresh fighting in Priboj between the Muslims and the Serbs during 1991 and 1992. Some 250 people had been killed. There were two schools now but there were no Muslim pupils in the Serbian school, just as there were no Serbian children in the Muslim school. Antonic spoke of the simmering resentments that continued to blight the region.

The Serbian school had been renamed after the second world war, in honour of Veljko. His bust stood on a wooden plinth at the school's entrance. We sat in the head teacher's office and drank coffee with another brandy which he produced from a store cupboard within arm's reach of his desk. He presented me with a Serbian book of history about the school which Alex inscribed in English at the head's dictation, 'a totem from your visit to our school'.

We drove on. 'Now we are in Turkish territory,' said Antonic, and suddenly the signs of recent warfare were all around us. Wrecked houses and buildings pocked and scarred by the damage from shells and bullets.

We reached Sarajevo in the late afternoon. We had not booked a hotel and many we now discovered, were full. The doctor was going out to the nearby town of Pale to stay with relatives and did not seem keen to hang around so Alex and I took our things from his car and hailed a taxi instead. Eventually we found a couple of rooms.

Nada had told us about the Christian Orthodox cemetery of St Mark's in Sarajevo where her father was buried along with the other 1914 conspirators. Vaso's will had expressly stated that he wanted to be buried there too, 'with his friends'. A small chapel had been built in one corner with a memorial plaque laid into its wall. Nada and her family had been unable to get into the chapel on a recent visit and were concerned it was not being properly looked after. There had been a stench of urine around the outside and traces of its use by people for taking drugs or drinking alcohol. We had promised we would try to find out who was in charge and do something about it.

But where was the cemetery? We got a tourist map but the cemetery was not shown. The hotel receptionist suggested we try the taxi rank on the far side of the river. We walked across and began to ask the taxi drivers waiting in a line in their cars if they knew where the 1914 assassins were buried. None of them knew, or if they did, they weren't going to tell us. Some were hostile to the very idea, 'If it hadn't been for them we'd still be in Austria,' barked one. Others feigned total lack of interest. They were of course all Muslims – Bosniaks.

Eventually we found a driver who, even though he too was Bosniak and didn't know where the cemetery was either, was at least willing to try and find it. I sat in the back as we set off and immediately saw that he had a hole in the back of his bald head like a miniature bomb crater. No one cares about these assassins, he said. It's a Serb thing not a Bosnian thing and they don't feel connected to it.

In 1914, Serbs had been in the majority, at about 40 per cent of the total Sarajevo population of around 60,000. By 1991, at the start of the notorious siege, there had been around 500,000 people living there, about half of them Bosniaks but still over 100,000 Serbians. By the late nineties the population had shrunk to 350,000 and hardly any of the Serbs were left – no more than 5 per cent.

Because of its location, settled at the foot of a valley around the Miljacka river, Sarajevo had lent itself perfectly to being besieged by Serb forces virtually non-stop from May 1992 until February 1996. The city had been blockaded from positions all around the surrounding hills, using snipers and artillery to keep supplies out and the population at bay. Over 10,000 had died there. People had been shot and killed trying to dart through exposed roads, known as sniper's alley, and terrible things had happened – schoolchildren dying outside their school, young lovers shot on a bridge over the river, lying there for days because their bodies could not be retrieved.

Both sides – Bosniaks and Serbs – had been embedded in positions sometimes a few yards apart, overlooking the town. In many cases they were childhood friends now on opposing sides. As they said in Sarajevo, after the war they sat down and drank coffee together again. Those who had survived.

Our taxi driver's father had been shot dead next to him in August

1992 as they lay together in a foxhole. The driver kept photographs of his shelled and ruined home in the sun visor. And of course, there was that shrapnel hole in the back of his head which had been made at the time of his father's death. He had been lucky not to die.

We drove for miles, crawling out along the valley through the early evening traffic to the place where the taxi driver thought he would find the cemetery. Alas, it wasn't there. We made various phone calls to different civic offices without success until, finally, we reached a tourist information desk and, by chance, the woman who answered the phone knew exactly where the cemetery was, right in the middle of a busy residential area, where people walked back and forth or queued for buses or got into or out of their parked cars apparently oblivious to the nearby monument to what was arguably the most significant moment in modern history.

One man, Gavrilo Princip, had fired the shots, but the planning and putting together of the assassination in Belgrade and Sarajevo had involved a conspiracy not unlike those perpetrated in recent times, in London and New York and elsewhere, by Islamic extremists.

Here too, in 1914, a loosely formed group of ascetic, devoted, single-minded young men had hoped to be remembered for their act of heroic self-sacrifice. They had planned to die, destroying an empire and creating a nation.

Instead, within a month of the assassination, in a consequence largely unforeseen by its perpetrators, the first world war had begun, marking the beginning of the end of several empires and causing the death of countless millions of people. It was either an unparalleled act of terrorism or a courageous strike against imperial oppressors.

The grey stone chapel in the cemetery looked neglected and unloved, the area around it stained, littered and untidy. We could find no one anywhere who was taking care of it, and could find no means of contacting anyone about it, either. But at least it was still standing. That in itself, in a town where so much had been damaged or destroyed, was a minor miracle.

Their names were etched into the memorial stone at the back of the chapel, an arch of inlaid black marble:

Gavrilo Princip, Nedeljko Cabrinovic, Danilo Ilic, Trifko Grabez, Veljko Cubrilovic, Misko Jovanovic, Mitar Kerovic, Nedjo Kerovic, Jakov Milovic, Marko Perin and Bogdan Zerajic. Missing were Cvjetko

Popovic and Vaso Cubrilovic, though Vaso's dying request had been to be buried with his friends in Sarajevo. Mehmed Mehmedbasic was also resting elsewhere, though as a Muslim his interment here would have been controversial, to say the least.

Above the names on the stone were the words 'Heroes of Vidovdan' and the inscription along the line of the arch:

'Blessed are those that live for evermore.'

Sources

There are dozens of books that examine or touch upon the events that led to the first world war but only a very few of them contain the results of original research into the group, or gang of young conspirators behind the Sarajevo assassination. One book towers above the others and that is Vladimir Dedijer's account of *The Road to Sarajevo* which was first published in English in 1967 by Macgibbon & Kee. Dedijer spent years pursuing both the participants and the paper trail left behind by them and by their contemporaries, and was fastidious in seeking out articles, papers, memoirs and assorted unpublished material in Belgrade, Sarajevo, Vienna and across Europe. In its time, based on what was then available, *The Road to Sarajevo* was a definitive study, albeit sometimes too thorough to be readily digestible.

It was not until the 1980s that a complete transcript of the trial of the Sarajevo conspirators was pieced together for the first time and then translated into English: *The Sarajevo Trial*, narrative by W.A. Dolph Owings; translation and editing by W.A. Dolph Owings, Elisabeth Pribic and Nikola Pribic was published in two volumes by Documentary Publications of Chapel Hill, North Carolina, in 1984. It is an immense work – the whole story is there for the meticulous, patient reader.

There were 25 defendants at the trial – a reminder, if one was needed, that the assassination was not simply the act of one man, Gavrilo Princip, even if he alone pulled the trigger. History might be excused for neglecting the role of, say, Blagoje Kerovic who once drove a horse and cart through the night to a town called Tuzla, smuggling guns and bombs and two key conspirators; but history should not be allowed to forget the part played by Nedjo Cabrinovic and the two brothers, Veljko and Vaso Cubrilović, one of whom was executed, while one survived.

When I began the research for this book it seemed highly unlikely there would be anyone still living who had been there and been touched by those events of that year, 1914, so it was an unexpected thrill to discover Nada, the daughter of Veljko, who was eight months old on the day the Archduke was assassinated and 93 years old when we met in Belgrade in the late autumn of 2006. She was a moving witness to the past and had kept for 90 years the collection of letters that had passed between her parents in the days before her father was hanged. Nada's story and her letters were unknown outside Serbia and offer an important new perspective on the conspirators.

I was introduced to Nada by Dr Zdravko Antonic, a warm, generous Belgrade historian who had been given exclusive access to the archives of the Cubrilovic family, especially those of his now dead colleague Vaso, the brother of Veljko. Vaso's unpublished account of the conspiracy and its aftermath had been written to his family while he was still in prison in 1918 and was discovered by Antonic, by chance, just a few years ago. The letter has never before been seen outside Serbia.

Dr Antonic drove me from Belgrade to Sarajevo, following the route taken by Gavrilo Princip and Trifko Grabez when they were smuggling the guns and bombs that were to be used in the assassination, with the help of poor Blagoje Kerovic and Veljko and others.

In Sarajevo, I was able, with the help of my colleague Alex Todorovic, to find Ranka Cabrinovic, the niece of Nedjo, who had much to offer in terms of elaborating on the family's troubles and her uncle's role in the plot. She spoke too of the romance between Gavrilo Princip and Nedjo's beautiful young sister, Vukosava, who seems to have been a significant influence in Princip's short life.

Also in Sarajevo we met Mirsad Avdic, the new curator of the newly reopened Sarajevo museum, who had done his best to salvage the exhibits of the former museum which had been thrown into chaos and disarray by the fighting and the siege of the 1990s. Avdic spoke with authority about Princip's shifting status in the city's history.

Back in Vienna, the curator at the museum of military history, Dr Christian Ortner, had an extraordinary, unexpected story to tell about the journey of the Princip gun and the intrigue that still surrounds it.

After that it was all libraries and books and journals, often following in the footsteps of Vladimir Dedijer (in London, Belgrade, Sarajevo and Vienna) trying to identify which materials were worth pursuing for useful information. I have read thousands and thousands of pages, and been briefed on thousands more by my Belgrade colleague Alex Todorovic. Here are the highlights:

SELECTED BOOKS

Albertini, Luigi, *The Origins of the War of 1914*, Volumes 1, 2 and 3 (Enigma Books, 2005)

Andric, Ivo, *Nemiri* (Naklada St Kugli, 1920)

Bogicevic, Vojislav, *Mlada Bosna* (Svjetlost, 1954)

Brook-Shepherd, Gordon, *Archduke of Sarajevo* (Little, Brown, 1984)

Cassels, Lavender, *The Archduke and the Assassin* (Frederick Muller, 1984)

Cistler, Rudolf, *Kako sam branio Principa I drugove* (Ljubljana, 1937)

Dedijer, Vladimir, *The Road to Sarajevo* (Macgibbon & Kee, 1967)

Durham, Edith, *The Sarajevo Crime* (George Allen & Unwin, 1925)

Fay, Sidney Bradshaw, *The Origins of the World War*, Volumes 1 and 2 (Macmillan, 1930)

Feuerlicht, Roberta Strauss, *The Desperate Act* (McGraw-Hill, 1968)

Gacinovic, Vladimir, *Ogledi i pisma*, edited by Todor Krusevac (Svetlost, 1956)

Gerolymatos, Andre, *The Balkan Wars* (Spellmount, 2004)

Gilbert, Martin, *A History of the Twentieth Century – Volume One: 1900-1933* (HarperCollins, 1997)

Glenny, Misha, *The Balkans* (Penguin, 2001)

Jevdjevic, Dobrosav, *Sarajevski Atentatori* (Binoza, 1934)

Jevtic, Borivoje, *Sarajevski Atentat* (P.N. Gakovic, 1923)

Jovanovic, Slobodan, *Moji savremenici* (Avale, 1962)

Kiszling, Rudolf, *Erzherzog Franz Ferdinand von Österreich-Este* (Graz, 1953)

Kranjcevic, Ivo, *Uspomene jednog ucesnika u sarajevskom atentatu* (Svetlost, 1954)

Ljubibratic, Drago, *Gavrilo Princip* (Prosveta, 1959)

Ljubibratic, Drago, *Vladimir Gacinovic* (Nolit Prosveta, 1961)

Maclean, Fitzroy, *Tito: A Pictorial Biography* (Macmillan, 1980)

Margutti, Albert von, *The Emperor Francis Joseph and His Times* (Hutchinson, 1921)

Mitchell, Lawrence, *Serbia* (Bradt, 2005)

Mousset, Albert, *L'Attentat de Sarajevo* (Payot, 1930)

Owings, W.A. Dolph, *The Sarajevo Trial* (Documentary Publications, 1984)

Pauli, Hertha, *The Secret of Sarajevo* (Collins, 1965)

Pfeffer, Leo, *Istraga u Sarajevskom atentatu* (Nova Evropa, 1938)

Reed, John, *The War in Eastern Europe* (Scribners, 1916)

Remak, Joachim, *Sarajevo* (Weidenfeld & Nicolson, 1959)

Seton-Watson, Robert William, *Sarajevo: a Study in the Origins of the Great War* (Hutchinson, 1926)

Stanojevic, Stanoje, *Ubistvo Austrikog Prestolonaslednika Ferdinanda* (Izdavacka Knjizarnica Napredak, 1923)

Stationery Office, *War 1914, Punishing the Serbs* (TSO, 1999)

Tuchman, Barbara W., *The Guns of August* (Ballantine Books, 1962)

West, Rebecca, *Black Lamb and Grey Falcon* (Canongate Classics, 1997)

SELECTED PAPERS AND ARTICLES

Armstrong, Hamilton Fish, 'Confessions of the Assassin Whose Deed Led to the World War' – the notes of Martin Pappenheim (*Current History*, New York, August 1927)

Bogicevic, Vojislav, 'Sarajevski Atentat' (Drzavni Arhiv Nrbih, 1954)

Cubrilovic, Vaso, 'The Expulsion of the Albanians' (Memorandum presented to the Serbian Cultural Club, March 1937)

DeVoss, David, 'Searching for Gavrilo Princip' (Smithsonian, August 2000)

Fabijancic, Tony, 'Following the Assassin' (*Toronto Star*, 31 July 2005)

Gacinovic, Vladimir, 'To Those Who Are Coming' (*Nova*, November 1910)

Jovanovic, M. Ljuba, 'The Murder of Sarajevo' (*Journal of the British Institute of International Affairs*, March 1925)

Judah, Tim, 'War In The Balkans, Ancient Hatreds' (*Observer*, 4 April 1999)

Matthias, John & Vuckovic, Vladeta, translators, 'The Battle of Kosovo', *Serbian Epic Poems* (Swallow Press/Ohio University Press, 1987)

Owings, W. A., 'Young Bosnia' (Balkanistika, 1975)

—— 'The Sarajevo Assassins on Trial' (Canadian Slavic Studies, 1980)

—— 'The Review of Mlada Bosna I Prvi Svetski Rat' by Ratko Parezanin (*Austrian History Yearbook*, 1977)

Remak, Joachin, 'Journey to Sarajevo' (*Commentary*, July 1968)

Werfel, Franz, 'Cabrinowitsch' (*Die Neue Rundschau*, May 1924)

West, Richard, 'Martyr Princip' (*The New Statesman and Nation*, 26 June 1954)

Zakula, S.T., 'From Terezin to Sarajevo' (pamphlet published 1930)

Endnotes

CHAPTER 1

'He would soon be … sleeping and dreaming …': Armstrong, Hamilton Fish, 'Confessions of the Assassin Whose Deed Led to the World War', the notes of Martin Pappenheim.

'Gavrilo said he chose to stay there because …': Owings, W.A. Dolph – *The Sarajevo Trial*, testimony of Gavrilo Princip.

CHAPTER 2

'It was said they had ploughed salt …': author interview with journalist David DeVoss.

'… where the baby was born.': Lebedev, Vladimir, 'Rodenje Gavrila Principa' in *Politika*, 28 September 1936 (cited in Dedijer, Vladimir, *The Road to Sarajevo*).

'In the old house the doors are small …': Tomic, Bozidar, 'Poreklo I detinjstvo Gavrila Principa' in *Nova Europa*, 26 October 1939 (cited in Dedijer, ibid).

'Father a peasant …': Armstrong, Hamilton Fish, 'Confessions of the Assassin Whose Deed Led to the World War', the notes of Martin Pappenheim.

'Was not much with other schoolboys …': Armstrong, ibid.

'The wet logs on the open fire …': Tomic, Bozidar, 'Poreklo I detinjstvo Gavrila Principa' in *Nova Europa*, 26 October 1939 (cited in Dedijer, Vladimir, *The Road to Sarajevo*).

'One biographer noted Gavro's exceptional childhood development …': Tomic, ibid.

'If he could force the whole Carsija into a box of matches …': Jevtic, Borivoje, *Sarajevski Atentat* (cited in Dedijer, ibid).

'Gavrilo would always say that no one knew literature better …': Owings, W.A. Dolph, *The Sarajevo Trial*, testimony of Dobrosav Jevdjevic.

'Ranka said Vukosava was like a peacock …': author interview with Ranka Cabrinovic, Sarajevo, 2005.

'… possessed the usual foundation of Slav beauty …': West, Rebecca, *Black Lamb and Grey Falcon*.

'… an upright girl …': Owings, W.A. Dolph, *The Sarajevo Trial*, testimony of Dobrosav Jevdjevic.

'He remains in my memory …': Jovanovic, M. Ljuba, 'The murder of Sarajevo' in *Journal of the British Institute of International Affairs*, March 1925.

'Look up on the map …': Bogicevic, Vojislav, *Mlada Bosna*.

'You are too small and too weak …' Dedijer, Vladimir, *The Road to Sarajevo*.

CHAPTER 3

'Let me die if I should lie to you!' Matthias, John & Vuckovic, Vladeta translators, 'The Battle of Kosovo', *Serbian Epic Poems*.

'In fact as others have pointed out …': Matthias & Vuckovic, ibid.

'O, Dearest God, what shall I do, and how?': Matthias & Vuckovic, ibid.

'The Miracle of Lazar's Head': Matthias & Vuckovic, ibid.

'… this fact fired me with zeal to carry out the attempt': Dedijer, Vladimir, *The Road to Sarajevo*.

'Nedjo's father had progressed under Austrian rule …': author interview with Ranka Cabrinovic, Sarajevo, 2005.

'In the 1930s Vukosava told Rebecca West …': West, Rebecca, *Black Lamb and Grey Falcon*.

'But he would never destroy them …': West, ibid.

CHAPTER 4

The opening narrative of this chapter is based on Dedijer, Vladimir, *The Road to Sarajevo*; Owings, W.A. Dolph, *The Sarajevo Trial*, testimony of witnesses and participants; Armstrong, Hamilton Fish, 'Confessions of the Assassin Whose Deed Led to the World War', the notes of Martin Pappenheim; author interview with Ranka Cabrinovic, Sarajevo 2005.

'Here was Milos Pura …': Owings, ibid, testimony of Milos Pura.

'Jovo Karic was only 17 …': Owings, ibid, testimony of Jovo Karic.

'The young men would gather on Appel Quay …': Owings, ibid, testimony of Kosta Kostic.

'The "servile loyalty" …': Owings, ibid, testimony of Nedeljko Cabrinovic.

'I gave her money because I love her …': Bogicevic, Vojislav, *Sarajevski Atentat*.

CHAPTER 5

This chapter is based on Dedijer, Vladimir, *The Road to Sarajevo*; Owings,

W.A. Dolph, *The Sarajevo Trial*, testimony of witnesses and participants; author interview with Ranka Cabrinovic, Sarajevo 2005.

'The pumpkin is ripe!': Owings, ibid, trial testimony of Svetozar Miljanic.

'One visitor from Sarajevo ...': Owings, ibid, trial testimony of Trifko Krstanovic.

'I don't know how to thank you for your kindness ...': Owings, ibid, trial evidence of Nedeljko Cabrinovic.

'Serbia would be empty ...': Owings, ibid, trial evidence of Nedeljko Cabrinovic.

'So he felt that he was dead to them, his parents ...': Owings, ibid, trial evidence of Nedeljko Cabrinovic.

CHAPTER 6

'When the grave of Bogdan Zerajic was opened ...': Ljubibratic, Drago, *Gacinovic* (cited in Dedijer, Vladimir, *The Road to Sarajevo*).

'He grabbed me in his arms ...': Gacinovic, Vladimir, 'To Those Who Are Coming' in *Nova*, November 1910 (cited in Dedijer, ibid).

'they do not exist, they do not exist ...': Grdjic, Vasilj, essay in *Pregled*, January 1927 (cited in Dedijer, ibid).

'It was noted that Zerajic was wearing a hand-made badge ...': Haus-Hof-Staatsarchiv, Vienna (cited in Dedijer, ibid).

'Nedjo Cabrinovic carved Zerajic's name into the cross ...': Owings, W.A. Dolph, *The Sarajevo Trial*, testimony of Nedeljko Cabrinovic.

'Schooling was still a novelty ...': Owings, W.A., 'Young Bosnia' in *Balkanistika*, 1975.

'I wonder if you can understand how mighty hatred can be?': West, Rebecca, *Black Lamb and Grey Falcon*.

'Our fathers, our dictators are real tyrants ...': Gacinovic, Vladimir, 'Ogledi I pisma' (cited in Dedijer, Vladimir, *The Road to Sarajevo*).

'In our organisation there is a rule of obligatory abstinence ...': Gacinovic, ibid.

'Yes, in Serbia we do not trust much to God ...': Reed, John, *The War in Eastern Europe* (cited in Dedijer, ibid).

'This caused a deep breach and hatred between us ...': Bogicevic, Vojislav, *Mlada Bosna* (cited in Dedijer, ibid).

'Anyone who spends one night in Sarajevo ...': Andric, Ivo, 'Story from 1920' in *Nemiri* (cited in Dedijer, ibid).

'this schoolboys' movement is not enough ...': Dedijer, ibid.

'Gavro described himself as a Yugoslav nationalist ...': Owings, W.A. Dolph, *The Sarajevo Trial*, testimony of Gavrilo Princip.

CHAPTER 7

The account of Ilic collecting the weapons is based in part on Dedijer, Vladimir, *The Road to Sarajevo* but is primarily based on the trial testimony of those involved.

'The idea of assassination as a means of revolution had taken hold of him.': Armstrong, Hamilton Fish, 'Confessions of the Assassin Whose Deed Led to the World War', the notes of Martin Pappenheim.

CHAPTER 8

'It had been a harsh winter and the snow was as high as a house, Gavro's mother Nana later told an interviewer ...': papers of Vladimir Lebedev at Gradski Muzej Sarajevo (cited in Dedijer, Vladimir, *The Road to Sarajevo*). Author's note: I could not find these papers nor very much else of relevance during a visit to the Sarajevo museum in 2006. The archivist acknowledged there was ongoing chaos and many losses as a result of the recent conflict.

'I know whence I arrive, unsatisfied like the flame.': Nietzsche, Frederick, *Ecce Homo*, 1908.

'... he would have liked to throw a bomb in the Sabor ...': Owings, W.A., *The Sarajevo Trial*, testimony of Nedeljko Cabrinovic; Dedijer, Vladimir, *The Road to Sarajevo*.

'After a short hesitation Nedjo agreed.': Owings, ibid, testimony of Nedeljko Cabrinovic.

CHAPTER 9

The narrative of this chapter is mainly based on Dedijer, Vladimir, *The Road to Sarajevo*; West, Rebecca, *Black Lamb and Grey Falcon*; Brook-Shepherd, Gordon, *Archduke of Sarajevo*; Cassels, Lavender, *The Archduke and the Assassin*; Feuerlicht, Roberta Strauss, *The Desperate Act* and author observation and research at Schloss Artstetten.

'The grand total of kills amounts to 272,439': author's observation during visit to Schloss Artstetten, 2006.

'The antlers of a Sandinavian elk ...': Dr Teuber article in *Pressburger Presse*, 1900 (cited in Brook-Shepherd, Gordon, *Archduke of Sarajevo*).

'Manifesto – to our people!': Brook-Shepherd, ibid.

CHAPTER 10

'the Russian emperor has just been killed': Jevdjevic, Dobrosav, *Sarajevski Atentatori* (cited in Dedijer, Vladimir, *The Road to Sarajevo*).

'One student who was not so fond of Gavro ...': Owings, W.A., *The Sarajevo Trial*, testimony of Dobrosav Jevdjevic.

'There, you see! It is true what they say, if any mother has lost her son ...': Jovanovic, M. Ljuba, 'The Murder of Sarajevo' in *Journal of the British*

Institute of International Affairs, March 1925.

'Nothing doing, Ciganovic was said to have told the plotters ...': Albertini, Luigi, *The Origins of the War of 1914*.

'Are you one of them? Are you ready?': Owings, W.A., *The Sarajevo Trial*, testimony of Trifko Grabez.

'One historian, himself a former Young Bosnian ... found in a Serbian archive ...': the historian was Drago Ljubibratic (cited in Dedijer, Vladimir, *The Road to Sarajevo*).

'Tankosic was a small, frail figure ...': portrait of Tankosic from sources cited in Dedijer, ibid and Albertini, Luigi, *The Origins of the War of 1914*.

'They were Belgian-made Brownings ...': information on the guns from another observation at Schloss Artstetten and the Museum of Military History, Vienna and author interview with Dr Christian Ortner, Vienna, 2006.

'One contemporary remembered him [Apis] ...': Stanojevic, Stanoje, *Die Ermordung des Erzherzoges Franz Ferdinand* (Societats-Drukerei, 1923) (cited in Albertini, Luigi, *The Origins of the War of 1914*).

'Another Serbian historian who knew him [Apis] ...': Jovanovic, Slobodan, *Moji savremenici* (cited in Dedijer, Vladimir, *The Road to Sarajevo*.

'Those officers became known as The White Hand ...': Albertini, ibid.

'I, Oskar Tartalja, swear by the sun that warms me ...': for Black Hand oath see Dedijer, Vladimir, *The Road to Sarajevo* and Remak, Joachim, *Sarajevo*.

'Hence when Tankosic came one day into the office ...': account given by Cedar Popovic to Luigi Albertini (cited in Albertini, *The Origins of the War of 1914*).

CHAPTER 11

This chapter is based on the trial testimony of all those who participated in, or assisted with, or were implicated in the smuggling of the weapons from Belgrade to Sarajevo.

CHAPTER 12

This chapter is based on the trial testimony of the participants and author interview with Nada Cubrilovic, Belgrade, 2006.

CHAPTER 13

This chapter is based on trial testimony of the participants, author interview with Nada Cubrilovic, on the letters of her father, Veljko Cubrilovic and the unpublished account of the plot written by Nada's uncle, Veljko's brother, Vaso Cubrilovic.

CHAPTER 14

This chapter is based on trial testimony of the participants.

CHAPTER 15

'Djukic told him it was hard to get weapons …': Owings, W.A., *The Sarajevo Trail*, testimony of Lazar Djukic and Danilo Ilic.

'After I gave my word to join the plot …': Popovic, Cvjetko, article in *Politika*, 3 April 1928 (cited in Dedijer, Vladimir, *The Road to Sarajevo*).

'If Gavro is first, said Popovic …': from the unpublished letter of Vaso Cubrilovic.

'Here entered 19-year-old, Ivo Kranjcevic …': Owings, W.A., *The Sarajevo Trail*, testimony of Ivo Kranjcevic.

'that's easy, there are weapons': Owings, ibid, testimony of Branko Zagorac.

'Vaso had bragged before that he was a kind of a hero …': Owings, ibid, testimony of Marko Perin.

'I can't do it because a detective is following me …': Owings, ibid, testimony of Dragan Kalember.

CHAPTER 16

'… a certain morbid yearning …': Haus-Hof-Staatsarchiv, Vienna (cited in Dedijer, Vladimir, *The Road to Sarajevo*).

'Gacinovic wrote about it for Leon Trotsky …': Gacinovic, Vladimir, *Ogledi I pisma* (cited in Dedijer, ibid).

'There was a kind of quarrelling between them': Gacinovic, ibid.

'In some accounts, Apis never informed the central committee of The Black Hand …': see Dedijer and Albertini for the contradictory theories surrounding attempts to stop the assassination.

'One source has Malobabic arriving in Sarajevo …': Ljubibratic, Drago, *Vladimir Gacinovic* (cited in Dedijer, ibid).

'It's fate, Rade': report of execution witness Ljubomir Dabic (cited in Remak, Joachim, *Sarajevo*).

'Mehmedbasic said there was no sign of Ilic's change of heart': Mehmedbasic interviewed by Luigi Albertini (cited in Albertini, *The Origins of the War of 1914*).

'These fellows were for the most part incapable of a great idea': Haus-Hof-Staatsarchiv, Vienna (cited in Dedijer, Vladimir, *The Road to Sarajevo*).

'because we are poets and futurists …': Borivoje Jevtic statement to police (cited in Dedijer, ibid).

CHAPTER 17

This chapter is based on Dedijer, ibid; Albertini, Luigi, *The Origins of the*

Great War; Brook-Shepherd, Gordon, *Archduke of Sarajevo*; Gilbert, Martin, *A History of the Twentieth Century*; West, Rebecca, *Black Lamb and Grey Falcon*; Cassels, Lavender, *The Archduke and the Assassin*; Feuerlicht, Roberta Strauss, *The Desperate Act*.

CHAPTER 18

The account of the assassination itself is primarily based on the trial testimony of participants and witnesses. In addition, I have relied on the unpublished letter of Vaso Cubrilovic.

'One writer, Joachim Remak …': Remak, Joachim, *Sarajevo*; Remak, Joachim, 'Journey to Sarajevo' in *Commentary*, July 1968.

'But Mehmedbasic then told the historian Albertini that, just as the procession was approaching …': Albertini, Luigi, *The Origins of the War of 1914*.

'That night two Sarajevo artists, Ludmila and Rudolf Valic …': Ludmila Valic interview in *Vreme*, 13 March 1938 (cited in Dedijer, Vladimir, *The Road to Sarajevo*).

CHAPTER 19

This chapter is substantially based on the trial testimony of participants and witnesses.

'Mehmed Mehmedbasic had run off when he heard Nedjo's bomb': Mehmedbasic interviewed by Luigi Albertini (cited in Albertini, *The Origins of the War of 1914*).

'According to Dusan's daughter Ranka …': author interview with Ranka Cabrinovic, Sarajevo, 2006.

'With his alert lively black eyes …': Pfeffer, Leo, *Istraga u Sarajevskom atentatu* (cited in Dedijer, Vladimir, *The Road to Sarajevo*).

'The young assassin exhausted by his beating …': Pfeffer, ibid.

'I am an adherent of the radical anarchist idea …': Haus-Hof-Staatsarchiv, Vienna (cited in Dedijer, ibid).

'The rioters were predominantly Catholic Croats and Muslims': see Dedijer, ibid and Remak, Joachim, *Sarajevo* for accounts of the riots.

'But the letter never existed …': Jevdjevic, Dobrosav, *Sarajevski atentatori* (see Dedijer, ibid and Albertini, Luigi, *The Origins of the War of 1914* for allegations of torture).

'One account has Ilic breaking down …': Albertini, ibid. This version of Ilic's betrayal also supported by Vaso Cubrilovic in his unpublished letter.

'… prompted Nedjo to devise a new system of communication': Dedijer, Vladimir, *The Road to Sarajevo* and the unpublished letter of Vaso Cubrilovic.

'the other young conspirators agreed to behave calmly …': Kranjcevic, Ivo, *Uspomene jednog ucesnika u sarajevskom atentatu* (cited in Dedijer, ibid).

CHAPTER 20

This chapter is primarily based on Dedijer, Vladimir, *The Road to Sarajevo*; Albertini, Luigi, *The Origins of the War of 1914*; Brook-Shepherd, Gordon, *Archduke of Sarajevo*; Remak, Joachim, *Sarajevo*; Gilbert, Martin, *A History of the Twentieth Century*.

CHAPTER 21

The account of the court proceedings is, of course, based on *The Sarajevo Trial*.

'An Archduke had been killed; someone had to hang': Owings, W.A. Dolph, introduction to *The Sarajevo Trial*.

The letters of Veljko and Jovanka Cubrilovic were initially disclosed to (and later generously shared with) me by Dr Zdravko Antonic, with the permission of the Cubrilovices' daughter, Nada.

CHAPTER 22

'Another priest who was there ...': the priest was Milan Mratinkovic. His account appeared in *Narodno jedinstvo*, 9 and 10 May 1919 (cited in Dedijer, Vladimir, *The Road to Sarajevo*).

'The executioner himself ... also left an account ...': the executioner's tale was told by Vojislav Bogicevic in the journal *Oslobodjenje*, 24 February 1952 (cited in Dedijer).

Again, I acknowledge the debt of gratitude to Nada Cubrilovic and Dr Antonic for access to the last letters of Veljko Cubrilovic and to the story of how the letters were saved from being destroyed.

'They proposed burying the bodies of the three hanged men secretly ...': Dedijer, Vladimir, *The Road to Sarajevo*.

CHAPTER 23

'One of the guards on the journey claimed afterwards ...': Dedijer, ibid.

'In an article published in 1924, Werfel wrote ...': Werfel, Franz, Cabrinowitsch in *Die Neue Rundschau*, May 1924.

'he took sparing notes ... and had no thought of publishing them ...': the story of the background to the publication of Pappenheim's notes was told by Ratko Parezanin in his book *Mlada Bosna* (cited in Will Owings's review of the book published in *Austrian History Yearbook*, 1977).

'His daughter Else had been born in Salzburg ...': author interview with Stephen Frishauf (husband of Else), 2006.

'An aide to the Archduke ...': Nikitsch-Boulles, Paul, *Vor dem Sturm*, Verlag für Kulturpolitik, 1925 cited in Dedijer, Vladimir, *The Road to Sarajevo*).

'These remarks were echoed by one of the doctors who treated him ...':

Marsch, Dr A., 'Princip In Theresienstadt' in *Die Zeit* (Prague), 29 June 1937 (cited in Dedijer, ibid).

CHAPTER 24

'I was told it was a common habit for the besieged citizens of Sarajevo to spit at the footprints ...': author interview Mirsad Avdic, Sarajevo, 2006.

CHAPTER 25

'The museum had a stroke of luck in 2004 ...': author interview with Dr Christian Ortner, Vienna, 2006.

Acknowledgements

A special note of admiration for his past work and thanks for his generous interest in this book to William 'Dolph' Owings, retired Professor of History at the University of Arkansas at Little Rock.

Thanks also to Charles Jelavich, Emeritus Professor of History at Indiana University; Tina Harrison of TB Alert; Father Thomas Neulinger SJ; Dr Else Pappenheim and Dr Stephen Frishauf; Father Leon Nicoll SJ, Associate Professor of History, Loyola University; Matty Leighton; Alex Todorovic; Bojan Pancevski; Dr Christian Ortner and Andreas Huber of the Vienna Museum of Military History – Heeresgeschichtliches; David DeVoss; Brian Cathcart; Dr Johannes Reichmayr; Nada Cubrilovic and her daughter Vera Vucic in Belgrade, Serbia; Dr Zdravko Antonic of the Serbian Academy of Science and Art; Ranka Cabrinovic in Sarajevo, Bosnia & Hercegovina; Heather Wood; Andrew Solomon; Allan Nazareth; Ashok Prashad; Steve Mason, Anthea Mason, Chris Williams; Pete Leutchford; Jamie Bruce; Tim Lott; Edith and the staff and trustees of the Mount Pleasant Retreat for Writers, Artists and Musicians in Reigate; Susan Sutovic; staff of the National Library, Belgrade, Serbia; the head teacher, staff and pupils of the Veljko Cubrilovic School in Priboj, Bosnia & Hercegovina; Mirsad Avdic, curator of the Sarajevo Museum, Bosnia & Hercegovina; Princess Anita von Hohenberg and staff of Schloss Artstetten, Austria; Tomas Rieger at the Terezin Memorial, Czech Republic; staff of the Humanities Room at the British Library; staff of the School of Slavonic and East European Studies, University College London; Robin Morgan, Cathy Galvin and Mark Edmonds at the *Sunday Times Magazine*; Georgina Capel at Capel Land; Alan Samson at Weidenfeld & Nicolson, and Carole Green his ever helpful assistant.

Finally, gold stars for tolerance of an absent father to my four adorable children Sitira, Kitty, Orealla and Mackenzie Felix-Smith, and a Kaiteur Falls of love and thanks to their mother, my inspiring and open-hearted partner, Petal Felix.

Index